The Security Development Lifecycle

SDL: A Process for Developing Demonstrably More Secure Software

*Michael Howard
and Steve Lipner*

PUBLISHED BY
Microsoft Press
A Division of Microsoft Corporation
One Microsoft Way
Redmond, Washington 98052-6399

Library of Congress Control Number 2006924466
978-07356-2214-2
0-7356-2214-0

Printed and bound in the United States of America.

1 2 3 4 5 6 7 8 9 QWE 1 0 9 8 7 6

Distributed in Canada by H.B. Fenn and Company Ltd. A CIP catalogue record for this book is available from the British Library.

Microsoft Press books are available through booksellers and distributors worldwide. For further information about international editions, contact your local Microsoft Corporation office or contact Microsoft Press International directly at fax (425) 936-7329. Visit our Web site at www.microsoft.com/mspress. Send comments to mspinput@microsoft.com.

Acquisitions Editor: Ben Ryan
Project Editor: Devon Musgrave
Technical Editor: Virgil Gligor; Technical Review services provided by
   Content Master, a member of CM Group, Ltd
Copy Editors: Bill Bowers & Shannon Leavitt
Indexer: Richard Shrout

Body Part No. X11-74982

For my patient and beautiful wife, Cheryl; my handsome little man, Blake; and my dazzling daughter, my little monkey, Paige. I love y'all.

—Michael

For Anne, with love and appreciation for her support and her patience during all the hours I've spent building secure systems.

—Steve

Contents at a Glance

Table of Contents

Foreword

Early one Monday morning, Steve Ballmer walked into his conference room carrying a desktop. He put it down on the table in front of me. "I want this fixed, and I want it fixed by tomorrow," he said. Over the weekend he had attended a wedding. The computer belonged to his friend, the groom. "I worked all weekend on this, and I couldn't fix it," he reported. "I want to send it back to him tomorrow."

We analzyed the machine, looking for the problem. We've diagnosed other machines, but this one was over the top—it was polluted through and through with viruses and other malicious software. Some we already knew about and could easily clean, but several others we had never seen before. Regardless, the machine was nearly a lost cause by the time the first virus was done with it. I had the opportunity to go through that virus's source code. The first thing it did was look around for and wipe out anything that had the word *virus* in it. This included, of course, anything with the moniker *antivirus*. It then disguised itself and turned off Windows Update as well as everything to do with group policy. The malware manipulated group policy facilities to disable all sorts of system capabilities. If you tried to run antivirus software on the machine, nothing happened. This machine was lost.

We did fix the machine—and some of Microsoft's new security and anti-malware products help protect against the kinds of issues we found that day—but more malicious software will follow in the future. Security attacks are no longer the purview of teenagers holed up in their bedrooms trying to gain bragging rights at the expense of the world economy—attacks are now a profitable criminal business. Make no mistake, when it comes to the security battleground, we are on a rapidly escalating path. This is a war that will last far into the future. Hackers have gone beyond attacking operating systems and network servers—they are going after databases and they're going after code associated with data types. If there's a parser in the code you write, they're going to go after it. Our research as well as other industry statistics show that attacks are moving farther up the stack from the operating system to the applications sitting on top. Everything, not just Microsoft Windows, is being attacked: Linux, Mac OS X, Solaris, server and client applications, and Web applications.

One of the best weapons you can have in your arsenal is clean code. Others include software configurations that are secure by default—so resilient that even vulnerable code can't be attacked successfully—and security products that block or recover from attacks. At Microsoft we have made two major sweeps to rid our operating systems of security problems: first with Microsoft Windows Server 2003 and then with Windows XP SP2. These were investments that took thousands of engineers months to complete. It also refocused our efforts around how we built Windows Vista. Our work in this area is ongoing, and through these projects we have learned a great deal. Sharing this learning with you is a high priority for us and the top priority of this book, *The Security Development Lifecycle*. No one course of action will cure all ills, but the information in this book will help you do much more to protect your customers when designing your products, managing your projects, writing code, assessing risk, and testing security scenarios.

The authors of this book, Michael Howard and Steve Lipner, have a great deal of experience in this arena—more than 45 years combined in software security. More than 80,000 copies of Michael's *Writing Secure Code*, co-written by David LeBlanc and first published in December of 2001, have reached developers' hands. It contains much of what we learned through the work we did on Windows XP SP 2. *The Security Development Lifecycle* is the result of knowledge we've gained from dealing with vulnerabilities reported to the Microsoft Security Response Center and from continually updating our development processes to eliminate the root causes of such vulnerabilities. It contains valuable how-to information on everything from educating your developers to conducting security reviews to handling emergencies.

The best advice I can give, based on all my years in the software industry, is to remind you that where security is concerned, lunch is expensive. If you don't pay for it now, you'll pay an order of magnitude more for it later. You'll have to dig out from under a cacophony of phone calls, PR problems, unhappy customers, and lost sales. Pay now or pay later—it comes down to the way you develop your code. By the time a vulnerability reaches the field, it's way too late. It's way too late if it gets into a beta release. It's too late if you find problems in testing. And it's too late if security holes make it into a build of the software. I hope the practices outlined in this book will help you more effectively address problems that might be found in your software, but more importantly, I hope it will help you prevent such problems in the first place.

Jim Allchin

May 2006
Redmond, WA

Introduction

Rewind back in time to the security landscape of 2001 and 2002—here are some security comments and headlines from that time:

- "Gartner Recommends Against Microsoft IIS" (eWeek 2001a)
- "IT Bugs Out Over IIS Security" (eWeek 2001b)
- "Microsoft's security woes" (CNET 2002a)
- "Microsoft's security push lacks oomph" (CNET 2002b)

Now fast-forward to 2005 and 2006:

- "We actually consider Microsoft to be leading the software [industry] now in improvements in their security development life cycle." (CRN 2006)
- "Oltsik gives Microsoft credit for implementing industry-leading security development processes saying, 'Microsoft is ahead of the pack in this area.'" (Enterprise Strategy Group 2006)
- "Overall, security bulletins from Microsoft have decreased in recent years" (eWeek 2005a)
- "Microsoft: Software Security Trendsetter?" (eWeek 2005b)

This change is not an accident. The improvement is due to only one thing: the development and adoption of software development processes designed solely to improve the security and privacy of Microsoft software. The sum of those processes is a 13-stage process called the Security Development Lifecycle (SDL), which is the subject of this book.

What makes this book unique is that the SDL is not theory; it works. And although there is no one silver bullet to address security and privacy issues, the SDL has had a large positive effect by significantly reducing the number of vulnerabilities in real-world code.

We want to stress the last point again. SDL is based on real-world experience and it works. You may hear of security consultants touting process improvements that will lead to more secure software. Perhaps they do. Perhaps they don't! Who knows? What we can categorically state is that the SDL *does* lead to more secure software. The SDL is not perfect, of course, but if you care about security and privacy, then you should look at the SDL.

The goals of the SDL are twofold; the first is to reduce the number of security vulnerabilities and privacy problems, and the second is to reduce the severity of the vulnerabilities that remain. You can never remove all security and privacy vulnerabilities, simply because when a product ships, it is built based on the security best practice of the day, but security research and the discovery of new attacks is never-ending.

Why Should You Read This Book?

It's probably best to start by explaining who is not the primary audience for this book; this is not a book for developers. That said, we don't mean that developers should not read this book. We mean there is very little code in this book and no real implementation best practices that would apply to developers. This book is more broadly aimed at two sets of people. The first group includes management and people who manage software development teams and the software development processes within their organizations. The second group includes designers and architects.

Organization of This Book

This book is divided into three parts, and each part is aimed at a different audience.

Part I, "The Need for the SDL"

This section addresses two issues: the first is why you should care about improving the security of your software in the first place, and the second is how to sell such improvements to management. Everyone should read Chapter 1, "Enough Is Enough: The Threats Have Changed," because it outlines why security and privacy are important and why trying to sell security is hard. Chapter 2, "Current Software Development Methods Fail to Produce Secure Software," which addresses the limitations with regard to security of current development methods, and Chapter 3, "A Short History of the SDL at Microsoft," which outlines Microsoft's experiences that led to the development of the SDL, give general and process managers a picture of "what doesn't work" in building more secure software. Chapter 4, "SDL for Management," is critical for upper-management and middle-management readers, because it explains the SDL in nontechnical terms and makes the reader aware of the costs and benefits of the process.

Part II, "The Security Development Lifecycle Process"

This 13-chapter section is the core of the book. Each chapter maps to one of the SDL's stages (Stage 0 through Stage 12) and lays out the requirements for that stage. If you are responsible for improving the security of your organization's software, if you are interested in process improvements in general, if you are a software development methodology person, or if you oversee the process work at your organization, you should read this section in its entirety.

Part III, "SDL Reference Material"

The last part of the book is a series of references that relate to SDL design and coding requirements. One chapter also covers infusing Agile development methods with the security requirements of the SDL. At the time of this book's publication, little or no literature addresses security and Agile methods. Chapter 18, "Integrating SDL with Agile Methods," is meant to start bridging this serious gap.

The Future Evolution of the SDL

The SDL is not static. No software development process that focuses on security could ever be static because the security landscape evolves quickly. At Microsoft we update the SDL twice a year in January and July. The change process is quite elaborate, but it is designed to ensure that the SDL incorporates only requirements that will be effective at improving the security of software. At a high level, the process order is as described in the following four paragraphs.

People from around Microsoft propose changes to the SDL. A change can be a requirement or a recommendation. A recommendation is just that, and a requirement is something that teams must adhere to in future products. It's not uncommon for a requirement to start out six months or a year earlier as a recommendation. The document describing the recommendation or requirement must include the proposed change to the SDL and the rationale for the change. Most importantly, the proposal for change must show demonstrable security improvement. We don't want SDL littered with well-intentioned but ineffective requirements, and that means identifying at least five Microsoft security bulletins that could have been prevented if the proposed change were in place. Also, if the change is to be a requirement, the document must include ways to verify that the requirement is adhered to. It is also worthwhile to identify a team to test the proposal to provide concrete and real-world feedback.

Next, the SDL steering group reviews the proposals and provides feedback to the authors. The authors are either members of the steering group or are invited to participate in the meeting where their proposal is reviewed.

Once the initial drafts are edited, the proposals are opened up to a larger team of security people within the company for comments.

Finally, the proposal is accepted, and goes into effect. All products covered by the SDL are now subject to the new requirements, and all should consider implementing recommendations.

Given the dynamic nature of the SDL, we expect some of the information in this book to be superseded in the coming years. Check *http://go.microsoft.com/fwlink/?LinkId=65489* for future updates about the material in this book.

What's on the Companion Disc?

The companion disc includes the following material:

- **"The Basics"**   In our opinion, every person contributing to software should have baseline security knowledge. This online video presentation and slide deck is what we believe to be a *reasonable* baseline. The presentation will not create security experts, but it serves as good entry-level education for anyone building software.

- **Security Risk Assessment document**   This document, riskassess.rtf, is referred to in Chapter 8, "Stage 3: Product Risk Assessment," and is used to find areas of risk within an application quickly, to help the security team focus in on potential weak spots.

- **banned.h**   This file—referred to in Chapter 11, "Stage 6: Secure Coding Policies"—is a C/C++ header file that can be included in any C and C++ code to find banned functions in your code quickly.

- **MiniFuzz file fuzzer**   Referred to in Chapter 12, "Stage 7: Secure Testing Policies," Mini-Fuzz is a set of C++ source code files that provides the starting point for a file fuzzer. The goal of the tool is not to provide a complete fuzzing solution, but to give developers and testers a feel for how fuzzers work and how you can use the Windows debug APIs to catch errors in the code being fuzzed.

- **Attack Surface Rationale document**   Referred to in Chapter 13, "Stage 8: The Security Push," this short document, AttackSurfaceRationale.rtf, helps security people understand why a product has attack surface elements (such as open network ports) that are enabled by default.

System Requirements

The two Word documents, attacksurface.rtf and riskassess.rtf, were created with Microsoft Word 2003 but have been read by Microsoft Windows WordPad in Windows XP SP2 and Microsoft Word 2000. The system requirements are the same for Microsoft Word.

The MiniFuzz software was written using Microsoft Visual C++ 2005, and the project file can only load into Microsoft Visual Studio 2005. The system requirements are the same as Visual Studio 2005.

Banned.h was written in Visual Studio 2005, but has been tested with Visual C++ 2002, Visual C++ 2003, and Visual C++ 2005 as well as GCC 3.4.x.

Finally, the "Basics" presentation requires Windows Media Player 7 or later, Windows Media 9 codecs, Internet Explorer 6, and XML Parser 4.0 Service Pack 1 (included on the disc).

Acknowledgments

This book would have been impossible to write without the help of many people inside and outside Microsoft. We'd like to thank the people who reviewed drafts, critiqued, and in some cases correctly criticized our work.

The following people are some of our peers in the Security Engineering and Communications group at Microsoft. These people work daily with engineering groups at Microsoft to execute on the vision of the SDL: Adel Abouchaev, Allen Jones, Bryan Nealer, Chris Walker, Dave Ross, David Ladd, Eric Bidstrup, George Stathakopoulos, Greg Wroblewski, John Lambert, Jon Ness, Matt Thomlinson, Mike Mitchell, Mike Reavey, Neill Clift, Nicholas Judge, Shawn Hernan, and Tina Knutson.

Other people from across Microsoft provided feedback, including Akshay Aggarwal, Amy Roberts, Bill Ramos, Bjorn Levidow, Christopher Budd, David LeBlanc, Irada Sadykhova, Jason Garms, JC Cannon, John Gray, Jon Wall, Manoj Mehta, Peter Torr, Rose Bigham, Talhah Mir, and Todd Webb.

Some of our customers tempered our views and comments with real-world pragmatism, including Adam Shostack, Alan Krassowski (Symantec), Charles Chandler (NetIQ), Hugh Thompson (Security Innovations), Kyle Randolph (Citrix), Michael Angelo (NetIQ), and Mukesh Kumar (SafeCo).

Virgil Gligor, professor of electrical and computer engineering at the University of Maryland, provided an outside technical review of the draft. The final text benefited greatly from Virgil's long experience in building secure systems, his wisdom, and his critical eye.

Microsoft's Trustworthy Computing Academic Advisory Board, of which Virgil is a member, played a significant role in motivating us to write this book. We asked the board to review a paper on the SDL (Lipner and Howard 2005), and in addition to providing us with helpful comments, several board members suggested that what we really needed to do was write a book on the SDL. Those suggestions were a major factor in our commitment to the project.

Finally, and most importantly, we would like to thank the executive staff at Microsoft, from Bill Gates down, for providing us with the mandate to carry out the SDL within the company, and the thousands of Microsoft employees who deliver more secure software every day and realize that security and privacy are just "part of getting the job done."

We sincerely thank you all.

Michael Howard

Steven B. Lipner

Redmond, WA
June 2006

References

(eWeek 2001a) *http://www.eweek.com/article2/0,1759,1240915,00.asp*. September 2001.

(eWeek 2001b) *http://www.eweek.com/article2/0,1759,97182,00.asp*. July 2001.

(CNET 2002a) *http://news.com.com/Commentary+Microsofts+security+woes/2009-1001_3-808870.html*. January 2002.

(CNET 2002b) *http://news.com.com/Microsofts+security+push+lacks+oomph/2100-1001_3-808010.html*. January 2002.

(CRN 2006) Rooney, Paula. "Is Windows Safer?" *http://www.crn.com/sections/coverstory/coverstory.jhtml;jsessionid=VV1Q351RM5A1YQSNDBOCKH0CJUMEKJVN?articleId=179103240*. February 2006.

(Enterprise Strategy Group 2006)   Oltsik, John, Senior Analyst, Enterprise Strategy Group. "Good security news to be in short supply in 2006," *http://news.com.com/Good+security+news+to+be+in+short+supply+in+2006/2010-1071_3-6028980.html*. CNET News.com, January 2006.

(eWeek 2005a)   Naraine, Ryan. "Microsoft Claims Security Win with New Development Rules," *http://www.eweek.com/article2/0,1759,1779769,00.asp*. March 2005.

(eWeek 2005b)   *http://www.eweek.com/article2/0,1759,1860574,00.asp*. September 2005.

(Lipner and Howard 2005)   Lipner, Steve, and Michael Howard. "The Trustworthy Computing Security Development Lifecycle," *http://msdn.microsoft.com/security/default.aspx?pull=/library/en-us/dnsecure/html/sdl.asp*. MSDN, March 2005.

Microsoft Press Support

Every effort has been made to ensure the accuracy of this book. Microsoft Press provides corrections for books through the World Wide Web at the following address:

http://www.microsoft.com/mspress/support/

To connect directly to the Microsoft Press Knowledge Base and enter a query regarding a question or issue that you may have, go to:

http://www.microsoft.com/mspress/support/search.asp

If you have comments, questions, or ideas regarding this book, please send them to Microsoft Press using either of the following methods:

Postal Mail:

> *Microsoft Press*
> *Attn:* Security Development Lifecycle *Editor*
> *One Microsoft Way*
> *Redmond, WA 98052-6399*

E-Mail:

> *mspinput@microsoft.com*

Part I
The Need for the SDL

Chapter 1

Enough Is Enough: The Threats Have Changed

The adage "Necessity is the mother of invention" sums up the birth of the Security Development Lifecycle (SDL) at Microsoft. Under the banner of Trustworthy Computing (Microsoft 2002), Microsoft heard the call from customers requiring more secure software from their software vendors and changed its software development process to accommodate customers' pressing security needs and, frankly, to preserve the company's credibility. This book explains that process in detail with the simple goal of helping you update your present software development process to build more secure software.

The first question that probably comes to mind is, "Why bother with security?" The answer is simple: the world is more connected now than it has ever been, and no doubt it will become even more connected over time. This incredible level of interconnectedness has created a huge threat environment and, hence, hugely escalated risk for all software users. The halcyon days of defacing Web sites for fun and fame are still with us to an extent, but the major and most dangerous attacks are now upon us: cybercrime has arrived. What makes these attacks so dangerous is that the cybercriminal can attack and exploit his target system silently without creating any obvious sign of a break-in. Now, the criminal can access private or sensitive data or use a compromised system for further attacks on other users, as in the cases of phishing (APWG 2006) and extortion.

The cost-benefit ratio for a criminal is defined by Clark and Davis (Clark and Davis 1995) as

$$M_b + P_b > O_{cp} + O_{cm}P_aP_c$$

where

- M_b is the monetary benefit for the attacker.
- P_b is the psychological benefit for the attacker.
- O_{cp} is the cost of committing the crime.
- O_{cm} is the monetary costs of conviction for the attacker (future lost opportunities and legal costs).
- P_a is the probability of being apprehended and arrested.
- P_c is the probability of conviction for the attacker.

If the left side of the equation is greater than the right side, the benefit of an attack outweighs the costs and a crime could ensue. Of course, this does not imply that all people will commit a crime given enough opportunity! Remember the old model of 10:80:10: 10 percent of people would never commit a crime, no matter what; 80 percent are opportunists; and 10 percent can't be deterred, no matter what. By raising the probability of getting caught and lowering the chance of success, you deter the 80 percent and make the task harder for the "evil 10."

The software development industry cannot easily control P_a or P_c, although the industry can work with the law-enforcement community to provide information that helps apprehend criminals. However, some countries have no cybercrime laws.

Users and administrators of computer systems could control M_b a little by not storing data of value to the attacker, but this solution is infeasible because much of the benefit of using computers is that they allow businesses to operate more efficiently, and that means storing and manipulating data of value to both the customer and the attacker. A well-designed and secure system will increase O_{cp}, making it expensive for an attacker to successfully mount an attack and motivating the attacker to move on to softer targets at other IP addresses.

From an Internet attacker's perspective, the element that influences this equation the most is P_a because the chance of being found and apprehended is too often very small. Admittedly, some miscreants have been apprehended (FBI 2005, CNN 2003), but most attacks are anonymous and go unnoticed by users and system administrators alike. In fact, the most insidious form of attack is the one that goes unnoticed.

As operating system vendors have focused on shoring up core operating system security, cybercriminals have simply moved to more fertile ground higher in the application stack (eWeek 2004)–such as databases (ZDNet 2006a), antivirus software (InformationWeek 2005), and backup software (ZDNet 2006b)–because there is a better chance of a successful attack and the reward is worth the effort. Attacking an operating system does not directly yield valuable data for a criminal, but attacking a database, a customer relationship management (CRM) tool, a health-care system, or a system management tool is like winning the lottery and is reflected in the O_{cm} variable in the equation previously mentioned. It doesn't matter how big or small your software or your company might appear to be; if the attacker thinks it's worth the effort, and the gains are many and the risk is low, then any insecure application you use might very well come under attack (Computerworld 2006).

Microsoft products are not the only targets of attack. That's why we wrote this book. A cursory glance at any security-bug tracking database will show that every platform and every product includes security bugs (OSVDB 2006a, OSVDB 2006b, OSVDB 2006c, OSVDB 2006d).

Furthermore, the skill required to reverse-engineer security updates (Flake 2004) and build exploitations is easier than ever (Moore 2006). As Mary Ann Davidson, Oracle Corporation's chief security officer, points out:

> *You don't have to be technically sophisticated to be a hacker anymore. Hacking isn't just for bragging rights and chest thumping. There's real money in it. (eWeek 2005)*

The implications of attacks on applications rather than on operating systems cannot be underestimated. Most software vendors build business-productivity or end-user applications, not operating system components. And most security-savvy administrators have focused their limited time on securing their operating system installations and putting network-level defenses such as firewalls in place.

One could argue that the software industry focused almost exclusively on securing operating systems when it should have considered the security of applications with just as much effort. One could also argue that the reason attackers are targeting applications is because the operating system vendors have, on the whole, done a reasonable job of securing the base operating systems in common use. Remember, everything is relative—we said "reasonable," not "good"—but regarding application security, most operating systems are in a better security state than applications.

To compound the problem, many application vendors are dangerously unaware of the real security issues facing customers (CNN 2002), which has led to a false sense of security within the user community and a lack of urgency within the vendor community. Many users and vendors see security as an operating system problem or a network perimeter and firewall problem, but it has become obvious that this is simply untrue.

In short, if you build software, and your software can be accessed by potentially malicious users inside or outside the firewall, the application will come under attack. But this alone is not a sufficient reason to consider security in the development life cycle. The following sections address additional considerations.

Worlds of Security and Privacy Collide

For security to be accepted within an organization, and for software developers to take security seriously, security must accommodate, or at least acknowledge, business needs and business problems. To be successful in an organization, secure software development requires a business benefit. In the case of Microsoft, the business benefit was pretty obvious—our customers demanded more secure software.

But for some people, the decision to make software more secure appears to be not so simple. This is where privacy enters the picture. Trying to sell security to project managers and to upper management can be difficult because there is little, if any, demonstrable return on investment (ROI) data for employing secure development practices. Frankly, upper management is tired of nebulous "we could be attacked" stories that are used to gain budget for security. This is often not a productive way to sell security. But privacy is another matter altogether. People understand what privacy is and what it means when personal, confidential, or personally identifiable information is leaked to miscreants. When users think of security, most often they think about credit card information or online banking passwords being stolen. This, to be pedantic, is not security; it is privacy. Administrators, Chief Information Officers (CIOs), and Chief Information Security Officers (CISOs) should think in terms of risk to business-critical data. Privacy plays a big part in risk calculations.

> ## Privacy and Security
>
> Many people see privacy and security as different views of the same issue. However, privacy can be seen as a way of complying with policy and security as a way of enforcing policy. Restrooms are a good analogy of this concept. The sign on a restroom door indicates the policy for who should enter the restroom, but no security prevents anyone who might want to enter. Adding a lock to the door would provide security to help enforce the privacy policy.

Note   Privacy's focus is compliance with regulatory requirements (Security Innovation 2006), corporate policy, and customer expectations.

Risk managers try to put a monetary value on risk. If, according to risk management, the value of protected data if exposed to attackers is, say, $10,000,000, it probably makes sense to spend the $200,000 needed by the development team to remove all known design and coding issues and to add other defenses to protect against such attacks.

Note   Risk management can assign a monetary value to the risk of disclosing data.

A security bug such as a SQL injection bug (Howard, LeBlanc, and Viega 2005) is a serious problem to have in your Web-based service-oriented application, but potential privacy issues are what make this class of bug so grave. A SQL injection bug allows an attacker to wreak havoc on an underlying database, including corrupting information and viewing sensitive data. In some instances, a SQL injection attack can be a steppingstone to complete takeover of a network (Johansson 2005). SQL injection vulnerabilities are reasonably common in database applications, but some have been discovered in database engines also (Red Database 2006).

SQL injection issues are not the only form of security bug that has privacy ramifications. Any bug that allows an attacker to run code of his bidding can potentially lead to privacy violations. Examples include some forms of buffer overflows, command-injection bugs, integer arithmetic issues, and cross-site scripting bugs. But more subtle issues that do not allow arbitrary code execution, such as cryptographic weaknesses and data leakage faults, can lead to privacy issues also.

> **Warning**   Much noise has been made about not running as an administrator or root account when operating a computer. We authors are vocal commentators about this issue, and this has helped force fundamental changes in Microsoft Windows Vista; users are, by default, ordinary users and not administrators. Even members of the local Administrators group are users until they are elevated to perform administrative tasks. Running as a normal user does indeed provide security benefits, but it may provide only a limited benefit for privacy protection. Malicious code running as the user can still access any sensitive data that can be read by the user.

The ability of an unauthorized person to view data, an information disclosure threat, can be a privacy issue. In some countries and United States, it could lead to legal action under U.S. state or federal or international privacy laws and industry-specific regulations.

In short, privacy is a huge driver for employing effective security measures and making applications secure from attack. Security is not the same as privacy, but effective security is a prerequisite for protecting the privacy of data about employees and customers.

It's also important to remember that, in some cases, security and privacy can be diametrically opposed to one another. For example, good authentication is a venerable and effective security defense, but it can also raise a privacy issue. Anytime you provide your identity to a computer system, any tasks you perform or any resources you access while you are logged on can be collected and used to model your computer habits. One way to defend against this is to not authenticate, but that's hardly secure.

A good example of privacy and security colliding is the design of Google Desktop version 3 beta. This product allows a user to upload his or her potentially personal or private documents to Google's servers. This design prompted a Gartner analyst to warn that the product posed an "unacceptable security risk" (ZDNet 2006c). It may seem like we're splitting hairs, but this is not a security risk; it's a privacy risk. It's very easy to mix the two concepts. Note that *Time* magazine ran a cover story on February 20, 2006, with the headline "Can We Trust Google with Our Secrets?" (Time 2006). Privacy issues can quickly yield negative headlines.

But wait, there's more!

Another Factor That Influences Security: Reliability

Additional aspects to consider are service-level agreements with your customers and maintaining uptime. Crashed or unresponsive software will probably not satisfy customers or meet their needs. Just as privacy and security are not the same, security is not the same as reliability. But like privacy and security, reliability and security share some goals. For example, any security mitigation that protects against denial of service (DoS) attacks is also a reliability feature.

However, like security and privacy, security and reliability can be at odds. Take a critical server on a protected network as an example. Once the computer's security audit log is full, the machine can no longer log security events, which means that an attacker has a window of opportunity to access sensitive resources on the computer without being audited. In this example, it is not unheard of to simply cause the computer to stop functioning *on purpose* when the audit log is full. For example, the U.S. government protection profiles (NIAP 2005) for evaluating the security of operating systems require the availability of the CrashOnAudit-Fail option in Microsoft Windows (Microsoft 2003). When this option is set, the computer will crash if the security log is full or if a security-related audit entry cannot be written successfully. Clearly, this is a reliability concern, but it's a valid security defense for some customers. In fact, in some legal-compliance scenarios, you might have no alternative but to crash a computer if auditing can no longer continue.

Another example of security working at odds with reliability is the ability of Windows to automatically restart a service if the service fails. This is an excellent reliability feature, but if it is configured incorrectly, it could be a security issue. Imagine that a service has a bad security vulnerability, like a buffer overrun, and an attacker attempts to compromise a system by exploiting the buffer overrun. If the attacker gets the attack wrong on the first attempt, the service crashes, and then, depending on the configuration, the service might restart. The restart would give the attacker another chance to get the attack right. Every time he gets it wrong, the service crashes and restarts!

Figure 1-1 shows the service recovery configuration dialog box for the print spooler. Configuration options present a tradeoff between security and reliability. The application can crash only twice in one day: if it crashes again, it will not restart. Also, there is a delay of one minute before the service starts up again. This will slow down an attacker substantially.

Many common security coding bugs and design errors can lead to reliability issues such as some forms of buffer overrun, integer arithmetic bugs, memory exhaustion, referencing invalid memory, or array bounds errors. All of these issues have forced software developers to create security updates, but they are reliability issues, too. In fact, the OpenBSD project refers to some of its security bugs as reliability bugs, although other vendors would call the fix a security fix. One such example is a bug fixed by OpenBSD in the BIND DNS daemon in late 2004 (OpenBSD 2004). This is clearly a DoS bug that most vendors would treat as a security fix, but OpenBSD treats it as a reliability fix. Technically, the OpenBSD team is correct, but no major OS vendor differentiates between reliability and security fixes.

Figure 1-1   Microsoft Windows XP service recovery configuration dialog box.

Note   Microsoft's Trustworthy Computing initiative has four pillars. Three of them are technical, addressing the issues we have discussed so far: Security, Privacy, and Reliability. The selection of these three technical pillars is not accidental. (For completeness, the fourth pillar is Business Practices.)

Figure 1-2 shows the results of an analysis of security bugs that were assigned a CVE number by Common Vulnerabilities and Exposures (CVE 2006) between 2002 and 2004. The authors analyzed the CVE bug categories (CVE 2005) to determine whether they had security, privacy, or reliability ramifications. Over this three-year period, CVE created entries for 3,595 security bugs from all corners of the software industry. Notice that the sum is greater than 3,595 because some bugs are both privacy and reliability issues.

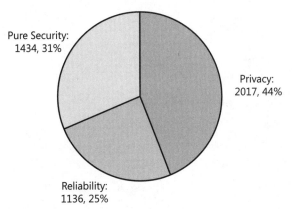

Pure Security:
1434, 31%

Privacy:
2017, 44%

Reliability:
1136, 25%

Figure 1-2   Analysis of CVE statistics showing a breakdown of security, privacy, and reliability issues. All the bugs are security bugs, but some also have privacy or reliability consequences, or both.

It's Really About Quality

Ultimately, all the issues we have mentioned are quality bugs. Figure 1-3 shows the relationship among quality, security, privacy, and reliability.

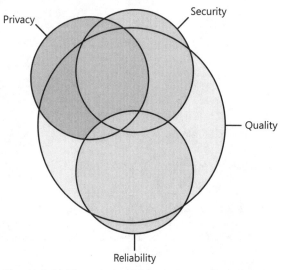

Figure 1-3   The relationship among quality, privacy, security, and reliability.

It is worth mentioning that some elements overlap, as noted in our description of the CVE analysis. Overlap can occur in the following combinations:

- **Security and privacy**   Examples include mitigation of privacy issues using encryption, which is a security technology.
- **Security and reliability**   For example, a DoS threat is also a reliability issue.
- **Reliability and privacy**   For example, an application might crash or otherwise fail, yielding sensitive information in an error message. This is also a security issue.

You'll also notice that portions of the privacy, security, and reliability elements extend beyond the quality circle:

- **Security**   If a user invites malicious software onto the computer, this is a security problem but not a security-quality issue.
- **Privacy**   If a user willingly divulges personal data to an untrustworthy attacker, through a phishing attack for example, this is not a privacy-quality issue.
- **Reliability**   If a person trips over and pulls out a computer's power cable, this is not a software reliability-quality issue.

What we're trying to say is that security should not be considered an isolated endeavor. Only when you start to think about security holistically—as the intersection of privacy, reliability, and quality—does it start to make business-value sense. At that point, you can better sell secure-software improvements to upper management.

Important   Security bugs that lead to disclosure of sensitive, confidential, or personally identifiable data are privacy issues and can have legal ramifications. Security bugs that lead to reliability issues could mean reduced uptime and failure to meet service-level agreements.

Why Major Software Vendors Should Create More Secure Software

Improving software security should be an easy sell if your software has a significant number of users; the sheer cost of applying security updates makes it worth getting security, privacy, and reliability right early in the process rather than putting the burden on your customers to apply updates. And frankly, if you have a large number of users, every security vulnerability in your product puts many customers at risk of attack—or worse, exploitation—because you will never have 100-percent patch deployment, and a deployment of less than 100 percent means that a large number of users are put at risk.

If your software is a business-critical application, improved security should again be an easy sell because of the business impact of a failed system.

The goal of creating more secure software and reducing customer pain is why Microsoft has adopted SDL. SDL is not free; it costs time, money, and effort to implement. But the upfront benefits far outweigh the cost of revisions, developing and testing security updates, and having customers deploy the updates. Microsoft has received a lot of criticism in the past about the insecurity of some of its products, and this criticism was a major factor in the company's commitment to improve its software development processes. A vocal critic of Microsoft's security problems was John Pescatore of Gartner. In September 2001, Pescatore advised Gartner clients to evaluate the cost of ownership of using Microsoft Internet Information Services (IIS) 5.0 Web server on Internet-facing computers and to seek alternatives if the costs were justified (Gartner 2001). After seeing the progress Microsoft has made since that date, Pescatore has stated, "We actually consider Microsoft to be leading the software [industry] now in improvements in their security development life cycle [SDL]," and "Microsoft is not the punching bag for security anymore" (CRN 2006).

In an interesting (almost perverse) turnaround, the main IIS competitor, Apache on Linux, is now, and has been for some time, the most frequently attacked Web server on the Internet. Not only does Apache on Linux (Secunia 2006a) have more security bugs than IIS 6.0 on Windows (Secunia 2006b), it is attacked and *compromised* more than IIS on Windows (Zone-H 2006). Admittedly, many attacks result from poor server administration and insecure configuration, but system management is a critical part of the security equation. We discuss this issue in more detail in Chapter 10, "Stage 5: Creating Security Documents, Tools, and Best Practices for Customers."

A Challenge to Large ISVs

We challenge *all* independent software vendors, especially those who have more than 100,000 customers, to change their software development processes. Pay close attention to what we say next: If you are not implementing a process similar to SDL, the processes you have now simply do not create more secure products. It's time to admit this and do something about it. Your customers demand it.

At Microsoft, our customers have benefited from a vulnerability reduction of more than 50 percent because of SDL. Admittedly, we still have a great deal of work ahead of us, and we are under no illusion that we're "done" with security. Jim Allchin, copresident of the Platforms and Services Division at Microsoft, stated, "At no time am I saying this system is unbreakable" (CNET 2006).

That said, Microsoft has taken on the challenge, and SDL has galvanized the company to deliver more secure products to customers. You must do likewise, or attackers will smell blood and the competition that offers products that are more secure than yours will take sales from you. Rebuilding customer trust and goodwill will be difficult at best. We say this from painful experience.

Numerous consumers are starting to ask what their vendors are doing to secure their products from attack. What will your answer be?

Why In-House Software Developers Should Create More Secure Software

The main benefits of SDL for in-house developers are reduced privacy and reliability exposure. Yes, there is a pure security benefit, but as we mentioned earlier, the benefits of security to in-house applications are hard to quantify. Privacy has a risk component that senior managers and risk managers understand, and reliability has an uptime and service-level agreement component that managers also understand. Sell security as privacy and reliability, with a security bonus!

Customer-facing e-commerce applications are, of course, high-risk components and should be developed with utmost care.

Why Small Software Developers Should Create More Secure Software

Creating more secure software is a harder sell for smaller companies because even a small amount of security work up front costs time and money. Although "hacking the code" is effective at creating code rapidly, it is also extremely effective at creating bugs.

Smaller development houses often have a lot of personal pride and ego tied up in their code; so look at security as a measure of quality. Most importantly, if you get it right up front, the cost of fixing bugs later diminishes rapidly. Many sources outline the benefits of building better-quality and more secure software early. One such example is in Chapter 9, "Stage 4: Risk Analysis."

It's fair to say that most people don't mind doing hard work; they just hate reworking. Fixing security bugs can be difficult and time consuming. You can pay now and increase the odds that you'll get it right, or you can pay much more later. As a small development house or an individual developer, you probably have little spare time, and implementing more secure software up front saves you time in the long run. Better-quality software means less reworking, which translates into more time to ski, work out, play with the kids, read a good book (not about software!), or go on a date with your significant other. You get the picture. We have observed at Microsoft that having fewer security vulnerabilities also means that there is more time to add useful features that customers want to our products, and this translates into more customers.

Summary

Selling security process improvements to upper management is not easy because security professionals have often focused on vague although troubling potential threats. Security experts are often seen as alarmists in the boardroom. Selling security as a means to mitigate risk—most notably privacy issues that could lead to legal action from affected customers and reliability issues that could lead to violation of service-level agreements and system downtime—is much more plausible and can be assigned monetary value by managers. Risks and potential costs are associated with the privacy issue and with downtime.

Threats have changed, and the security and privacy landscape is not what it was in 2001. Everything is connected today, and criminals are being lured to the online community because that's "where the money is." There is no indication that this trend will abate any time soon.

The software industry's past is littered with security bugs from all software vendors. If our industry is to protect the future and deliver on the vision of Trustworthy Computing, we need to update our processes to provide products that are more secure, more private, and more reliable for customers.

Microsoft has learned from and has adopted the SDL to remedy its past mistakes. You should, too. Microsoft has seen vulnerabilities reduced more than 50 percent because of the SDL. You will, too.

References

(Microsoft 2002)   Trustworthy Computing site, *http://www.microsoft.com/mscorp/twc/default.mspx.*

(APWG 2006)   Anti-Phishing Working Group, *http://www.antiphishing.org/.*

(Clark and Davis 1995)   Clark, J. R., and W. L. Davis. "A Human Capital Perspective on Criminal Careers," *Journal of Applied Business Research*, volume 11, no 3. 1995, pp. 58–64.

(FBI 2005)   "FBI Announces Two Arrests in Mytob and Zotob Computer Worm Investigation," *http://www.fbi.gov/pressrel/pressrel05/zotob_release082605.htm*. August 2005.

(CNN 2003)   "Teenager arrested in 'Blaster' Internet attack," *http://www.cnn.com/2003/TECH/internet/08/29/worm.arrest/*. August 2003.

(eWeek 2004)   "App Developers Need to Redouble Security Efforts," *http://www.eweek.com/article2/0,1759,1663716,00.asp*. September 2004.

(ZDNet 2006a)   Ou, George. "Oracle from unbreakable to unpatchable," *http://blogs.zdnet.com/Ou/?p=151&tag=nl.e622*. January 2006.

(InformationWeek 2005)   Keizer, Gregg. "Bug Bites McAfee Antivirus," *http://www.informationweek.com/showArticle.jhtml?articleID=175007526*. December 2005.

(ZDNet 2006b)   Evers, Joris. "Backup software flaws pose risk," *http://news.zdnet.com/2100-1009_22-6028515.html*. January 2006.

(Computerworld 2006)   Vijayan, Jimkumar. "Targeted attacks expected to rise in '06, IBM study says," *http://www.computerworld.com/securitytopics/security/story/0,10801,107992,00.html*. January 2006.

(OSVBD 2006a)   Open Source Vulnerability Database. Oracle, *http://www.osvdb.org/searchdb.php?action=search_title&vuln_title=oracle*.

(OSVDB 2006b)   Open Source Vulnerability Database. CRM software, *http://www.osvdb.org/searchdb.php?action=search_title&vuln_title=crm*.

(OSVDB 2006c)   Open Source Vulnerability Database. Lotus Domino, *http://www.osvdb.org/searchdb.php?action=search_title&vuln_title=lotus+domino*.

(OSVDB 2006d)   Open Source Vulnerability Database. Firewalls, *http://www.osvdb.org/searchdb.php?action=search_title&vuln_title=firewall*.

(Flake 2004)   Flake, Halvar. "Structural Comparison of Executable Objects," *http://www.sabre-security.com/files/dimva_paper2.pdf*.

(Moore 2006)   Moore, H. D. Metasploit Project, *http://www.metasploit.com*.

(eWeek 2005)   Fisher, Dennis, and Brian Fonseca. "Data Thefts Reveal Storage Flaws," *http://www.eweek.com/article2/0,1759,1772598,00.asp*. March 2005.

(CNN 2002)   Evers, Joris. "Ellison: Oracle remains unbreakable," *http://archives.cnn.com/2002/TECH/industry/01/21/oracle.unbreakable.idg/index.html*. January 2002.

(Security Innovation 2006)   Security Innovation, Inc. "Regulatory Compliance Demystified: An Introduction to Compliance for Developers," *http://msdn.microsoft.com/security/default.aspx?pull=/library/en-us/dnsecure/html/regcompliance_demystified.asp*. MSDN, March 2006.

(Howard, LeBlanc, and Viega 2005)   Howard, Michael, David LeBlanc, and John Viega. *19 Deadly Sins of Software Development*. New York, NY: McGraw-Hill, 2005. Chapter 4, "SQL Injection."

(Johansson 2005)   Johansson, Jesper. "Anatomy of a Hack," *http://www.microsoft.com/ australia/events/teched2005/mediacast.aspx*. Microsoft Tech.Ed, 2005).

(Red Database 2006)   Red Database Security. "Published Oracle Security Alerts," *http:// www.red-database-security.com/advisory/published_alerts.html*.

(ZDNet 2006c)   Espiner, Tom. "Google admits Desktop security risk," *http:// news.zdnet.co.uk/0,39020330,39253447,00.htm*. February 2006.

(Time 2006)   "Can We Trust Google with Our Secrets?" *Time*, February 20, 2006.

(NIAP 2005)   National Information Assurance Partnership, National Security Agency. "Protection Profiles," *http://niap.nist.gov/pp/index.html*.

(Microsoft 2003)   Microsoft Help and Support. "How To Prevent Auditable Activities When Security Log Is Full," *http://support.microsoft.com/kb/140058/*. Last Review: May 2003.

(OpenBSD 2004)   OpenBSD 3.6 release errata & patch list. "002: Reliability Fix," *http:// www.openbsd.org/errata36.html*. November 2004.

(CVE 2006)   Common Vulnerabilities and Exposures. *http://cve.mitre.org*.

(CVE 2005)   Christey, Steven M. "Re: Vulnerability Statistics," *http://seclists.org/lists/ webappsec/2005/Jan-Mar/0056.html*. January 2005.

(Gartner 2001)   Pescatore, John. "Nimda Worm Shows You Can't Always Patch Fast Enough," *http://www.gartner.com/DisplayDocument?doc_cd=101034*. September 2001.

(CRN 2006)   Rooney, Paula. "Is Windows Safer?" *http://www.crn.com/sections/coverstory/ coverstory.jhtml;jsessionid=VV1Q351RM5A1YQSNDBOCKH0CJUMEKJVN?articleId= 179103240*. February 2006.

(Secunia 2006a)   "Vulnerability Report: Apache 2.0.x," *http://secunia.com/product/73/*.

(Secunia 2006b)   "Vulnerability Report: Microsoft IIS 6.0," *http://secunia.com/product/1438/*.

(Zone-H 2006)   Zone-H, the Internet Thermometer. *http://www.zone-h.org*.

(CNET 2006)   Evers, Joris. "Allchin: Buy Vista for the security," *http://news.com.com/ Allchin+Buy+Vista+for+the+security/2100-1012_3-6032344.html?tag=st.prev*. January 2006.

Chapter 2

Current Software Development Methods Fail to Produce Secure Software

Software engineering companies and companies creating their own lines of business software have been looking forever for the classic "silver bullet" to deliver great quality software on time and under budget. As Fred Brooks mentions in the classic text *The Mythical Man-Month*, there is no such thing as the software silver bullet (Brooks 1995). The same lack of an easy solution applies to software security. In fact, we're going to go one step further and say that present software engineering practice in the industry does not lead to secure software at all. If any of the current state-of-the-art processes did create secure software, we'd simply see fewer security errata and bulletins from software vendors. But the industry suffers a huge security problem; everyone has security bugs, often very bad security bugs. This leads us to conclude that present security practices don't create secure code.

In this chapter, we'll look at a number of software development and certification processes to outline why they do not create code that is secure from attack. We'll look at the following:

- "Given enough eyeballs, all bugs are shallow"
- Proprietary software development methods
- Agile software development methods
- Common Criteria (CC)

Let's look at these in detail, outlining why each method does not produce more secure software.

"Given enough eyeballs, all bugs are shallow"

First discussed by Eric Raymond in his well-known paper "The Cathedral and the Bazaar," this is the battle cry of the open source movement (Raymond 1997). The more formal definition of the slogan, as expressed in the paper, is as follows:

> *Given a large enough beta-tester and co-developer base, almost every problem will be characterized quickly and the fix obvious to someone.*

Now before we start a religious debate, we want to explain something. Both authors have a deep respect for the open source software community; we both believe that opening source code is of value to some customers and users and that the ability to change code also has benefits for a few customers. But the software produced by the open source community is not secure from attack, and it most certainly is not secure simply because the code can be reviewed by many people. The concept of "Given enough eyeballs, all bugs are shallow" is wrong on many fronts: it assumes that people reviewing the code are motivated to review the code, that the people doing the reviews know what security bugs are, and that there is a critical mass of informed and motivated reviewers. But more important, and as we'll see, it just misses the point altogether. Let's look at each aspect in detail.

Incentive to Review Code

The author of this chapter (Michael) has worked with thousands of developers, teaching them how to review code and designs for security bugs. He has also reviewed more code than he cares to remember. And if he's learned one thing from all that experience, it's that most people don't enjoy reviewing code for bugs and vulnerabilities. Given the choice of reviewing code for bugs—including security bugs—or working on the newest feature in an upcoming software product, developers will choose writing new code. Developers are creative, and creating new features is the epitome of inventiveness. Another reason for not wanting to review code is that the task is slow, tiresome, and boring.

> **Note**   Based on analysis at Microsoft, at most an average developer can review about 1,500 lines of C code a day or 1,100 lines of C++ code a day looking for deep security bugs. It is, of course, possible to review code more quickly than this, but the quality of the review might suffer.

We have seen evidence of the distinct lack of will to review code in the open source community. For example:

> *The promise of open source is that it enables many eyes to look at the code, but in reality, that doesn't happen.*
> *—Crispin Cowan (Cowan 2002)*

Also, do not lose sight of a very simple maxim: the quality of code review—in other words, the ability to find real bugs versus finding false positives or missing bugs—is proportional to the code size under review. More code to review means you must have even more knowledgeable and motivated people reviewing the code.

Understanding Security Bugs

Understanding security vulnerabilities is critically important and is covered in detail in Chapter 5, "Stage 0: Education and Awareness." If your engineers do not know what constitutes a security bug, they will find none when reviewing the design of a component or the code underlying the design. As an example, unless you know what an HTTP Response Splitting attack is (Watchfire 2005), you won't see the security bug in the following code:

```
<% @ LANGUAGE=VBSCRIPT CODEPAGE = 1252 %>
<!--#include file="constant.inc"-->
<!--#include file="lib/session.inc"-->
<% SendHeader 0, 1 %>
<!--#include file="lib/getrend.inc"-->
<!--#include file="lib/pageutil.inc"-->

<%
'<!-- Microsoft Outlook Web Access-->
'<!-- Root.asp : Frameset for the Inbox window -->
'<!-- Copyright (c) Microsoft Corporation 1993-1997. All rights reserved.-->
On Error Resume Next
If Request.QueryString("mode") <> "" Then
    Response.Redirect bstrVirtRoot + _
        "/inbox/Main_fr.asp?" + Request.QueryString()
End If
```

This coding bug in the Microsoft Outlook Web Access component of Microsoft Exchange Server 5.5 is what led Microsoft to release a security bulletin, MS04-026 (Microsoft 2004). This kind of bug can lead to numerous security issues.

By the way, the coding bug is in the line that starts *Response.Redirect*.

Critical Mass

Next, the issue of critical mass: there must be enough knowledgeable people reviewing enough of the code often enough. Yes, there might very well be many people with security expertise working on some of the larger projects such as Apache and the Linux kernel, but that's an incredibly small number of people compared to the sheer volume of software being created that needs reviewing.

But let's assume for a moment that there *is* a critical mass of people who understand security bugs and are prone to audit code for security errors. You would think that it would be appropriate to change the "many eyes" mantra to "A critical mass of experienced and willing eyes makes all bugs shallow," but again, it misses the point of software engineering processes, our next topic.

"Many Eyeballs" Misses the Point Altogether

The goal of a good development process that leads to quality software is to reduce the chance that a designer, an architect, or a software developer will insert a bug in the first place. A bug that is not entered during the development process is a bug that does not need removing and that does not adversely affect customers. Make no mistake, there is absolutely a critical need for code review, but simply "looking for bugs" does not lead to a sustainable stream of secure software. Throwing the code "over the wall" for others to review for security bugs is wasted effort. A goal of the Security Development Lifecycle (SDL) is to reduce the chance that someone will enter security bugs from the outset.

In late 2004, the author of this chapter made a point in his blog about the number of security bugs in Microsoft Internet Information Services (IIS) 5 and IIS 6 and Apache 1.3.x and Apache 2.0.x, noting that because of the SDL, IIS 6 has had substantially fewer security bugs than IIS 5, but Apache 2.0.x had more than Apache 1.3.x (Howard 2004). A comment entered by an open source advocate named "Richard" (on blog page *http://blogs.msdn.com/ michael_howard/archive/2004/10/15/242966.aspx*) was, "Apache 2 is new. It is an immature product and is less secure because of it."

Apache 2.0.35 was the first "General Availability" release of Apache 2.0.x and was made available April 2002. It may be new relative to Apache 1.3.x, but it most certainly is not new. The belief that, over time, open source code quality will improve is a pretty typical view in the open source community. It may be true, but it is a naïve viewpoint: customers don't want code that will be of good quality in due course; they want more secure products from the outset.

Finally, most security professionals agree that the concept of "many eyeballs" leading to secure code is incorrect. Following are some quotes from well-known open source security experts.

> *"Experience shows this simply isn't true," the research firm states, calling it "the myth of more eyes," citing case after case where no one spotted critical flaws in open source code.*
> –Network World, *citing a Burton Group report (Burton 2005)*

> *Now, I'm not going to throw any of that "many eyeballs" nonsense at you–much of the code we use never gets audited.*
> –Jay Beale, Bastille Linux *(Beale 2002)*

> *Unless there's a great deal of discipline underlying the development, there's no difference in the security. Open source is not inherently more secure.*
> –Peter Neumann, principal scientist, SRI International *(eWeek 2002)*

In short, there is no empirical evidence whatsoever that "many eyes" lead to secure software. There is a great deal of opinion–but no hard facts–to back up the claim. In fact, a great deal of evidence exists to show that the "many eyes" concept *does not* lead to secure software. Take the preceding scenario—Apache 2.0 versus Apache 1.3 and IIS 5 versus IIS 6—as an example. A lack of motivation to review old code (instead of developing new code) and a lack of systematic security training for developers and testers has helped create this reality, as well as a lack of discipline in the profession to exploit lessons learned and discovered vulnerabilities.

Finally, numerous security bugs have existed in open source software for years, such as the following:

- **15 years**   Sendmail e-mail server (CVE-2003-0161)
- **10 years**   MIT's Kerberos authentication protocol (CVE-2003-0060)
- **7 years**   SAMBA file and print (CVE-2003-0085)
- **5 years**   MIT's Kerberos authentication protocols (CVE-2005-1689)
- **5 ½ years**   Eric Raymond's Fetchmail e-mail server (CVE-2002-0146)

> **Important**   Each bug in the preceding list is identified using a unique value assigned by MITRE Corporation. Some IDs start with CVE and some with CAN, so if you can't find, for example, CVE-2002-0146, try CAN-2002-0146. A link to each of these bugs is given at the end of this chapter in the "References" section.

Admittedly, closed source software security bugs can linger unseen for years. But it's not the closed source developers making the "many eyes" claim.

Again, we want to stress that this is not a slam against the open source community; "many eyes" is simply a myth that needs dispelling for the open source community to move onto producing better, more secure products. Why? Again, the skills aren't there, the motivation isn't there, and there is little sign of process improvement. Until the development processes improve in the open source community, no major decrease in the staggering number of security bugs will occur. And that's simply not good for customers.

Proprietary Software Development Methods

Each commercial software company has its own development method; some follow a classic waterfall model (Wikipedia 2002a), some use a spiral model (Wikipedia 2002b), some use the Capability Maturity Model, now referred to as Capability Maturity Model Integration (CMMI) (Carnegie Mellon 2000), some use Team Software Process (TSP) and the Personal Software process (PSP) (Carnegie Mellon 2003), and others use Agile methods. There is no evidence whatsoever that any of these methods create more secure software than another internal development method, judging by the number of security bugs fixed by commercial software companies such as IBM, Oracle, Sun, and Symantec each year that require customers to apply patches or change configurations. In fact, many of these software development methods make no mention of the word "security" in their documentation. Some don't even mention the word "quality" very often, either.

CMMI, TSP, and PSP

The key difference between the SDL and CMMI/TSP/PSP processes is that SDL focuses solely on security and privacy, and CMMI/TSP/PSP is primarily concerned with improving the quality and consistency of development processes in general—with no specific provisions or accommodations for security. Although certainly a worthy goal, this implicitly adopts the logic of "if the bar is raised on quality overall, the bar is raised on security quality accordingly." Although this may or may not be true, we don't feel that sufficient commercial development case study evidence exists to confirm or refute this either way. Our collective experiences from SDL are that adopting processes and tools specifically focused on demonstrably reducing security and privacy vulnerabilities have provided consistent examples of case study evidence testifying to improved security quality. Although we feel the verdict is still out on how effective CMMI/TSP/PSP are in improving security quality in software as compared to SDL, we'd assert that SDL is, at a minimum, a more optimized approach at improving security quality.

There is information about TSP and security (Over 2002), but it lacks specifics and offers no hard data showing software is more secure because of TSP.

Agile Development Methods

Agile development methods (Wikipedia 2006) such as Extreme Programming attempt to reduce the overall risk of a software development project by building software in very rapid iterations, often called timeboxes or sprints. These short turnarounds potentially allow for better customer feedback and interaction, time management, and schedule prediction.

The Microsoft Solutions Framework (MSF) for Agile Software Development (MSF 2006) adds some security checklists and threat modeling, and the latest version of Extreme Programming adds some security best practice, but it's very shallow and weak, focusing only on some programming practices for security. Having a list of security best practices and secure coding checklists is certainly better than nothing and will reduce the chance that some security bugs enter the design and the code, but it's not deep enough and it will catch only shallow security bugs. With all that said, there's no reason why SDL cannot be adopted by Agile methods, and we'll discuss this in Chapter 18, "Integrating SDL with Agile Methods."

Common Criteria

The Common Criteria (CC), also referred to as *ISO/IEC 15408* (Common Criteria 2006), is an international standard for computer security to assess the presence and assurance of security features. Its goal is to allow users to define their security requirements, have developers specify the security attributes of their products, and, finally, allow third-party evaluators to determine whether the products meet the stated claims. Common Criteria does not define standards for quality of design or code quality.

CC defines sets of assurance requirements, called Evaluation Assurance Levels (EALs), numbered from one (EAL1) to seven (EAL7). Higher numbers mean more evaluation effort, time, and money. The CC, at EAL4 and below, does not define standards for code or design quality. EAL5 and EAL6 do specify standards for design but not for code. The highest assurance level, EAL7, specifies both. A higher EAL does not necessarily mean that a product is more secure—it just means that the product under evaluation (called the Target of Evaluation, or TOE) has been more extensively analyzed and evaluated.

Important   A higher evaluation level, for example, EAL4 versus EAL3, does not necessarily imply "more secure."

Many people mistakenly associate CC with quality and therefore assume the software is resilient to attack. This is not true. Indeed, many products with CC certifications have had numerous successful attacks, including the following:

- Microsoft Windows 2000 (EAL4) (Microsoft 2000)
- Red Hat Enterprise Linux 4 (EAL3, in evaluation for EAL4) (Red Hat 2005)
- Oracle9i Release 9.2.0.1.0 (EAL4) (Oracle 2005)
- Trend Micro InterScan VirusWall (EAL4)

What CC does provide is evidence that security-related features perform as expected. For example, if a product provides an access control mechanism to objects under its control, a CC evaluation would provide assurance that the monitor satisfies the documented claims describing the protections to the protected objects. The monitor might include some implementation security bugs, however, that could lead to a compromised system. No goal within CC ensures that the monitor is free of all implementation security bugs. And that's a problem because code quality does matter when it comes to the security of a system.

Important   Design specifications miss important security details that appear only in code.

Summary

Present software development methods lack in-depth security awareness, discipline, best practice, and rigor, and this is evidenced by the sheer quantity of security patches issued each year by all software vendors. To remedy this, the industry must change its present engineering methods to build more secure software.

References

(Brooks 1995)   Brooks, Frederick P. *The Mythical Man-Month: Essays on Software Engineering,* 20th Anniversary Edition. Reading, MA: Addison-Wesley Publishing Co., 1995.

(Raymond 1997)   Raymond, Eric S. "The Cathedral and the Bazaar," *http://www.catb.org/ ~esr/writings/cathedral-bazaar/.* February 2006.

(Cowan 2002)   Cowan, Crsipin, quoted in "Group to boost code review for Linux," *http:// news.zdnet.com/2100-3513_22-830255.html.* February 2002.

(Watchfire 2005)   Watchfire Whitepapers. "HTTP Response Splitting, Web Cache Poisoning Attacks, and Related Topics," *http://www.watchfire.com/news/whitepapers.aspx.*

(Microsoft 2004)   "Vulnerability in Exchange Server 5.5 Outlook Web Access Could Allow Cross-Site Scripting and Spoofing Attacks (MS04-026)," *http://www.microsoft.com/ technet/security/bulletin/ms04-026.mspx.* August 2004.

(Howard 2004)   Howard, Michael. "Follow-up on IIS 6 and Apache Security," *http:// blogs.msdn.com/michael_howard/archive/2004/10/18/244181.aspx.* October 2004.

(Burton 2005)   Messmer, Ellen. "Open source vs. Windows: Security Debate Rages," *http:// www.networkworld.com/supp/2005/opensource/070405-open-source-security.html.* July 2005.

(Beale 2002)   Gross, Grant. "Bastille's Beale: How to Avoid Security Problems," *http:// newsforge.com/article.pl?sid=02/10/25/1728232.* November 2002.

(eWeek 2002)   Fisher, Dennis. "Open-Source Security Comes Under Fire," *http:// www.eweek.com/article2/0,1759,1656652,00.asp.* November 2002.

(CVE-2003-0161)   Common Vulnerabilities and Exposures. "Sendmail prescan() buffer over-run," *http://cve.mitre.org/cgi-bin/cvename.cgi?name=CVE-2003-0161.*

(CVE-2003-0060)   Common Vulnerabilities and Exposures. "MIT Kerberos v5 format-string bug," *http://cve.mitre.org/cgi-bin/cvename.cgi?name=CVE-2003-0060.*

(CVE-2003-0085)   Common Vulnerabilities and Exposures. "Buffer overrun in SAMBA," *http://cve.mitre.org/cgi-bin/cvename.cgi?name=CVE-2003-0085.*

(CVE-2005-1689)   Common Vulnerabilities and Exposures. "Double free in MIT Kerberos v5," *http://cve.mitre.org/cgi-bin/cvename.cgi?name=CVE-2005-1689.*

(CVE-2002-0146)   Common Vulnerabilities and Exposures. "Fetchmail buffer overrun," *http://cve.mitre.org/cgi-bin/cvename.cgi?name=CVE-2002-0146.*

(Wikipedia 2002a)   "Waterfall model," *http://en.wikipedia.org/wiki/Waterfall_model.*

(Wikipedia 2002b)   "Spiral model," *http://en.wikipedia.org/wiki/Spiral_model.*

(Carnegie Mellon 2000)   Carnegie Mellon Software Engineering Institute. Capability Maturity Model Integration, *http://www.sei.cmu.edu/cmmi/.*

(Carnegie Mellon 2003)   Carnegie Mellon Software Engineering Institute. "The Team Software Process (TSP) and the Personal Software Process (PSP)," *http:// www.sei.cmu.edu/tsp/*.

(Over 2002)   Over, James W. "Team Software Process^{SM} (TSP^{SM}) for Secure Systems Development," *http://www.sei.cmu.edu/tsp/tsp-secure-presentation/*.

(Wikipedia 2006)   "Agile software development," *http://en.wikipedia.org/wiki/ Agile_software_development*.

(MSF 2006)   Microsoft Corporation. "MSF for Agile Software Development," *http:// lab.msdn.microsoft.com/teamsystem/Workshop/msfagile/default.aspx*. March 2006.

(Common Criteria 2006)   Common Criteria Project. Common Criteria portal, *http:// www.commoncriteriaportal.org*.

(Microsoft 2000)   "The New Common Criteria Security Evaluation Scheme and the Windows 2000 Evaluation," *http://www.microsoft.com/technet/security/prodtech/windows2000/ secureev.mspx*. TechNet, 2000.

(Red Hat 2005)   "Red Hat Enterprise Linux 4 in Evaluation for Common Criteria Controlled Access Protection Profile Compliance (CAPP/EAL4+)," *http://www.redhat.com/ solutions/industries/government/commoncriteria/*.

(Oracle 2005)   Oracle Common Criteria press release, *http://www.oracle.com/corporate/ press/2005_feb/oid%20evaluation_0.html*. February 2005.

Chapter 3
A Short History of the SDL at Microsoft

This chapter describes the path that Microsoft followed in developing the Security Development Lifecycle (SDL) and offers a brief overview of the recent history and evolution of computer security practices. This history also makes clear why some current approaches to building more secure software don't work or don't work well enough to respond to evolving threats to software security.

First Steps

Microsoft designed MS-DOS, Microsoft Windows 3.1, and Windows 95 as single-user operating systems whose user would own and control all of the resources on the computer. Such a system doesn't require internal security controls that can protect one user from another because there is only one user on a system, and he or she controls everything. Windows 95 was designed to connect to corporate networks that provided shared file and printer infrastructures and to connect to the Internet as a client system, but the primary focus of security efforts was the browser—and even there, the understanding of security needs was much different from what it is today.

So Microsoft Windows NT 3.1 was the first Microsoft product for which operating system security was a significant design consideration. The core team that designed Windows NT largely came from Digital Equipment, where the team members had gained years of experience and had successfully developed large time-sharing systems used in major enterprises. They knew that any server or multiuser operating system would have to address security threats and protect one user from another, one application from another, and one process from another. In fact, many members of the Windows NT team had previously worked at Digital Equipment on a system that was targeted at a relatively high "B2" security evaluation by the United States government; they initially planned to seek B2 evaluation for Windows NT and reflected many of the security assurance requirements for B2 evaluation in the initial design of Windows NT. See the following sidebar for more information.

Security Evaluation

In the early 1980s, the United States government's National Security Agency (NSA) began the development of a set of evaluation criteria intended to characterize the security features and security assurance—or resistance to attack—of operating system software. These criteria—known as the Trusted Computer System Evaluation Criteria (TCSEC) or Orange Book after the color of its cover (DOD 1985)—guided the efforts of vendor operating system development teams from the early 1980s to the late 1990s. Most commercial operating systems of the period achieved "Class C2" evaluations. The higher levels of evaluation—Classes B2, B3, and A1—required high levels of modularity and structure at the design level, extensive documentation, and the implementation of an access control model that met the needs of defense and national security users. One of this book's authors (Lipner) was deeply involved during the early 1980s in the review of the NSA's drafts of the TCSEC and subsequently led a project at Digital Equipment to develop a system targeted at TCSEC Class A1 (Karger 1991).

By the late 1980s, other governments, including those of Canada and several European countries, had begun the development of their own security evaluation criteria applicable to operating system software and to other classes of products. Most of those countries' evaluation processes converged on the European Information Technology Security Evaluation Criteria, or ITSEC (ITSEC 1991). The structure of the ITSEC differed from that of the TCSEC in that security feature requirements and assurance requirements were treated separately.

By the mid-1990s, it had become obvious to vendors that neither commercial nor government customers were willing to make buying decisions based on compliance with the higher levels of evaluation specified by the TCSEC or ITSEC, and commercial product evaluations were thus limited to TCSEC Class C2 and the (roughly) equivalent ITSEC Class E3. In an effort to offer a wider market for evaluated products and to improve efficiency, the United States government and the European supporters of the ITSEC agreed in the late 1990s to support the Common Criteria for Information Technology Security Evaluation or, simply, the Common Criteria (Common Criteria 2005). The Common Criteria have received formal international recognition as ISO Standard 15408.

Microsoft products have undergone numerous evaluations under a variety of evaluation regimes. Because it became evident across the industry that customers did not require and would not buy systems that incorporated the features required by TCSEC Class B2,

Microsoft submitted Windows NT Versions 3.51 and 4.0 for evaluation at TCSEC Class C2 and at ITSEC Class E3. Microsoft SQL Server 2000 was also evaluated at Class C2 under the "database interpretation" of the TCSEC (NCSC 2000; ITSEC 1999). Recent Microsoft products, including Windows 2000, Windows XP, Microsoft Windows Server 2003, ISA Server 2004, and Exchange Server 2003, have completed evaluation at Class EAL4 of the Common Criteria, which is the highest evaluation level achieved by high-volume commercial products (Common Criteria 2006). Other Microsoft products are undergoing evaluation as this book is being written.

Although the basic design of Windows NT was structured similarly to a multiuser time-sharing system, by the time the system was widely deployed, it was used as a desktop client in applications that required a more robust operating system than Windows 95, and it was used as a file, print, or Internet server (HTTP, FTP, DNS, DHCP, etc.) system. Windows NT was designed with a high degree of modularity and consideration for security, and the resulting system was relatively secure compared to other multiuser systems of its day. However, as server applications gained in popularity, Windows NT quickly came face to face with the evolving threat environment of the Internet.

New Threats, New Responses

The mid-1990s saw the explosive growth of the Internet and, with it, the evolution of a new cottage industry specializing in discovering security vulnerabilities. Internet infrastructure components for UNIX, including Sendmail, BIND, and X Windows, were early targets of this industry, and Web browsers and Web servers did not lag far behind as targets. Discoveries of vulnerabilities in Netscape and Internet Explorer received wide publicity (CERT 1997). In this early stage of research into the vulnerability of Internet software, the vulnerability finders, for the most part, confined themselves to demonstrations aimed at building credibility for their security product companies or consulting practices, although there were instances of hostile attacks as early as the dawn of the commercial Internet (CERT 1994). Some security researchers chose to release "exploit code" that could be used to make use of the vulnerabilities, and in some cases, "script kiddies" took advantage of the exploit code to attack unpatched systems.

Because it became evident that discovery and disclosure of software vulnerabilities would be a continuing feature of the Internet-connected world, Microsoft took multiple steps to deal with the new realities. Prior to 1998, Microsoft had taken an ad hoc approach to dealing with discoveries of software vulnerabilities. Individual product teams handled communications with vulnerability finders. Product teams released fixes as security updates through their support organizations and on Microsoft's Web site, and the Windows marketing organization handled questions from the press concerning the discovery of new vulnerabilities in Windows.

In mid-1998, Microsoft created its Security Response Team to centralize the process of dealing with software vulnerabilities. Early team members included Jason Garms, Scott Culp, and coauthor of this book Steve Lipner. Security researchers were encouraged to report to a single well-known e-mail address (*secure@microsoft.com*), security updates were made public at a single Web site (*www.microsoft.com/security*), and the team handled press response to security issues associated with any Microsoft product. The new team's charter was to improve communications and relations with security researchers and communications with customers. The Security Response Team—predecessor of today's Microsoft Security Response Center (MSRC)—was widely acknowledged to have made a significant contribution to these objectives.

In parallel with the launch of the Security Response Team, Microsoft formed an internal Security Task Force to examine the underlying causes of vulnerabilities and to plot a course that could help to reduce vulnerabilities over time. That task force's set of recommendations forms the earliest precursor of the SDL. Viewed from a perspective seven years later, the task force's report appears prescient. Some of its key components included these recommendations:

- Focus on the need for management commitment

- Focus on the need for engineer awareness and training

- Use processes that are the precursors of today's threat modeling

- Apply tools and code review to detect and remove common coding errors that lead to potential security vulnerabilities

- Emphasize the importance of security testing, including "thinking like a hacker"

- Focus on the need for a post-release security response process

- Suggest that product groups organize for better security, including

    ❑ Establishing a dedicated security team within the product group

    ❑ Defining a consistent "security bug bar" to help evaluate the criticality of potential security vulnerabilities

    ❑ Tracking security bugs found and fixed and internalizing lessons learned from new kinds of security bugs

The Security Task Force pointed the way to the SDL, but it could not know and thus did not prescribe the level of resources or effort that would be required. Discovering how the process should work, identifying and committing the necessary resources, and coming to terms with the continuing evolution of security and threats required the next five years and launched a process that will never be static or "done."

Windows 2000 and the Secure Windows Initiative

The Security Task Force report coincided with the final stage of fixing bugs before the release of Windows 2000. Windows 2000 incorporated a great many new security features, including the use of Kerberos as the primary authentication protocol for Windows domains, integration of smartcards for user authentication, integration of a public key infrastructure and certificate server, integration of the IETF IPSEC protocol for network authorization and encryption, and the introduction of an Encrypting File System (EFS) to protect data stored on hard drives. However, it was clear that the value of the new security features could be put in jeopardy by a growing number of vulnerability reports. The management of the Microsoft Windows division took three key steps to implement the recommendations of the report:

- The deployment of an automated static analysis tool (PREfix) that could detect some classes of security vulnerabilities in source code, including some buffer overruns

- The deployment of a dedicated security penetration test team to find potential vulnerabilities in the Windows 2000 code base

- The creation of a dedicated security program management team—the Secure Windows Initiative (SWI) team—that was chartered to conduct design and code reviews and to work with component development teams to improve design and implementation before the product shipped

- Treatment of security vulnerabilities as a "ship-stopper" issue

PREfix was Microsoft's first static analysis tool. The PREfix-related technology was acquired when Microsoft acquired a startup company named Intrinsa. Many of the Intrinsa personnel joined the Programmer Productivity Research Center at Microsoft Research. In the late 1990s, PREfix could detect a few classes of stack-based buffer overruns by tracing the flow of input from an untrusted source to a stack buffer. Although the PREfix technology that was applied to Windows 2000 made a positive contribution and led to the removal of some classes of security vulnerabilities, it took several years of additional development—and additional discovery of new classes of vulnerabilities in a partnership between Microsoft Research and the SWI team—to evolve the tool into a highly effective one for writing more secure code. Nonetheless, the Windows 2000 experience introduced Windows developers to the notion that their code would be subject to automated analysis and that they'd be presented with automatically filed "security bugs" requiring analysis and correction.

The penetration test team was assembled of experienced Microsoft developers and testers who had shown an interest in security and talent for finding security vulnerabilities. The team reviewed the code of Windows components that they believed were security-critical or highly exposed to attack, found potential vulnerabilities, and filed bug reports to ensure that the bugs were fixed. The team was initially a small one—fewer than 10 engineers—and they developed their approaches to finding vulnerabilities as they went, based on their own experience with the security of older systems and on the lessons learned from vulnerability reports to the Security Response Team. The team established a good track record in the sense that many vulnerabilities that were externally reported against Windows NT had already been found by the penetration team, fixed in the evolving Windows 2000 code base, and scheduled for correction in an upcoming Windows NT service pack.

The initial SWI team was chartered to work with product teams by reviewing component designs and code and making recommendations (or filing bugs) that would lead to improved security. Initially, this team was even smaller than the penetration team (fewer than five members), and it was made up of Microsoft engineers with expertise in software security design and analysis as demonstrated by their accomplishments and contributions while working in Microsoft product development groups. The team's operational concept was to move from component team to component team, meeting with developers and program managers, making recommendations, and filing bugs. The limitation of this incarnation of the SWI team is obvious in retrospect—the team was too small to review all the Windows components.

The determination by Windows division management to treat security as a ship-stopper issue constituted a visible management commitment to security. Although the processes and resources applied during the development of Windows 2000 were a significant first step in improving the security of Microsoft software, the management commitment sent a message to middle managers and individual contributors that Microsoft's focus on security was changing and that the company was committed to improving it.

Seeking Scalability: Through Windows XP

After the release of Windows 2000, the penetration team and the SWI team continued to focus on the security of the Windows code base, turning their attention to Windows XP, the next planned release. Windows 2000 was shipping to customers, and vulnerability reports continued to arrive at a growing pace as security researchers turned their attention to the new product version. It was evident that the work done before Windows 2000 shipped, although useful, did not have sufficient impact on the product's security.

The SWI team of 2000–2001, in particular, revisited its operational concept and recognized that it was simply not going to be possible for a small team to conduct sufficient design and code reviews to materially improve the security of the next Windows release. After considering alternatives, the team made a fundamental change: SWI engineers would still be available to consult on specific security design and coding issues, but their focus would be on helping the engineers in product groups build more secure code. Instead of fishing for security vulnerabilities on behalf of the product groups, the SWI team would teach them how to fish. This change coincided with a broadening of the SWI charter to cover all "major" or enterprise Micrsosoft products, and it seemed likely to constitute a "scalable" approach to improving product security.

To implement their new approach, the SWI team focused on component team–wide "security days" or "bugbashes." Typically, such a day would begin with two to four hours of security training, followed by the component team spending the remainder of the day or more reviewing code and conducting penetration or other security testing. The team would file bugs against vulnerabilities that had to be eliminated and areas where the component design should be made more resistant to attack. Often, the SWI team presented prizes for the "best security bug" filed during the day.

The Windows penetration team continued its code reviews, finding additional vulnerabilities and other issues and filing bugs to ensure that they were fixed. More significantly, Microsoft's tool developers (the Programmer Productivity Research Center [PPRC]) continued to enhance PREfix to improve its ability to detect buffer overrun vulnerabilities and also developed a new tool known as PREfast, which is very effective at detecting buffer overruns in individual modules.

> **Note**   The major difference between PREfix and PREfast is that PREfix can find errors that span multiple programs or components, whereas PREfast is especially effective at finding errors in a single program. PREfix is maintained and operated by a central team that scans an entire product code base periodically. PREfast is executed by individual developers before they check in their code. PREfast has been released as the /Analyze feature of Microsoft Visual Studio 2005.

The Windows development organization continued its commitment to addressing security vulnerabilities when found, as evidenced by the fact that the Windows XP release was delayed to address a security bug (in the handling of encryption keys) discovered late in the development process.

Security Pushes and Final Security Reviews

The second half of 2001 was not a good time for Microsoft's reputation with respect to security issues. Mid-July saw the release of the Code Red Internet worm, which exploited a vulnerability in Windows 2000 systems running an Index Server Internet Server Application Programming Interface (ISAPI) filter within the Internet Information Services (IIS) 5 Web server component (CERT 2001a). In September, the Nimda worm exploited another vulnerability in IIS as well as a vulnerability in the Internet Explorer Web browser component (CERT 2001b). Although the vulnerabilities exploited by Code Red and Nimda had been addressed by security updates released before the worms were launched, the worms affected significant numbers of customer systems. Finally, late in the year, news of a buffer overrun vulnerability in the Universal Plug and Play (UPnP) component of Windows XP made headlines, although the vulnerability itself was never successfully exploited (CERT 2001c).

Even as the worms prowled the Internet and researchers continued to discover Windows vulnerabilities, Microsoft's top management was working on plans to make fundamental changes in the ways that Microsoft addressed security and privacy. The Trustworthy Computing (TwC) initiative was planned as a way of mobilizing Microsoft's staff and markedly improving the quality of Microsoft software. Trustworthy Computing was planned during late 2001 and launched with a January 2002 e-mail message from Bill Gates to all Microsoft employees (Microsoft 2002).

While Microsoft executives were working on the plans for the broad TwC effort, members of the SWI team were working with product groups to devise immediate steps that would improve the security of product versions nearing release. Microsoft's Developer Division was nearing release of the initial version of the Microsoft .NET Framework common language runtime (CLR), and in an effort to make the release as secure as possible, division management decided to delay the release and turn all of the engineers in the division to the task of reviewing code for security vulnerabilities and conducting penetration and other security tests. This effort—the first case of an effort that would come to be known as a security push—lasted for about six weeks and ended when the rate of discovery of security vulnerabilities dropped so much that further searching was unproductive. The outcome of this work was that a number of security bugs were fixed and extra defensive methods were added to the CLR and Microsoft ASP.NET to compensate for any missed security bugs (Paul and Evans 2006). The introduction of extra defensive methods led the SWI team to formalize the notion of measuring attack surface (Attack Surface Analysis [ASA]) and to advocate Attack Surface Reduction (ASR) as a way of compensating for the fact that you can never get the code one hundred percent correct (unless the code is trivially small in size). We'll discuss ASR in more detail in Chapter 7, "Stage 2: Define and Follow Design Best Practices."

Given the experience of the .NET Framework security push, the SWI team recommended that the management of the Windows division proceed with a similar security push focused on what was known at the time as Windows .NET Server and later would be renamed Windows Server 2003. At the time, Windows Server 2003 was in beta test and relatively close to its planned release date. This security push posed significant challenges: the Windows code base was roughly ten times larger than that of the .NET Framework, and it included legacy code (unlike the .NET Framework, which was a version 1 product) and associated constraints to maintain compatibility with former Windows versions. The Windows division also employed an engineering staff more than five times as large as that of the Developer division, so even logistics for the security push posed a major challenge.

Despite the challenges, and spurred on by the TwC commitment, the Windows division proceeded with its security push. The push began with training for more than 8,000 Windows division engineers (in late January 2002). Two members of the SWI team (author Michael Howard and his colleague David LeBlanc) had recently completed the first edition of *Writing Secure Code* in an effort to make lessons learned by the SWI team widely available to engineers inside and outside of Microsoft, and copies of *Writing Secure Code* were issued to all engineers who attended the security push training (Howard and LeBlanc 2002). Once the training was completed, the engineering staff turned to a series of activities planned by the SWI team and the Windows program management organization:

- Developing threat models to identify components and interfaces that might be vulnerable to attack.

- Devising design changes to improve default security and reduce the product's attack surface.

- Performing special runs of PREfix, PREfast, and other automated tools to detect potential vulnerabilities. Because PREfix and PREfast are extensible, the security push included iterative additions of code to these tools to enable them to detect new classes of potential vulnerabilities.

- Reviewing code to find and remove both identified vulnerabilities and dangerous coding constructs that might lead to vulnerabilities.

- Bad-parameter checking and penetration testing to identify vulnerabilities and areas where the code might be unreliable or unstable.

The Windows security push was initially planned to take place through February 2002. As the scope of the work involved became clear, the duration of the push was extended through the end of March 2002. At the end of the push, many security bugs had been filed and many design changes were specified, including those affecting attack surface. In the following months, Windows division engineers went on to fix the bugs and code and test the design changes.

By late 2002, Windows Server 2003 was largely ready to ship. The product was in the Release Candidate stage, which involves final testing by customers and the Microsoft IT organization. Around that time, the Microsoft executive responsible for Windows Server 2003 development asked members of the SWI team how they felt about the outcome of the security push and the other work that had been done on the new release. To answer this seemingly simple question, the SWI team launched a series of actitivies, including a review of bugs that had been filed as security bugs, an evaluation of the server release in the context of externally discovered vulnerabilities affecting prior Windows versions and competing products, and penetration tests by SWI team members and outside contractors.

The activities undertaken to assess the security of Windows Server 2003 led the SWI team to the conclusion that the work of the security push had largely been successful, and that Windows Server 2003 was on track to set a new standard for Microsoft operating system security. However, in reviewing the security of the Windows Server 2003 code base, the team discovered a few new classes of vulnerabilities (which were fixed before the software was released) and found that there were a few areas of the system where additional work would produce additional security benefits. They also determined that the browser component of Windows (Internet Explorer) needed significant security work before its security would be comparable to the rest of Windows Server 2003. Because the product was a server release, browsing arbitrary Web sites was not a primary usage scenario, so the SWI team and the product team worked together to "lock down" the browser, blocking most scenarios in which vulnerabilities might occur by default. (More fundamental changes to improve the security of Internet Explorer without requiring configuration lockdown were undertaken for Windows XP Service Pack 2 and Windows Server 2003 Service Pack 1, and even more significant changes aimed at further improving security are reflected in Internet Explorer 7, the browser component of the forthcoming Windows Vista.)

In addition to the browser changes, the Windows development team changed to a new compiler that incorporated enhanced run-time detection of attempts to exploit buffer overruns. This was the second security-related compiler change for Windows Server 2003—the first was made at the time of the Windows security push. Windows Server 2003 was launched in April 2003 and has had a much better security track record than its predecessors or competing products: roughly a factor of two in reduction of security vulnerabilities rated "critical" or "important" by MSRC.

The discussions in this section have focused on the Windows security push and the activities taken to improve the security of Windows Server 2003. The initiation of Trustworthy Computing in early 2002, in fact, mobilized product groups across Microsoft and led to security pushes—and, in some cases, prerelease security reviews—for a number of products or product service packs. Key among these products were Microsoft Office 2003, SQL Server 2000 Service Pack 3, and Exchange 2000 Server Service Pack 3. In every case, the result of these efforts was improved security. In some cases, the improvements were especially dramatic. For example, Microsoft issued 16 security bulletins addressing vulnerabilities in SQL Server 2000 from its initial release in late 1999 through the release of Service Pack 3 in January 2003. In the subsequent three years, through March 2006, Microsoft issued only three security bulletins related to SQL Server 2000.

Through most of 2003, the SWI team continued to work with product groups to provide training, help organize security pushes, and conduct pre-ship reviews—originally referred to as "security audits" but now called Final Security Reviews (FSRs) to avoid confusion with financial or operational audits—on software that was close to release. These efforts were effective, and the products shipped during this period showed reduced vulnerability rates, but the process that the SWI team followed was still ad hoc. The team was guided by documents that were produced (especially by Michael Howard) at the end of the Windows Server 2003 security push, and it was guided by an "oral tradition" of effective practices and issues to watch out for. It was clear that the process was effective, but it was less clear what the process itself was!

Formalizing the Security Development Lifecycle

In late 2003 and early 2004, members of the SWI team held a series of meetings with senior managers across Microsoft's product development organizations. The focus of these meetings was to review the results achieved since the first security pushes and to revisit the requirements that would have to be met to put in place a consistent and effective security engineering process. These meetings culminated in a decision at high levels of the management at Microsoft to replace the ad hoc process of training, security pushes, and FSRs with a mandate declaring that essentially all Microsoft products must meet the requirements of a formally defined Security Development Lifecycle. The SDL mandate applies to any software that meets these criteria:

- The software is regularly used in an enterprise, business, government agency, or other organization.

- The software is regularly used to process personal or sensitive information.

- The software is regularly used to connect to the Internet. (This requirement is not met by software that interacts with the Internet only to update its code or databases by connecting to a Microsoft-operated Internet server.)

The formal definition of the SDL—which has evolved into the process described in Part II of this book—proceeded in parallel with the series of meetings that established the SDL mandate and informed senior management across Microsoft of the existence of the mandate and its implications for product groups. The formal version of the SDL was designated as SDL Version 2.0 in recognition of the fact that many product versions had undergone an earlier (and less formal) SDL process during the era of security pushes and the first FSRs.

> **More Info**   Part II of this book, "The Security Development Lifecycle Process," describes the SDL stage by stage—from "Stage 0: Education and Awareness" through "Stage 12: Security Response Execution."

The transition to SDL Version 2.0 was completed by 1 July 2004. By that time, well over half of Microsoft's engineering population had completed the new security training mandated by SDL, and the formal requirements for SDL compliance were posted on an internal Web site. The staffing of the SWI team grew significantly between January and June of 2004 to provide the level of effort needed to

- Conduct security training.
- Develop and update the definition of the SDL itself.
- Develop and support tools the use of which was mandated by the SDL.
- Provide advice and consultation on the SDL to product teams.
- Conduct Final Security Reviews before product release.

The SWI team has continued to grow since July 2004 as the process has evolved and the requirements of implementing it have become clearer. The SWI team updates the SDL itself at six-month intervals. SDL Version 2.1 went into effect in January 2005, and Version 2.2 became effective in July 2005. SDL Version 3.0, a major revision that incorporated privacy requirements for Microsoft products, went into effect in January 2006.

A Continuing Challenge

This chapter has summarized the history of the SDL at Microsoft from earliest attempts to improve software security to a formally defined process that is supported by a relatively large staff and subject to regular updates. The reference to updates might prompt the reader to ask, "When will you be done?" Neither of the authors believes that the process of building secure software will ever be "done." That's why the SDL process includes security responses. See Chapter 14, "Stage 9: The Final Security Review," and Chapter 16, "Stage 11: Security Response Execution."

We expect the discovery of new ways to attack software—and new classes of vulnerabilities—to go on forever. Security researchers will continue to seek new classes of vulnerabilities at the design and implementation levels that are not addressed by current security techniques. People who try to build more secure software will continue their efforts by finding new ways to make software more resistant to attack and by developing tools and techniques that respond to new classes of attack when they are discovered. Although the people working on more secure software will make the security researchers' and attackers' jobs harder and will reduce the set of products and features that can be attacked, the combination of new classes of products and new classes of vulnerabilities means that the problem of making software secure will never go away.

We know that applying the techniques of the SDL can make the attacker's job harder—the vulnerability statistics for software versions that were developed with the SDL process (and its immediate predecessors) show that. But better is not the same as perfect. We also know that new discoveries of classes of vulnerabilities will require new techniques and tools. That's why we continue to update the SDL, and security response is an integral part of the process. We've written this book to give other development organizations a framework for making their software more resistant to attack and for organizing their own process to respond to the continuing challenge of software security.

References

(DOD 1985)   Department of Defense Standard. Department of Defense Trusted Computer System Evaluation Criteria, (DOD 5200.28-STD, Supercedes CSC-STD-001-83, dtd 15 Aug 83), *http://www.radium.ncsc.mil/tpep/library/rainbow/5200.28-STD.html*. 26 December 1985.

(Karger 1991)   Karger, P. A., M. E. Zurko, D. W. Bonin, A. H. Mason, and C. E. Kahn. "A Retrospective on the VAX VMM Security Kernel," *Transactions on Software Engineering*, 17(11):1147–1165. November 1991.

(ITSEC 1991)   Commission of the European Communities. Information Technology Security Evaluation Criteria, Provisional Harmonised Criteria, Version 1.2, *http://www.oc.ccn.cni.es/pdf/ITSEC.pdf*. 28 June 1991.

(Common Criteria 2005)   Common Criteria Project. Common Criteria for Information Technology Security Evaluation, Version 2.3, *http://www.commoncriteriaportal.org/public/developer/index.php?menu=2*. August 2005.

(NCSC 2000)   National Computer Security Center. Trusted Product Evaluation Program, Evaluated Products List by Vendor, *http://www.radium.ncsc.mil/tpep/epl/epl-by-vendor.html#Microsoft*. August 2000.

(ITSEC 1999)   Information Technology Security Evaluation Criteria, E3–F/C2 Evaluation, *http://www.microsoft.com/technet/archive/security/topics/issues/e3-fc2ev.mspx*. April 1999.

(Common Criteria 2006)   Common Criteria Project. List of Evaluated Products, *http://www.commoncriteriaportal.org/public/consumer/index.php?menu=4*.

(CERT 1997) Carnegie Mellon Software Engineering Institute, CERT Coordination Center. "CERT Advisory CA-1997-20 JavaScript Vulnerability," *http://www.cert.org/advisories/CA-1997-20.html*. July 1997.

(CERT 1994) Carnegie Mellon Software Engineering Institute, CERT Coordination Center. "CERT Advisory CA-1994-07 wuarchive ftpd Trojan Horse," *http://www.cert.org/advisories/CA-1994-07.html*. April 1994.

(CERT 2001a) Carnegie Mellon Software Engineering Institute, CERT Coordination Center. "CERT Advisory CA-2001-19 'Code Red' Worm Exploiting Buffer Overflow in IIS Indexing Service DLL," *http://www.cert.org/advisories/CA-2001-19.html*. July 2001.

(CERT 2001b) Carnegie Mellon Software Engineering Institute, CERT Coordination Center. "CERT Advisory CA-2001-26 Nimda Worm," *http://www.cert.org/advisories/CA-2001-26.html*. September 2001.

(CERT 2001c) Carnegie Mellon Software Engineering Institute, CERT Coordination Center. "CERT Advisory CA-2001-37 Buffer Overflow in UPnP Service on Microsoft Windows," *http://www.cert.org/advisories/CA-2001-37.html*. December 2001.

(Microsoft 2002) Microsoft Corporation. Executive E-mail, "Trustworthy Computing," *http://www.microsoft.com/mscorp/execmail/2002/07-18twc.asp*. July 2002.

(Paul and Evans 2006) Paul, Nathaniel, and David Evans. University of Virginia, Department of Computer Science, "Comparing Java and .NET Security: Lessons Learned and Missed," *http://www.cs.virginia.edu/~nrp3d/papers/computers_and_security-net-java.pdf*.

(Howard and LeBlanc 2002) Howard, Michael, and David LeBlanc. *Writing Secure Code*, 1st ed. Redmond, WA: Microsoft Press, 2002.

Chapter 4
SDL for Management

This chapter tells managers what they need to know about the Security Development Lifecycle (SDL). Our major focus is the role of managers in making the SDL succeed: what the manager or executive must do to ensure that his or her team can build more secure software.

Another purpose of this chapter is to prepare the manager or executive to deal with the impact of the SDL on development projects: what kinds of resources will be required, what impact the SDL will have on costs and schedules, and how the manager should assess whether the project is on track to comply with SDL requirements.

Commitment for Success

It is very important that managers understand the SDL's impact on the software they produce and the expectations that SDL places on the stakeholders in their organizations. SDL is not free—it requires time, money, and the strong commitment of senior managers to prioritize security over other factors such as time to market and compatibility with older, less secure software versions. One key measure of success for this chapter is if a senior executive reads it and walks away saying: "Yes, that makes perfect business sense."

Commitment at Microsoft

In their "day jobs," the authors often brief Microsoft customers and partners on the inner workings of the SDL, explaining how Microsoft is using the process to create more secure products. One question that we frequently hear is: "What component or aspect of the SDL has been most important to its success?" There is no easy answer to this because the SDL is an integrated process that comprises a large number of individual and equally important phases. The viability of the SDL within an organization such as Microsoft is intimately tied to the fact that each phase is necessary and contributes to improved product security. If any phase were unimportant, the SDL team would have to remove or modify it or face a loss of credibility for the entire process. Training, which is not so much a discrete phase as a cross-cutting component that affects all phases, usually makes the "extremely important" list, as does threat modeling.

> **Note**   Every task within SDL is there for a reason: it leads to more secure software. If any task were deemed ineffective, it would be removed from SDL.

Still, executive commitment to the SDL process is the key factor for success. Bill Gates sent e-mail committing Microsoft to a sustained drive toward Trustworthy Computing, telling individual contributors, middle managers, and senior executives throughout the company that the rules and priorities for Microsoft's development teams had changed. And the fact that the group and senior vice-presidents responsible for Microsoft Windows Server 2003 (and other products) decided to stop development and delay schedules in order to conduct security pushes and complete Final Security Reviews told everyone concerned that Microsoft was willing to do what was necessary—in terms of longer product schedules and extra staff effort—for improved security. Of course, shipping on time is extremely important at Microsoft (and in most other software companies), so this was a very significant change and one that managers might be expected to resist. The commitment of the most senior executives in the company to delaying products as needed to improve security told all concerned that Trustworthy Computing was a reality and not just a slogan. And the continued commitment by Microsoft's top management to Trustworthy Computing and the SDL has led to a culture change at Microsoft— today, everyone knows that product groups must do what it takes to meet security requirements before they ship their products.

In the authors' view, managers' and executives' most important contribution to the SDL is support for the process. And executive support for the SDL has been the key factor in making the process successful and effective.

> **Important**   The biggest single factor in the success of SDL is executive support.

To lead effectively at Microsoft, managers must understand and get involved in the issues and challenges that confront their organizations. This means that managers must understand the security problems that their products pose and commit to resolving those problems. The facts that motivated this commitment at Microsoft were discussed briefly in Chapter 3, "A Short History of the SDL at Microsoft Corporation":

- Customers were complaining about the frequency and cost of patching for security vulnerabilities.

- Actual attacks manifested in the form of worms and viruses were disrupting customers' IT operations to an extent that made the attacks very visible to both operations staffs and end users.

- Press coverage was focusing on security problems to the point of overshadowing product improvements.

- The need for frequent patching diverted Microsoft developers' time and attention away from new features and new code and toward responding to security vulnerabilities. Although the costs of patch development were not great in absolute terms, the frequent need to divert developers to patching made development schedules less predictable—and conveyed to teams and their managers the dimensions of the security challenge.

In sum, real-world business considerations dictated that Microsoft address customers' needs for improved security and more than justified the investment in the SDL. Not only is it more efficient to build watertight boats than to divert the shipwrights to plugging leaks, but the customers are much happier with the results.

Is the SDL Necessary for You?

Because implementing the SDL is expensive—and the authors have already made it pretty clear that it's not cheap—any effective manager is going to ask whether the SDL is really necessary. The answer is, of course, "It depends." If customers rely on the security of your software, then it behooves you to ensure that the software you supply is up to the challenge. Platform products—operating systems, database systems, e-mail and collaboration servers—obviously fall into this category because they must protect the confidentiality and integrity of user data and because the computing resource provided by the platform must remain available even in the face of hostile attack. But security is equally vital in other kinds of products, including e-commerce (Web) applications and many of the line-of-business applications that are used within organizations (where sensitive data must be handled and not all users are equally trusted or authorized). Many applications developed by government contractors handle sensitive information, which demands stringent security measures. Although the security of these applications could be circumvented if the underlying platform were insecure, attackers will target the applications themselves if security measures at the platform level make attacks there costly or infeasible.

The extent of the challenge that any particular software product or package faces depends on how exposed the software is to potential threats and on the value of the information that it is used to process. In Chapter 3, we summarized Microsoft's tests for the applicability of the SDL to software products—software that is used in a business or organization, software that is exposed to the Internet, or software that is used to process sensitive or personal information. When considering the application of the SDL to in-house (line-of-business) applications, it's important to focus on the impact on the business if the data were disclosed, modified, or destroyed. Recent attention in the media and by government and consumer advocates to disclosures of customer data have reemphasized the potential impact of security failures in e-commerce and line-of-business applications.

The security of Microsoft software has historically (at least since the mid-1990s) been exposed to special scrutiny because of its wide deployment in personal , business, and organizational environments. A researcher who discovers a vulnerability in Microsoft software might have found a way to attack millions of systems and their users! And the popularity of vulnerability research on Microsoft software has provided a degree of "cover" for smaller development organizations. However, recent (as of 2005 and 2006) trends in the discovery and publication of software vulnerabilities have demonstrated that if the work required to attack a Microsoft software product increases, the vulnerability seekers will look elsewhere.

> **Note**   As Microsoft enhances the default security of its products, attackers are turning their attention to lower-hanging fruit—other software in which security best practices have not been followed.

In one case that the authors consider a significant success for the SDL, vulnerability finders radically reduced their attention to Microsoft SQL Server software–which had previously been a prime target–and focused their efforts on Oracle database products (Mogull 2006). Even if vulnerabilities remain in SQL Server–and we are sure that it has not yet achieved perfection–users of this particular Microsoft product are safer because new vulnerabilities are not being discovered or exploited. In a similar development, the SysAdmin, Audit, Networking, and Security (SANS) Institute reported that vulnerability finders were increasingly focusing on security and backup software that users had acquired with the expectation that such software would keep their systems and data safe (SANS 2005).

The fact that vulnerability finders will seek alternative targets whose vulnerabilities are easier to find than those in Microsoft software has a direct bearing on the priority of the SDL for both software vendors and enterprises' internal IT development organizations. Vulnerability finders have never confined themselves exclusively to Microsoft software, and it's clear that their attention to other vendors' products is increasing: this trend is evident from the National Vulnerability Database maintained by the U. S. National Institute of Standards and Technology (NIST 2006). There have already been comments in the media to the effect that enterprise line-of-business IT systems are the next target for security researchers and security attacks. The developing trend toward targeted attacks focused on financial gain rather than on Internet vandalism also makes enterprise applications an appealing target.

You might want to know where it's *not* necessary to apply the SDL in software development. The answer is that most software sold to customers or used by an organization or business should go through the process! Some standalone games or other entertainment products that don't handle sensitive information or touch the Internet are exceptions, as are applications developed by an organization for very limited use (such as one-time data analysis applications). However, even software that does not otherwise qualify for application of the SDL should be reviewed to ensure that it does not somehow compromise or expose the platform on which it's run–for example, by installing unprotected user accounts or modifiable executable files.

In summary, we believe that the rules that Microsoft uses (enterprise application; exposure to the Internet; sensitive information) to determine applicability of the SDL can serve as a guide for other organizations that are trying to decide whether they need to apply the SDL to their development efforts. Of course, we leave the precise determination of need to each product vendor or IT organization, but as a general principle, we believe that most software development organizations—whether vendors of packaged software, developers of e-commerce applications, or in-house line-of-business developers—will need to deploy a process similar to the SDL at some point.

Effective Commitment

If you have decided that it's necessary to apply the SDL to some or all of the software that your organization develops, what do you as a manager have to do to ensure that your organization's efforts are effective? The next few paragraphs summarize actions that we believe a manager should take to support the application of the SDL in his or her organization.

Make a Statement

If you believe that it's important for your development teams to implement the SDL and produce more secure software, you have to make that belief clear. At Microsoft, Bill Gates sent his Trustworthy Computing e-mail, but that was not all. Jim Allchin (then the group vice-president of the Platforms Group) personally kicked off the briefing/training session when we started to engage component team managers in the planning of the Windows security push, and Brian Valentine (the senior vice-president of the Windows Division) sent division-wide e-mails telling his employees what we were about and why it was important. The same story applies to the Microsoft Exchange and SQL Server products.

> **Note**   Contrary to what you might read in the press, the various security pushes across Microsoft were not the method by which we shipped more secure software—they were simply the start of a long journey.

The preceding examples are specific to Microsoft, and although experience has shown that the methods introduced in this book are much more effective than conducting a one-shot security push, the need for an executive statement remains. The people who are designing, writing, and testing the code need to hear from you and understand that you believe the changes to their work involved in implementing the SDL are important, and why.

Be Visible

It is not sufficient to make a single statement about the importance of the SDL and expect your subordinates to follow through on their own. As with everything that managers do, follow-up is important. During the Microsoft Windows security push, Brian Valentine and the vice-presidents who worked for him sent status e-mails, held periodic meetings, and engaged with people across their organizations to remind them of how important security was to the success of their products. We identified the teams and individuals who were doing the best jobs of finding security bugs and recognized them with public statements and prizes. Today, with the SDL a normal part of product development at Microsoft, executives continue to communicate, in e-mails and team meetings, the importance of security and the necessity of meeting the requirements of the SDL. It's very important for you to provide reminders, recognition, and rewards consistent with the culture of your organization to encourage effective execution of the SDL.

Again, our task of organizing and executing visible recognition during the many product security pushes was relatively simple. Security was the only thing the teams were working on, and the duration of each push was finite. But there are many milestones and deliverables in the SDL (threat models built, legacy code or interfaces removed or disabled, tests completed, bugs found) that offer opportunities for statements, recognition, and reinforcement by management. You should take advantage of these opportunities to ensure that your teams know what you expect and know that you are watching and intend to encourage behaviors that lead to more secure software.

Provide Resources

Earlier, we mentioned that implementing the SDL had a significant impact on product schedules at Microsoft, and we'll talk about how significant later. But you should know that there is a cost to implementing the elements of the SDL, and if you're serious about shipping more secure software, you'll need to pay that up-front cost. (We know that customer satisfaction with the security of Microsoft products that have undergone the SDL has improved, and we are confident that the SDL has more than paid for itself in improved customer satisfaction and reduced impact of vulnerabilities on customers and on Microsoft teams.) When you look at development schedules and tools budgets—to take two examples—elements of the SDL are almost certain to be visible if your teams are executing the process "right," especially if they are just introducing the SDL to your development organizations. You'll have the choice of signing off on those resources and making it clear that you believe they're important, or "pushing back" and expecting your organization to implement the SDL on the cheap. Software security is an area in which you get what you pay for; if your teams are asking for the resources to implement the SDL in an honest and effective way, support them.

The most striking example of providing resources that we've seen came, again, during the Windows security push. As we were starting to plan the push, we held an initial meeting with one of the Windows Server 2003 project managers and got an offer to stop development for two working days while the teams working on the server product attended training, did code reviews, ran tools, built threat models, and did penetration testing. Given the magnitude of the product and that this was our initial security push, that offer was woefully inadequate to the need, and we persevered with a request for a longer security push. Eventually, we got a commitment for a four-week security push and began executing it. As the scope of the work became clear, it was evident that even a four-week push would not accomplish what was needed, and the senior management of the Windows Division (with the complete agreement of the project manager who'd initially made the offer of a two-day push) extended the duration of the push from four weeks to eight. Of course, we all had to do our homework regarding what kind of effort was needed, how long it would take, and why it was important—but the point was that management provided the resources that the work really demanded. The key aspect of this commitment is that the security push was finished when the work of the push was complete, not when some arbitrary date arrived.

Stop Products

We wish that this last component of effective commitment were never necessary, and in your organization it might not be. But one aspect of management support for the SDL is being prepared to recognize when a product is not ready to ship and making the decision to delay until it is. The suggestion to "stop products" might make you think of getting close to shipping and then realizing that the product isn't secure enough, and that is indeed one possibility. But in reality, a decision to stop or delay shipping can come in a variety of flavors, at a variety of times, and for a variety of reasons.

- The rates of discovery of security bugs might be unacceptably high, and you might need to allow more time for the rate to drop to the point at which your security review and penetration testing teams are being frustrated by the high level of security of the product they are reviewing and testing.

- It might become evident that a feature not only is insufficiently secure, but that it will never be made sufficiently secure. You might have to make the hard decision to remove the feature from the product.

- Your internal security team, or an outside security researcher, might discover a new class of vulnerability that neither you nor anyone else had previously known about. You might have to decide whether to ship with vulnerable code or to delay the product and eliminate the root cause of the problem.

- Finally, a component or an entire product might fail the Final Security Review (FSR) that comes toward the end of the SDL and assesses "fitness to ship." You might have to support the FSR team and delay the product until it can pass.

The best example we know of stopping a product—and one that took considerable commitment to security—was the case of the Microsoft .NET Framework and .NET common language runtime (CLR). Before there even was an SDL, and without knowing precisely what steps would address their security concerns, the management of the Framework team decided that the rate of discovery of security vulnerabilities in their code was too high and delayed their ship schedule, and they launched the first security push, at that time called a "security stand-down." Not only were security bugs found and fixed, but the default configuration of the .NET Framework and CLR were made more conservative to maximize the chance of mitigating any defects that might be left in the code. (In the four years since its release—after the stand-down—the .NET Framework and CLR have been the subject of only three security updates addressing externally discovered vulnerabilities, and none of these was in the core framework runtime software.) We wish that the need to "stop ship" never arose, but we've lived through examples of each of the cases listed here and seen product group executives at Microsoft make the right decisions for security at the cost of schedule and/or features.

Managing the SDL

In this section, we provide you with some thoughts on the resources you'll have to commit to implementing the SDL in your organization. Unfortunately, this section won't give you prescriptive guidance about resource requirements for the SDL. The reason is that almost everything we can say about resources begins with "it depends . . ." We'll also suggest how a manager or executive can tell whether a development project is on track in implementing the SDL.

Resources

We know from experience that there are a great many variables that determine the resources needed to implement the SDL, and we have a good idea of the ways in which they affect the resources needed to implement the SDL successfully. But we can't yet give you a set of equations that says, for example: "For this code size and this implementation language and this level of exposure to the Internet, here's the factor that you should apply to the planned development resource level to get to SDL compliance." One reason is that we don't really collect fine-grained resource data at Microsoft. Unlike defense contractors or other services firms that do development at an hourly rate, Microsoft typically assigns a team to own one or more products and allocates the cost of the team to the product. There's no attempt to identify the finer-grained costs of individual activities within the development process. So the salaries of testers on Windows are charged to the current Windows release, whether those testers are testing new features for application compatibility or doing security "fuzz testing" as part of the SDL.

Factors That Affect the Cost of SDL

Despite our lack of quantitative guidance on the costs of the SDL, we can identify some of the factors that we know to make a difference in implementing the SDL effectively. We believe that most of these factors will be just common sense, but we hope that a few will surprise some readers:

- Implementing the SDL is cheapest if it's being applied to a project that is building a product or application from scratch. Your ability to choose languages, coding standards, and tools with security in mind—and to avoid mistakes rather than fix them—makes for efficiency in time and effort.

- Similarly, applying the SDL to a mass of "legacy code" (written before security was a consideration) is expensive. The teams have to find problems, make changes, and then ensure that their changes don't cause any problems, such as backward compatibility, with the correct functioning of the product or component.

■ From the two preceding items, it follows that the second and subsequent releases of code that has gone through the SDL should be less costly than the first. The first SDL release pays the price, in time and schedule, to clean up most of the latent problems, and subsequent releases can concentrate on preventing defects from being entered in the first place and on looking for newly discovered classes of vulnerabilities.

■ All things being equal, it will be easier to apply the SDL to a language that produces managed code—such as C#, Microsoft Visual Basic .NET, or Java—than to an unmanaged one such as C or C++. Although it's absolutely *not* the case that managed code is guaranteed to be secure, there are classes of security vulnerabilities that developers can't introduce in managed code. For example, it's not possible to write a buffer overrun in C#, as it is in C or C++, although it is still possible for a developer to write an application in C# that is vulnerable to a SQL injection attack. The fact that it's not possible to include certain kinds of vulnerabilities in an application written in managed code saves the effort that would otherwise be required to look for, find, and remove them.

■ It is often both better—that is, more secure—and cheaper to remove a feature than to fix it. Obviously, if you applied this rule in an extreme way, you would ship nothing at all, and it would be perfectly secure. That is not what we are suggesting. But if you are faced with a feature or component that presents significant security problems and is either not widely used or obsolete, it might be better to remove it or disable it by default than to bring it up to a level of security appropriate to the current threat environment. Note that disabling by default can be—but should not be—a crutch for shipping an insecure design or security bug–ridden code. If a feature or component is insecure and off by default, but you know that many users will enable it, you should either pay the price to fix it or bite the bullet and remove it.

■ Tools are almost always more effective and more efficient than a manual search for implementation vulnerabilities. This does not mean, however, that such tools are a panacea and find all security bugs. Tools can parse vast quantities of code rapidly, faster than a human could, but tools are no replacement for humans. You may have read or heard of the major Microsoft tools, such as PREfast, that we use to scan unmanaged code for buffer overruns and some other kinds of vulnerabilities. But we also build tools as needed when a new kind of vulnerability is discovered and we believe that it might occur throughout a product or set of products. For example, we've built testing tools to find and report classes of remote procedure call (RPC) vulnerabilities and scanning tools to find and report common errors in system configuration.

■ A product or component with a long history of security vulnerabilities, or a product that has exhibited security vulnerabilities resulting from design (rather than code) errors, is likely to be costly to bring to an acceptable level of security. It might be tempting to say that you have "done enough" to such a product, but this is the area in which you can easily deceive yourself. It's much better to pay what it costs to find and remove vulnerabilities than to watch the new vulnerability reports keep rolling in!

■ Training helps to reduce the cost of security. This might sound obvious, but it's still worth emphasizing: an effective training program will motivate your designers and developers to produce more secure software in the first place. The code reviews, tools, and testing will find fewer problems, and implementing the SDL will be quicker and cheaper.

■ Secure designs reduce the number of code-level errors that result in security vulnerabilities and reduce the severity of the vulnerabilities that remain. As a result, code reviews, tools, and testing will find fewer security vulnerabilities that need to be addressed.

Rules of Thumb

As stated earlier, we don't have solid guidance on the cost of implementing the SDL, but we do have a rough idea of what the SDL, as implemented on several products that have undergone the process, has cost Microsoft. Our best guess is that the SDL for a product that has *significant legacy code* and is going through the SDL for the first time might cost as much as 15 to 20 percent in schedule (and thus engineering effort). As you'd expect, the presence or absence of the factors outlined in the previous section can drive this resource level up or down.

We are confident that the "steady state" resource level required to implement the SDL on a product that was initially developed under the SDL, or has gone through one or two prior SDL releases, is significantly less than the 15 to 20 percent previously estimated. However, our experience with the SDL is not yet extensive enough for us to provide a confident estimate of how low the steady state cost will go. And we are also confident that the cost—in impact on customers, in impact on our reputation, and in lost sales—of *not* implementing the SDL would have significantly exceeded the costs of implementing it.

Is the Project on Track?

This section provides some suggestions for managing the execution of the SDL. How do you know whether the product team is executing the SDL effectively and building a more secure product?

Beginning with Chapter 5, "Stage 0: Education and Awareness," and throughout Part II, "The Security Development Lifecycle Process," we'll discuss in detail the activities that make up the individual stages of the SDL. Each of the SDL's stages requires the conduct of specific activities and the production of specific outputs, either in the form of documents (in a few cases) or of bugs in the project's workflow system, that must be investigated and (in many cases) fixed. A manager or executive who is committed to applying the SDL to his or her products should pay close attention to those outputs to determine how the effort is actually going. The following list outlines some of the key measures that are helpful in assessing the quality of SDL implementation "on the way," so that managers won't be surprised when the product ships.

■ Track training attendance for your teams. If your training includes tests or qualifying exams, you should track scores also.

- Track threat model production and quality early in development. You'll have to have a specialized security team analogous to Microsoft's Secure Windows Initiative team. One of their tasks should be to review threat models to ensure that they are not only present but effective in identifying potential vulnerabilities early in the process.

- Monitor the rates and types of security bugs found during product design, development, and testing. Overall, is the number of real or potential security vulnerabilities dropping as the project reaches completion? Are there specific classes of vulnerabilities (either by type, such as buffer overrun or cross-site scripting, or by component) that are not dropping with the rest?

- Track the impact of externally discovered vulnerabilities that affect your product. If there are earlier versions of your product in the field, or if there are similar products in the field, ask whether vulnerabilities similar to those discovered by outside vulnerability finders would have been present in your product if it had shipped under the current "plan of record." Of course, you'll find and fix such vulnerabilities before your product ships. But if your only clue to their presence was the "external find," this suggests that your SDL process is not doing what it should.

Following these suggestions will give you a lot of data to review and should help you assess both the effectiveness of your process and the trend of your product toward readiness to ship. The keys to effective management and monitoring are to watch the numbers and trends and learn what they mean in terms of effective execution of the SDL—and the development of more secure software.

Summary

Executives and managers play a vital role in the implementation of the SDL in a software development organization. Management commitment is vital to a team's success at implementing the SDL and producing more secure software. Measuring both costs and benefits of the SDL is difficult. Although there are not yet any authoritative guidelines about the impact of the SDL on project cost and schedule, monitoring the deliverables and activities associated with each phase in the SDL can give managers a clear idea whether the project is on track and how much the SDL is costing. Tracking external measures, such as customer satisfaction with security and the rate of security incidents affecting products and services, can give managers a similar understanding of the benefits of implementing the SDL.

References

(Mogull 2006)   Mogull, Rich. "Flaws Show Need to Update Oracle Product Management Practices," *http://www.gartner.com/resources/137400/137477/flaws_show_need_to_update_or_137477.pdf.* January 2006.

(SANS 2005)   "SANS Top 20 Internet Security Vulnerability Shows Attackers Are Using New Approaches for Which Users Are Not Prepared," SANS NewsBites, Vol. 7 Num. 55, *http://www.sans.org/newsletters/newsbites/newsbites.php?vol=7&issue=55#200.* November 2005.

(NIST 2006)   National Institute of Standards and Technology. NIST National Vulnerability Database, *http://nvd.nist.gov.*

Part II
The Security Development Lifecycle Process

Chapter 5
Stage 0: Education and Awareness

We are often asked why the Security Development Lifecycle (SDL) has been so successful at reducing vulnerabilities in Microsoft software. There are two very simple answers: executive support, and education and awareness. Getting Bill Gates and Steve Ballmer 100 percent committed to SDL was critical (Microsoft 2002), but nearly as critical in security work is an educated engineering workforce.

If your engineers know nothing about basic security tenets, common security bug types, basic secure design, or security testing, there really is no reasonable chance that they will produce secure software. We say this because, on average, software engineers know very little about software security. By security, we don't mean understanding *security features*; we mean understanding what it takes to build and deliver *secure features*. It's unfortunate that the term *security* is overloaded in this manner because these are two very different security realms. Security features refer to how defensive mechanisms work—for example, the inner operations of the Java sandbox or of the Microsoft .NET common language runtime—or how encryption algorithms, such as Data Encryption Standard (DES) or Rivest-Shamir-Adleman (RSA), work.

Although these are interesting and useful topics, knowing that the DES encryption algorithm is a 16-round Feistel network isn't going to help people build software that is more secure. On the other hand, knowing the limitations of DES, and that its key size is woefully small for today's threats, is very useful, and this kind of detail is the core tenet of how to build secure features. The real concern is that most schools, universities, and technical colleges teach security features but not how to build secure software. Year after year, these schools churn out legions of software engineers who believe they can build secure software because they know how a firewall works. In short, you cannot assume that anyone you hire understands how to build security defenses into your software.

In this chapter, we'll explain how to build a security education and awareness program for your engineering staff. But first we want to outline how we evolved this program at Microsoft.

A Short History of Security Education at Microsoft

Microsoft has always created a great deal of excellent internal technical education for its employees. This education has focused on such diverse subjects as the following:

- Software engineering principles
- Lessons learned from past projects
- Software architecture
- Testing methods
- Transaction technology
- Reliability
- Scalability
- Understanding future technical directions
- Various technologies, such as XML, ASP, SOAP, and so on
- Programming languages
- Interface design
- Accessibility

There have always been security sessions, too, but again, most of them focused on how security technologies work, not on how to build secure software.

As discussed in Chapter 3, "A Short History of the SDL at Microsoft Corporation," in 1999 and 2000, the Secure Windows Initiative team started holding a series of security "bug bashes" across the company to hunt for security bugs before products or features shipped to customers. A typical bug bash day would follow an agenda something like that shown in Table 5-1.

Table 5-1   A Typical Security "Bug Bash" Day

Time	Event
9:00 A.M.–9:10 A.M.	Kickoff by the group's vice-president
9:10 A.M.–11:00 A.M.	Basic security training pertinent for the group
11:00 A.M.–5:00 P.M.	Hunt for security bugs, build threat models, and perform basic penetration testing
5:00 P.M.–5:30 P.M.	Hand out prizes for the largest number of bugs found, the bug found written by the most senior person, and so on

Although the apparent purpose of the bug bashes is to find security bugs, the real, underlying purpose is to simply raise awareness within the product group. The up-front basic security training is simple and covers the following topics:

- **Common excuses for not fixing security bugs**   This list appears in Appendix B, "Ridiculous Excuses We've Heard," of *Writing Secure Code, Second Edition* (Howard and LeBlanc 2003). This tended to be a humorous litany of war stories, but the humor is important because it makes the stories stick in people's minds.

- **Design issues that can lead to compromise**   A look at design errors such as leaving ports open, erroneous key storage, bypassing authentication and authorization schemes, evading logging methods, and so on.

- **Understanding threats to software**   We'll cover this topic in more detail—and with the benefit of five years of threat-modeling research—in Chapter 9, "Stage 4: Risk Analysis."

- **Insecure coding techniques**   A quick romp through common coding errors such as buffer overruns, cross-site scripting, structured query language (SQL) injection, and weak encryption. In the early days, there was no discussion of integer arithmetic errors because they were virtually unheard of at the time.

The security bug bashes were pretty low-tech and somewhat entertaining, and although real security bugs were found, simply hunting for security bugs in this manner is not a sustainable process. But perhaps more importantly, the bug bash education started to form the basis of all security education at Microsoft.

Following Bill Gates's Trustworthy Computing memo, our group started working on ongoing security education for all engineering disciplines within the organization. This culminated in a four-hour, lecture-style awareness presentation dubbed "The Basics of Secure Software Design, Development, and Test" (or, simply, "The Basics"). The goal of this lecture was not to turn people into security experts; rather, it was to raise awareness of security issues and to let people know what was (and currently is) expected of them.

 On the CD   An updated version of the "The Basics" class is available on the companion disc that accompanies this book.

The outline of "The Basics" presentation is as follows:

- Overview of Trustworthy Computing

- Short Introduction to SDL

- Basics of Secure Design

    - Attack Surface Reduction

    - Defense in Depth

- ❑ Least Privilege
- ❑ Secure Defaults
- ■ Threat Modeling
  - ❑ Designing to Threat Model
  - ❑ Coding to Threat Model
  - ❑ Testing to a Threat Model
- ■ Introduction to Fuzz Testing
- ■ Secure Coding Best Practices
  - ❑ Buffer Overruns
  - ❑ Integer Arithmetic Issues
  - ❑ Cross-Site Scripting
  - ❑ SQL Injection
  - ❑ Weak Cryptography
  - ❑ Microsoft .NET–Specific Issues

Again, it's important to point out that "The Basics" presentation does not make anyone in the audience a security expert, although it does outline the need for security and quickly makes people realize how little they know about security. Acknowledging that there's a lot that they don't know about software security makes people willing to have their ideas, designs, code, and test plans reviewed by others who do understand the security issues in depth.

Ongoing Education

All Microsoft engineering staff must attend security training at least once a year. At first, the only class available was the "The Basics" presentation, but attendance is not appropriate once a person has taken the course, even though the content does change substantially. In fact, the content changes every month to reflect new threats, research, and mitigations. With this in mind, we hired another person and started working on a more in-depth security curriculum to address the needs of specific disciplines. At the time of writing, the following classes are either complete or being developed:

- **The Basics of Secure Software Design, Development, and Testing**   This class introduces all engineers to the basics of security.
- **Fuzz Testing in Depth**   Explained in detail in Chapter 12, "Stage 7: Secure Testing Policies," this class is an effective way to find certain classes of security bugs. This class explains how fuzz testing works, how to build effective fuzz tests, and how to identify fuzz-testing failures.

- **Threat Modeling in Depth**   Explained in detail in Chapter 9, threat modeling is a method for uncovering design flaws in a software component before the component is built. This class, which includes a small exercise at the end, outlines the process.

- **Implementing Threat Mitigations**   This class begins where the threat-modeling class leaves off. The original threat-modeling class covered the threat-modeling process as well as development tasks and test tasks. This turned out to be a great deal of content, spanning many disciplines, and was simply too unwieldy. The present threat-modeling class covers just the threat-modeling process, and the "Implementing Threat Mitigations" class is aimed mainly at developers and helps them to decide how to choose the appropriate mitigations or countermeasures.

- **Security Design and Architecture: Time-Tested Design Principles**   We touch on this subject in Chapter 7, "Stage 2: Define and Follow Design Best Practices." Most software developers focus solely on best practice to lift themselves out of the security pit, but we need to go much further than simple best practice. Engineers should learn some of the basic security models, such as the Bell-LaPadula Disclosure model (Wikipedia 2006a) and the Biba integrity model (Wikipedia 2006b), and secure design principles such as Saltzer and Schroeder (Saltzer and Schroeder 1975).

- **Introduction to the SDL and Final Security Review (FSR) Process**   This class covers the end-to-end SDL process, but most important, it prepares development groups for the final security review, outlining what they can expect during an FSR. The target audience is more senior employees because these folks need to build SDL time into their schedules. A key facet of the class is explaining the importance of building time into the schedule for all the SDL requirements.

- **Security Tools Overview**   There are many security tools available inside and outside Microsoft. This class covers some of the most important tools for performing code analysis, design analysis, attack surface reviews, penetration testing, threat modeling, and fuzz testing.

- **Performing Security Code Reviews**   Very few people know how to review code correctly for security bugs. This class teaches some of the critical skills, such as understanding lack of trustworthiness of most incoming data, as well as ranking system entry points by potential "attackability." This in part is driven by the threat model, which identifies the dangerous interfaces into the application.

- **Secure Coding Practices**   Going beyond "The Basics," this class teaches developers how to create secure software not simply by applying best practice, but also by using good, sound security discipline and secure coding patterns.

- **Security Bugs in Detail**   This class covers a catalog of security bugs along with their causes, mitigations, and defenses. The class then examines security bugs in more detail, showing specific bugs in various software products.

■ **Attack Surface Analysis (ASA) and Attack Surface Reduction (ASR)**   This class outlines what defines attack surface for common applications and platforms and how to drive attack surface down while trying to keep the application useful for customers. ASA is covered in detail in Chapter 7.

■ **Exploit Development**   This advanced class outlines how to create exploit code to take advantage of vulnerabilities. Obviously, the purpose of the class is to educate, not to attack real systems. When it comes to showing how dangerous security bugs can be, there is nothing quite as effective as seeing an exploit in action.

■ **Build Requirements**   The target audience for this class is people involved in creating the daily build. Admittedly, most companies don't need this class, but for companies like Microsoft, it's important because the build process must be protected, and the correct security tools must be run on the build.

■ **Security Response**   There will be security bugs in products, and it's important that your team understands what the security response is going to be. This subject is covered in detail in Chapter 15, "Stage 10: Security Response Planning."

■ **Cryptography by Example**   This class takes a scenario of two people wishing to communicate securely and builds up to a secure solution using cryptographic primitives to mitigate real threats. The second part of the class covers cryptographic best practice.

■ **Customer Privacy**   This online training class focuses on protecting customer data, most notably protecting private user data maintained by some of the Microsoft online properties, such as MSN (Microsoft 2006a). The basics taught include legal aspects of privacy, privacy statements, the data lifecycle, and privacy-enhancing technologies (PETs), as well as global privacy policy such as notice, choice, access, security, onward transfer, data integrity, and enforcement.

Important   If your company creates or uses software that stores and maintains private user data or sensitive or confidential data, your engineers must understand the basics of privacy.

Note that this is a partial list of classes, and it will be augmented and modified in coming years as threats evolve.

Important   Any education you require for your employees must provide new specific skills that they can apply "on the job."

Types of Training Delivery

We have found that live training sessions are very effective, but they do not scale to the thousands of Microsoft employees. With about 100 people per session, putting about 25,000 engineers through training would mean holding 250 training sessions a year. Microsoft is a software company, not a training company, and we're not staffed to conduct so many sessions. This means that we have to change the way we present educational material. With this in mind, we always try to have live training recorded so that it can be placed on the internal network for engineers to access whenever they wish.

> **Tip**   Recorded or online educational material (Microsoft 2006b) helps with geographically dispersed development teams and acquisitions.

Here is the general path that we follow for developing a new class:

- Objectives and target audience are determined for the class.

- A security expert builds the new class.

- Other experts review the class material for technical accuracy and applicability.

- Training (not security) experts edit the class material, looking for consistency and typographical errors.

- We deliver a beta class. The main goal of this class is to fine-tune timing and get feedback on content.

- We update the class material with the feedback on content.

- We deliver the class at least once a month for six months.

- After six months, we record the class and put it on the intranet.

In our experience, more people "attend" online training, but live training tends to be more effective, mainly because there are often questions that need answering by the presenter, and this can be done only in a live setting.

Exercises and Labs

Exercises and labs are incredibly important to help cement concepts in the students' minds. Let us give you an example. For a long time at Microsoft, we had a very hard time teaching people how to make good threat models. This was in part due to the complexity of the threat-modeling process, so we made the process simpler and more definable, but we also added a small exercise at the end of the class. The exercise takes only 30 minutes to complete. Feedback from the new threat-modeling class has been very positive mainly because of the exercise.

> **Tip**   Consider adding short exercises to your classes.

Tracking Attendance and Compliance

For a product at Microsoft to comply with the SDL, all engineers must have attended security training within the past year. When students go to a training session, they swipe their Microsoft identity badges on the way in, and this information is entered automatically in a database of training attendance that goes on the employees' education record. We then use that data to roll up security class attendance by manager or VP. For example, in the Windows group, we could get a percentage of attendance for all employees under Brian Valentine (Senior Vice-President), or, perhaps, a manager can determine the attendance of his subordinates. Keep in mind that Microsoft counts only people who participate in product development. We do this by matching each employee's official title against a list of engineering titles. For example, an administrative assistant does not need to attend the training. Of course, they are certainly welcome at the security class!

As an employee's one-year anniversary approaches, an e-mail message is automatically sent, reminding the employee that he or she must attend another security class. If they don't refresh their attendance, the figures for the employee's group are affected and the employee's manager can take appropriate action.

Notice that we use the word *compliance*. To be SDL-compliant, product teams must have 100 percent security training attendance.

Other Compliance Ideas

As this goes to print, the security engineering team at Microsoft is looking into other ways of measuring compliance. For example, what if someone attends a security conference, delivers security educational material, or perhaps writes a paper on security? Shouldn't these people be credited for that work and the credit go toward their yearly educational quota? We think the answer is yes, but we have not finalized how this will be measured. One possibility is to create a program a little like the Certified Information Systems Security Professional (CISSP) Continuing Professional Education (CPE) credit program from $(ISC)^2$. Individuals who attain CISSP status must earn a minimum of 120 CPE credits during the three-year certification cycle to ensure that they stay current with security trends and issues $((ISC)^2$ 2006). Examples of CPE include the following:

- Attendance at a security conference (1 CPE credit per hour of attendance)
- Security vendor presentation (1 CPE credit per hour of attendance)
- Providing security training (4 CPEs per hour of preparation)
- Publication of a security article (10 CPEs)
- Publication of a security book (40 CPEs)
- Read a security book (5 CPEs)

This kind of program is effective because it allows for greater flexibility than simply requiring security course attendance. One proposal underway at Microsoft is to require a certain number of points per year for compliance. For example, the policy might be something like the following:

> To be in compliance with SDL, each person involved in a product engineering discipline must attain 25 credits per year. Attending Microsoft security training yields 25 credits, reading a security book yields 5 credits, publishing a security article external to the company yields 10 credits, an internally published paper yields 5 credits . . . .

> **Note**   Within Microsoft product groups, *Writing Secure Code, Second Edition*, is required reading as a baseline knowledge prerequisite. This book has also been turned into an instructor-led class created by Vigilar, Inc. (Vigilar 2005).

Measuring Knowledge

On the surface, knowledge measurement seems easy, but for a company that develops software, it's actually a complex subject. It's complex because it's hard to determine what do to with the results. Is the goal simply to determine whether people can work on specific portions of the code? What do you do if someone fails or, worse, fails again and again? Do you fire them? As you can imagine, there are many legal issues involved with measuring folks for security expertise. Then, of course, there is the issue of how to measure people's knowledge. Do you measure by way of an exam immediately after the training, or at some later date? Is the exam online? Is it an open-book exam? How do you prevent cheating? Again, Microsoft is a software company, not a university.

Microsoft does not presently measure employees' security expertise, but we are constantly looking at ways to address these issues.

One promising and easy-to-implement way to measure knowledge acquisition (although not knowledge retention) is to use an online training session and then, at various times throughout the course, to ask a series of short, multiple-choice questions. If the question is answered correctly, we move to the next stage of the training material. If not, we inform the student of the correct solution and move on.

Implementing Your Own In-House Training

It is *imperative* that you have a baseline security class focusing on good security and privacy engineering practice for all people involved in software development. This is the reason behind the "Security Basics" class at Microsoft. All engineering personnel must attend this training session so that we can set a minimum security baseline. Making people security experts is not the goal of a class like this. The core goal is simply to raise awareness and provide engineers with basic security knowledge, let them know what's expected of them, and tell them where they can go for more security-related and privacy-related information. This is an important point: we teach engineers enough so that they know when they are in trouble and know whom they need to contact to get help.

Creating Education Materials "On a Budget"

If, like Microsoft, your organization is not an educational institution, you should also consider encouraging security experts to present their knowledge to your people. But don't stop there. Record the session for posterity and place the slide deck and the video on an easily searchable internal Web site. A simple Microsoft Office PowerPoint presentation, although useful, is not as beneficial as a PowerPoint presentation with audio or video from the instructor. In its simplest form, this could be a presentation using the Record Narration option with a microphone attached to the computer. In Office PowerPoint 2003, you can find the Record Narration option under the Slide Show menu item, as shown in Figure 5-1. When a person views the presentation, she will see the slides and hear the presenter at the same time.

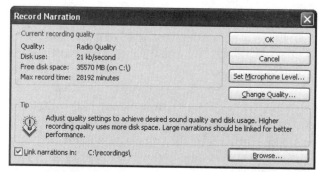

Figure 5-1   The Record Narration dialog box in Office PowerPoint 2003.

Key Success Factors and Metrics

There are three main requirements for successful security education and awareness:

- Executive support
- Experienced presenters
- Ongoing education

Let's look at each requirement in more detail.

Like all aspects of SDL, executive support is critical, but gaining executive support for security awareness and education should not pose much of a challenge. It's fair to say that most technology and business executives understand the importance of security education as a way to reduce risk to their companies. But there's more than just risk at stake. Better-quality code—and more secure code *is* better-quality code—leads to increased user satisfaction and, possibly, competitive advantage.

The next piece of the puzzle is experienced presenters. At Microsoft, the presenters are usually people from the security "trenches" rather than people trained to teach. The reason is simple: invariably there will be many questions from the audience, and although the presenter might not know all the answers, a software security expert is more likely to know an answer. Of course, we have to balance this with the potential for an excellent and seasoned security professional to be a dull presenter! In our experience, it's better to err on the side of security expertise.

The third aspect of SDL is ongoing education. Track who attends the training sessions and when, and tie this information to the engineer's annual review. Ongoing attendance is also a core metric.

> **Important**   100 percent of engineering staff should attend security training every year.

Summary

Education and awareness are critical to creating secure software. Unfortunately, today's software engineering workforce often lacks skilled security professionals, and there is no end in sight to this dilemma. This means that the software industry must pick up the slack and make a point of educating its engineers about security and privacy issues. Build a security and privacy curriculum within your company for all engineers. At a minimum, you should require a basic security course—or use the course on the companion disc for this book—for everyone involved in designing, developing, testing, and documenting your software. Track security training attendance, and insist on updated training at least once a year.

References

(Microsoft 2002)   Microsoft Corporation. Bill Gates's Trustworthy Computing memo, *http://news.com.com/2009-1001-817210.html*. January 2002.

(Howard and LeBlanc 2003)   Howard, Michael, and David LeBlanc. *Writing Secure Code, Second Edition*. Redmond, WA: Microsoft Press, 2003.

(Wikipedia 2006a)   "Bell-LaPadula Model," *http://en.wikipedia.org/wiki/Bell-LaPadula_model*.

(Wikipedia 2006b)   "Biba Model," *http://en.wikipedia.org/wiki/Biba_model*.

(Saltzer and Schroeder 1975)   Saltzer, J. H., and M. D. Schroeder. "The Protection of Information in Computer Systems," *http://www.cs.virginia.edu/~evans/cs551/saltzer/*. April 1975.

(Microsoft 2006a)   Microsoft Corporation. "Microsoft Online Privacy Notice Highlights," *http://privacy.msn.com*. January 2006.

(Microsoft 2006b)   Microsoft E-Learning, Security Catalog, *https://www.microsoftelearning.com/security/*.

((ISC)² 2006)   CISSP CPE Credit Requirements, *https://www.isc2.org/cgi-bin/cissp_content.cgi?page=89*.

(Vigilar 2005)   Vigilar, Inc. "Vigilar Launches 'Writing Secure Code' Training Class for Programmers," *http://www.vigilar.com/press48.html*. August 2005.

Chapter 6

Stage 1: Project Inception

As a project starts—perhaps it's a new version, iteration, or a brand new product—it's important to get all the security ducks lined up correctly. From our experience, a good project start leads to a much smoother final security review and a more secure product.

The project inception phase has a number of discrete and important steps:

- Determine whether the application is covered by the Security Development Lifecycle (SDL).

- Assign the Security Advisor.

- Build the Security Leadership team.

- Make sure the bug-tracking process includes security and privacy bug fields.

- Determine the "bug bar."

Let's look at each of these steps in detail.

Determine Whether the Application Is Covered by SDL

The first course of action is to determine whether the product is covered by SDL. Ultimately, all software will benefit from the processes described by the SDL, and managers are always encouraged to follow the SDL. However, products that meet any of the following criteria listed *must* follow this software development process:

- Any product that is commonly used or deployed within a business—for example, e-mail and database servers.

- Any product that regularly stores, processes, or communicates personally identifiable information (PII). Examples include financial, medical, and sensitive customer information.

Because of various child online protection laws, such as the Children's Online Privacy Protection Act (COPPA 1998), any products or services that target or are attractive to children are of particular concern.

- Any product that regularly touches or listens on the Internet:

    - Always online: services provided by a product that involves a presence on the Internet—for example, instant messaging software

    - Designed to be online: browser or mail applications that expose Internet functionality—for example, Web browsers and e-mail clients

    - Exposure online: components that are routinely accessible through other products that interact with the Internet—for example, mobile code or games with multiplayer online support

- Any product that automatically downloads updates.

Note The SDL applies to both new products and major updates such as "dot" releases or service packs.

Assign the Security Advisor

The next course of action is to nominate a security person to guide the development team through the SDL process with the aim of successfully completing the Final Security Review (FSR). (See Chapter 14, "Stage 9: The Final Security Review," for more on the FSR.) Historically, Microsoft has referred to this individual as a Security Advisor.

If your company has a central security team, or an engineering quality team, it makes sense to nominate someone from that team to be the security point person. Specific skills are required to fulfill this role, however. Following is a sample job description used within Microsoft:

Do you enjoy probing and analyzing product security, finding holes in assumptions, and working with product teams to make our products as secure as possible for our customers? Are you interested in a job that provides incredible opportunities for learning and visibility? The Secure Windows Initiative (SWI) team is looking for a stellar PM to continue to drive the adoption of good security practices across Microsoft. You will own working with teams such as Office, Windows, Visual Studio, or SQL Server to help them develop secure products from beginning to end and finally verify the security of each product before it ships.

We are looking for a Program Manager with a strong technical and security background, strong cross-group and communication skills, attention to detail, and solid process skills. Coding skills are helpful but not required; security-mindedness is a must.

Candidates should have 3–5 years' experience building and shipping software and have solid PM skills. A Bachelor's degree in Computer Science is preferred.

Come and help the company ship secure products to customers.

We have noticed that although deep security skills are important, it's even more vital that the Security Advisor have good project and process management skills. Having both security and project management skills is a bonus. Having neither skill is obviously a disqualifier.

> **Best Practices**   Large software development houses should assign similar products to the same security point person so that the Security Advisor can pass on lessons learned from one group to other groups.

The tasks of the security advisor include:

- Acting as a point of contact between the development team and the security team.
- Holding an SDL kick-off meeting for the development team.
- Holding design and threat-model reviews with the development team.
- Analyzing and triaging security-related and privacy-related bugs.
- Acting as a security sounding board for the development team.
- Preparing the development team for the FSR.
- Working with the reactive security team.

We want to delve briefly into each of these areas. But before we do, do not lose track of the high-level goal of the security advisor: it is to help product teams become self-sufficient and "good at security."

Act as a Point of Contact Between the Development Team and the Security Team

Before the creation of the SDL process, security communication between product groups and the security team was unstructured and prone to miscommunication. To remedy this, the Security Advisor acts as the central point of contact for the development team. Most notably, a person is selected from the development group to be the security point person for the development group, and that person and the Security Advisor act as a conduit for security information. Of course, there is nothing stopping *anyone* on the development team from communicating with the Security Advisor, or vice versa, but it's important that the advisor and the security point person are made aware of all security- and privacy-related communication.

> **Best Practices**   People from different development groups within Microsoft often e-mail us, asking security questions. When this happens, we make a point of including the Security Advisor on the reply.

Holding an SDL Kick-Off Meeting for the Development Team

Before the development project gets fully underway, the Security Advisor presents the goals of the SDL and the key points about the SDL process to the engineering staff. Often this is simply a one-hour presentation. It's imperative that, at a minimum, the development, test, and program management leadership staff attend. It's also important that management and the people building the schedule understand that the SDL tasks and deliverables must be built into the development schedule.

> **Important**   It's important that SDL tasks and deliverables be built into the software development schedule.

Holding Design and Threat Model Reviews with the Development Team

At the point during the design phase when the designs are nearly complete, the Security Advisor should sit down with the development team to discuss the design and system architecture. At this stage, the Security Advisor will critique the design to see if she can find security issues within it. For example, the Security Advisor will make sure that:

- The application has a low attack surface.

- The application uses the appropriate development best practices.

- The application follows secure design best practices.

- The threat models are complete and reflect how the system will defend itself.

- There is appropriate testing and test coverage.

Attack-surface analysis and reduction and secure design best practices are both covered in Chapter 7, "Stage 2: Define and Follow Design Best Practices"; appropriate secure development best practices are covered in Chapter 11, "Stage 6: Secure Coding Policies," and Chapter 12, "Stage 7: Secure Testing Policies"; and threat models are discussed in Chapter 9, "Stage 4: Risk Analysis."

Analyzing and Triaging Security-Related and Privacy-Related Bugs

Invariably, security and privacy bugs will be detected in the product during development, and such bugs must be triaged accordingly. Reviewing these kinds of bugs requires a great deal of expertise to make sure the correct course of action is taken for each. Some may be fixed with code or design changes; others might not be fixed at all because the risk is very low and the amount of work required to perform a correct fix may be large. Whatever the outcome, it's important that the Security Advisor review the list of unfixed security and privacy bugs.

Acting as a Security Sounding Board for the Development Team

The Security Advisor should address security and privacy questions and ideas as they arise from the product group. Indeed, the advisor should encourage this kind of discourse and have ideas evaluated and verified as soon as possible. At Microsoft, this process is usually handled in the manner shown in Figure 6-1 (on the next page), but many software development houses may not have the luxury of a central, dedicated security team. In this case, the advisor will probably be the security contact and problem solver for all security issues.

Security Advisors also serve as great sources of security wisdom and education for the software development team.

Preparing the Development Team for the Final Security Review

Before a product ships, it must successfully complete an FSR as defined in Chapter 14, "Stage 9: The Final Security Review." An important task for the Security Advisor is to make sure that all the required SDL tasks are completed so that the FSR goes smoothly. You don't want surprises at the FSR stage because they could hold up the final product release to customers.

Working with the Reactive Security Team

If an externally reported security bug is found in a product you create, it saves a great deal of time for the Security Advisor to be in the loop when triaging the issue because she will have a great deal of background knowledge that may aid in determining the most appropriate way to fix the issue.

Build the Security Leadership Team

In all software development endeavors, there is a person or team that leads the development process. At Microsoft, there is a central project management team driving the day-to-day coordination of team communication, scheduling, and features. This team should also handle security leadership for the project. The team's tasks include

- Regular communication, usually by e-mail, to the development team about security and privacy bug counts.
- Communication of security and privacy policy updates.

This role is different from the development team contact; the development team security contact is technical in nature, whereas the security leadership team sets policy and communicates status to the team.

Here's a real example of how this communication system works. In late 2004, I (Michael) learned of a security bug that affected the Java programming language from Sun Microsystems (Huwig 2004). To my surprise, it was an integer overflow problem. As I dug deeper, I found that this bug could affect C# or Microsoft Visual Basic .NET code. So I spoke to the Security Advisor for the Microsoft .NET Framework about the issue, and he then talked to both the security contact on the .NET Framework team and the .NET Framework security leadership team. Between them, they decided that this kind of error could indeed affect managed code and should be fixed prior to shipping the .NET Framework 2.0. The .NET Framework security contact then created some prescriptive guidance, and the leadership team made the entire product team aware that this guidance must be adhered to. Three bugs of this nature were found and eradicated from the code base before the product shipped.

This may seem like a lot of communication overhead—and for some software development teams it certainly is—but for larger software projects it works well because there is a combination of security and privacy technical expertise (the security team, Security Advisor, and security contact) and policy setting to make sure that it happens. Figure 6-1 shows the relationship between these roles discussed previously.

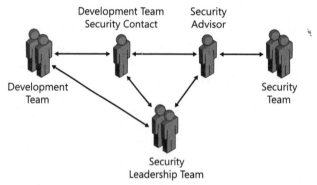

Figure 6-1   The communication relationship between the Security Advisor, the development team contact, and the security leadership team.

Make Sure the Bug-Tracking Process Includes Security and Privacy Bug Fields

It is critically important that security and privacy bugs be tracked correctly in your bug-tracking database. Even more important, such bugs must be tracked in a consistent manner. Here are the SDL-required bug-tracking fields that should be added to your bug-tracking software:

- Security/Privacy Bug Effect
- Security/Privacy Bug Cause

The Security/Privacy Bug Effect field should then have these predefined values:

- Not a Security Bug
- Spoofing
- Tampering

- Repudiation
- Information Disclosure
- Information Disclosure (Privacy)
- Denial of Service
- Elevation of Privilege
- Attack Surface Reduction

Note that Attack Surface Reduction is akin to defense in depth and is not necessarily a true security bug. Rather, it's a bug that identifies a task that should be triaged like any other security or privacy bug.

> **Note**   Defense in depth employs multiple security defenses to help mitigate the risk of one defense failing.

Information disclosure threats can also be privacy threats if the data exposed is personally identifiable or confidential data, so there is a separate bug category to make it easy to search for privacy bugs. Privacy issues are almost always high-impact bugs, and this should be reflected in the severity rating of the bug.

The Security/Privacy Bug Cause field should then have these predefined values:

- Not a Security Bug
- Buffer Overflow or Underflow
- Arithmetic Error (for example, integer overflow)
- SQL/Script Injection
- Directory Traversal
- Race Condition
- Cross-Site Scripting
- Cryptographic Weakness
- Weak Authentication
- Weak Authorization/Inappropriate ACL
- Ineffective Secret Hiding
- Resource Consumption (DoS)
- Incorrect/No Error Messages
- Incorrect/No Pathname Canonicalization
- Other

Determine the "Bug Bar"

At the outset, you should decide what types of bugs you will fix within the project development lifecycle, including security and privacy bugs. Defining the bar up front reduces confusion about what should be fixed, what should be mitigated, and what can be left unfixed. The SDL mandates that critical, important, and moderate security and privacy bugs be fixed prior to releasing the product. You can get a feel for the relative risk rankings by looking at Figure 9-6 through Figure 9-10 in Chapter 9.

Summary

Having a Security Advisor, security contact, and security leadership team in place as the project begins can make the process of building more secure software easier because expert security advice is available via a defined channel, and security communication flows well. More important, this level of communication makes it harder for important data to fall between the cracks.

Setting the bug-tracking system and bug bar at the outset also helps to streamline the process by establishing a consistent and well-understood bug standard. This reduces friction during development by defining the nomenclature and what will and will not be fixed prior to product release.

References

(COPPA 1998)   U.S. Federal Government. "The Children's Online Privacy Protection Act of 1998," *http://www.ftc.gov/ogc/coppa1.htm*. October 1998.

(Huwig 2004)   Huwig, Kurt. "DoS (Denial of Service) Against Java JNDI/DNS," *http://archives.neohapsis.com/archives/bugtraq/2004-11/0092.html*. Neohapsis, November 2004.

Chapter 7

Stage 2: Define and Follow Design Best Practices

The software industry abounds with security software coding best practices (few of which are followed), but there is a dearth of pragmatic secure-design guidance. Microsoft has spent considerable time working to make secure design accessible to the average non-security expert. Saltzer and Schroeder's classic paper "The Protection of Information in Computer Systems" (Saltzer and Schroeder 1975, Computer Security Resource Center 2002) offers many time-tested secure-design principles that apply today as much as they did in 1975. Secure design is necessary for all computer software, from operating systems to online computer games (Yan and Randell 2005). This chapter offers brief ideas for applying secure-design principles to modern application software.

Extensive coverage of these principles is beyond the scope of this book; for more information, please refer to one or more of the many references (Anderson 2001, Bishop 2002, Howard and LeBlanc 2003) on the subject.

Internet Engineering Task Force (IETF) requests for comments (RFCs) must also include security information. Rescorla and Korver's "Guidelines for Writing RFC Text on Security Considerations" (Rescorla and Korver 2003) offers some ideas on how to think about the security implications of software, firmware, and hardware features.

 Best Practices   When you expect engineering staff to execute on security-related initiatives or to adhere to a security or privacy policy, it is imperative that you provide prescriptive guidance about how to achieve your goals. Don't just say, "This is bad." Instead, say, "This is the way you should do it." In our experience, engineering staff are happy to adhere to security and privacy policies as long as you explain how to attain the desired objectives.

All products should follow appropriate secure-design best practices. These are not the same as threat modeling; threat modeling and secure design are different but complementary. Threat modeling determines appropriate mitigations based on threats to the system, and secure design best practices focus on "good security hygiene" within the application. For example, if you identify a threat to a system and then select mitigations, your mitigations could be compromised if the application's design is insecure. Secure-design principles can help prevent such potential errors.

Another important best practice of the design phase is reducing a software product's attack surface, which is the sum of all code and functionality accessible to users and potential attackers. For example, a Transmission Control Protocol (TCP) socket opened by an application is part of the application's attack surface. Attack surface might appear to be an operating system characteristic only, but all applications have it, even if some applications measure it differently. A goal of any product should be to reduce the attack surface.

> **Note**   Remember the two major goals for the Security Development Lifecycle (SDL): reduce the number of vulnerabilities in the software as you develop it, and reduce the severity of any undiscovered security bugs. The first principle is the high-level goal of *Secure by Design*, and the second is the high-level goal of *Secure by Default*. Securing the design and the code is paramount, but mistakes will be made, and research into new vulnerabilities that may affect the software continues long after a product has been shipped to customers. It is therefore imperative that the product have a minimal attack surface to reduce the severity of any security bugs in the code. This is what secure by default is all about; secure by design is about getting things right, and secure by default is recognizing you never will!

Common Secure-Design Principles

Of the numerous secure-design principles, the classic and most quoted are those in the list created by Saltzer and Schroeder in their seminal paper, "The Protection of Information in Computer Systems." These principles, although written in 1975, are still valid today and apply especially to security software:

- **Economy of mechanism**   Keep the code and design simple and small. The more complex the software, the greater the likelihood of bugs in the code. When the code is small, less can go wrong.

- **Fail-safe defaults**   The default action for any request should be to deny the action. Thus, if the user request fails, the system remains secure.

- **Complete mediation**   Every access to every protected object should be validated. Follow the best practice of performing the check as close to the protected object as possible. For example, if your Web-based application protects a file, operating system file system access control lists (ACLs) are a more robust protection mechanism than an access check within your Web-based code.

- **Open design**   Open design, as opposed to "security through obscurity," suggests that designs should not be secret. The most well-known embodiment of this principle is Kerchoff's Law, which applied to cryptographic designs states, "The system should not depend on secrecy, and it should be able to fall into enemy hands without disadvantage" (Wikipedia 2006).

- **Separation of privilege**   Do not permit an operation based on one condition. Examples include two-factor authentication, and, at a higher level, separation of duties.

- **Least privilege**   Operate with the lowest level of privilege necessary to perform the required tasks. This subject is covered in more detail later in this chapter.

- **Least common mechanism**   Minimize shared resources such as files and variables. You can more easily control individual processes manipulating private files than two processes manipulating the same file. Furthermore, code that uses only local variables is more robust and maintainable than code that uses global variables.

- **Psychological acceptability**   Is your secured product easy to use? If not, it won't be used. You should always ask yourself, "Can I implement this system in a way that makes the product easier to use?" Never forget about your users. Psychological acceptability requires a great deal of skill and user interface design expertise.

Caution   Psychological acceptability is hard to get right; if a very secure system is difficult to use, users might abandon the security features of the product. As we developed Microsoft Windows XP SP2, we carefully balanced security, the main focus of the service pack; usability; and backward compatibility. We recognized, for example, that if the firewall prevented too many applications from working or if some defenses made the system hard to use, users would simply disable the defenses, making their systems more susceptible to successful attack and rendering all the protective work useless. A key lesson is to be wary of security for the sake of security.

Various resources address secure design; we urge you to consider the references listed at the end of this chapter for further study.

A product's security features do not necessarily secure the product from attack. Any feature, whether or not it's a security feature, must be implemented as a "secure feature" and be engineered correctly, with appropriate attention to security and quality. All input must be rigorously validated for correctness.

Best Practices   Remember, even the most secure design is rendered pointless by a low-quality and insecure implementation, regardless of the number of security features the product employs.

"Bolting on" security or privacy later in the schedule, or after the features are complete, is not an option. The only way to deliver robust security and privacy consistently to customers is by including those qualities in the application during the design phase.

Complexity and Security

We want to spend a few moments on complexity—a critically important part of secure design that is covered in Saltzer and Schroeder's "Economy of Mechanism." All things being equal, complex software is likely to be less secure than simpler software, so you should always strive to produce "simple enough" software. Numerous methods that measure complexity can help immensely in your code reviews. Make yourself aware of some of these complexity metrics, such as McCabe's cyclomatic complexity (McCabe and Watson 1994, VanDoren 2000) and Halstead's complexity (VanDoren 1997).

Attack Surface Analysis and Attack Surface Reduction

Any useful application employs code accessible to end users and attackers alike. Code almost always has bugs, some of which are security related. Accessible code might be vulnerable to malicious users.

Note   The inspiration for Attack Surface Analysis (ASA) and Attack Surface Reduction (ASR) comes from Saltzer and Schroeder's principles, most notably, least privilege and economy of mechanism.

Attack Surface Analysis and Attack Surface Reduction are all about understanding what constitutes the attack surface of your application and how you can effectively reduce it to prevent an attacker from taking advantage of potentially defective code. The software industry worries a lot about improving code quality. But although code quality is exceptionally important, new classes of vulnerabilities may affect even the best code, so we cannot focus exclusively on getting the code right. Even if your code happens to be perfect, it's only perfect by today's standards—a snapshot of best practices at development time. Yet the vulnerability research landscape is constantly evolving. Five or so years ago, integer overflow vulnerabilities were almost unknown; today they are an extremely common attack.

Best Practices   The software industry needs to change its outlook from trying to achieve code perfection to recognizing that code will always have security bugs. We must therefore focus on extra defense mechanisms. But of course, we should never stop trying to achieve software perfection.

The attack surface of a software product is the union of code, interfaces, services, and protocols available to all users, especially what is accessible by unauthenticated or remote users.

ASA is the process of enumerating all the interfaces and protocols and executing code. The rest of this chapter will give you an idea of elements you need to consider during the ASR phase. Code that is part of the attack surface is more vulnerable to attack. For example, the code behind a remotely accessible socket is more at risk of attack than, say, the code behind a closed socket.

How ASA and Threat Modeling Relate

ASA focuses on reducing the amount of code accessible to untrusted users. You can usually achieve this reduction by understanding the system's entry points and the trust levels required to access them. Threat modeling can help feed the ASA process and hence the ASR process because key components of the threat model include the entry points and trust levels.

The core tenet of ASR is that all code has a nonzero likelihood of containing one or more vulnerabilities. Some vulnerabilities result in customer compromises. Therefore, the only way to avoid customer compromises is to reduce code usage to zero. ASR compromises between perfect safety and unmitigated risk by minimizing code exposed to untrusted users. Code quality and ASR can help produce software that is more secure; striving to write perfect code alone will not.

Best Practices   Code with a large attack surface—that is, a large amount of code accessible to untrusted users—must be extremely high-quality code. It must be extensively hand-reviewed and tested.

At a high level, ASR focuses on:

- Reducing the amount of code that executes by default.
- Restricting the scope of who can access the code.
- Restricting the scope of which identities can access code.
- Reducing the privilege of the code.

Figure 7-1 shows the steps you should follow when considering the attack surface of your application.

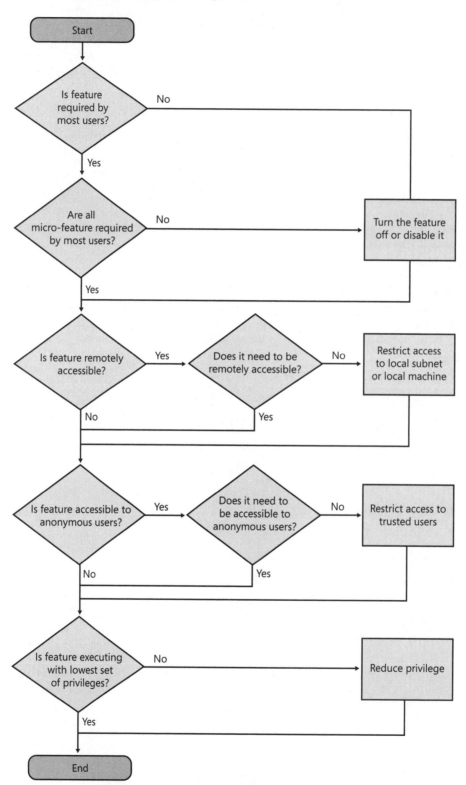

Figure 7-1 Follow these steps to reduce attack surface.

Step 1: Is This Feature Really *That* Important?

The first task is incredibly important. For each of the product's features (especially services, daemons, mobile code such as ActiveX controls and Java applets, running applications, and so on), you should ask, "Is this feature needed by at least 80 percent of our users?" If the answer is no, the feature should be turned off, not installed, or disabled by default.

A good example of this kind of ASR is the Internet Information Services (IIS) 6.0 Web server in Microsoft Windows Server 2003. It is not installed by default, unlike IIS 5.0 in Microsoft Windows 2000, which is installed by default.

> **Important**   Disabling a feature by default does not mean that you can ship a poor-quality feature. Disabling a feature will reduce, not prevent, the likelihood of many users being impacted by a potential bug.

Next, you should consider all the sub-features that make up the overall feature. This is probably best explained through example. A Web server, such as Apache or IIS, ships with a lot more functionality than just HTTP 1.0 or HTTP 1.1 processing. These servers can parse and respond to

- Various HTTP verbs (GET, POST, HEAD, and so on).
- WebDAV requests (PROPFIND, PROPPATCH, SEARCH, and so on).
- SOAP Web service requests (all exposed SOAP methods).
- Requests to Java Server (.jsp files), CGI (.pl or .cgi), PHP (.php), ASP (.asp), or ASP.NET (.aspx) applications.
- Requests to ISAPI filters and applications or Apache modules (such as mod_rewrite).
- SSL and non-SSL requests (including SSL2, SSL3, PCT, and TLS variants).

Remember, each of the preceding sub-features is a separate code path, and that code probably has security bugs. Hence, you have to determine whether it makes sense to enable all this micro-functionality by default. Again, IIS 6.0 is a great example of micro-ASR; when the Web server is enabled, it responds only to requests for static files, and that code path is relatively small. If you want to enable, say, WebDAV, you must opt in for that functionality. Two years after the release of IIS 6.0, Microsoft had issued only one security bulletin for the Web server; the bug was a denial-of-service vulnerability in WebDAV, which was shared with IIS 5.0. The bulletin MS04-030, "Vulnerability in WebDAV XML Message Handler Could Lead to a Denial of Service" (Microsoft 2004), is an update rated as important for Windows 2000 users and moderate for Microsoft Windows Server 2003 users because in Windows 2000, WebDAV is enabled by default, and in Windows Server 2003, it is an "opt-in" feature and hence is less severe.

Step 2: Who Needs Access to the Functionality and from Where?

A viable application must have some useful functionality enabled by default, so the next step is to determine who can access the code and from where. As you see in Figure 7-2, code that is accessible remotely by anonymous users has a larger attack surface than code that is accessible only to local administrators.

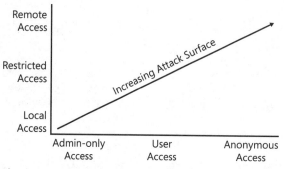

Figure 7-2   Accessibility increases attack surface.

What follows is a good example of reducing the attack surface of a network-facing component. Windows Server 2003 users were unaffected by the Sasser worm (Microsoft 2005a) even though the code included the vulnerable security bug because the network endpoint that the worm attacked was accessible only to administrators seated at the keyboard. Microsoft developers had introduced an explicit "local administrator only" check in the remote procedure call (RPC) code during design reviews of the product. In Windows 2000 and Windows XP, this network interface was remotely accessible to anonymous users. Likewise, the Zotob worm did not affect Windows XP SP2 users (Microsoft 2005b) because in Windows XP SP2 and later versions of Windows, all RPC traffic must be authenticated before full communication can occur. Moreover, because malicious code such as Zotob is not authenticated (there is no valid user name and password associated with the payload), the attack could not penetrate to the vulnerable code. Lessons learned from the Blaster worm prompted the change in RPC attack surface in Windows XP SP2. Also, Windows XP SP2 explicitly enabled the firewall by default, blocking the RPC ports at the computer's IP network layer. This is a great example of multi-layer defenses.

You should consider each piece of functionality individually in your application to determine who needs to access the code by default (anonymous, user, or a specific group of users or administrators) and from where they should access it (remote, remote but only from a specific set of addresses or a subnet, site-local or link-local [IPv6], or local-only).

You can require valid user account access by using authentication and authorization techniques. Use techniques provided at the lowest possible level of your system, such as those in the operating system or those in a class library your application relies on, such as the Microsoft .NET Framework or the Java Runtime libraries.

Caution   Do not create your own authentication or authorization mechanisms unless the underlying mechanisms absolutely do not provide what you need. And if you still think you need to create your own mechanisms, think again!

You can often restrict network accessibility by using a firewall, but you should consider adding another layer of defense in case the firewall is disabled.

Important   Never depend on a firewall as your sole defense. Firewalls are exceptionally good perimeter defenses, but too often they are turned off or left open. How many stories have you heard of users being told to turn off their firewalls because an application didn't work correctly? The firewall is always the first suspect.

Perhaps the better way to restrict network accessibility is by a configuration switch that defaults to the local machine, the local subnet (such as 192.168.x.x, 10.x.x.x, or an internal corporate address), or site-local or link-local for IPv6 networks. You can then set network accessibility to "no restrictions" for users or environments that require this added level of connectivity.

Tip   In .NET code, you can use the *IPAddress.IsLoopback* function to determine whether a connection is from the local machine and whether it works with IPv4 and IPv6.

Best Practices   If your application is to analyze IP addresses, make sure the code can parse IPv6 as well as IPv4 addresses; Microsoft has a tool named checkv4 that can check WinSock C/C++ code for IPv4-specific dependencies (Microsoft 2006).

Step 3: Reduce Privilege

The last step in reducing attack surface is to ascertain the privilege level under which the code operates. This applies mainly to long-running processes such as Windows services or *nix daemon processes. Processes that are exploited when running in a Local System or root context can create catastrophic failure because the exploit code will also run in the same context, and these accounts have access to all resources on the compromised computer. It is therefore imperative that you run code with just enough privilege to get the job done, and no more.

In Windows, "privilege" has two aspects that must be evaluated: the privileges associated with the account (Microsoft 2005c) and the group membership associated with the account. Privileges allow an account to do computer-wide tasks such as debug an application or backup files. Sun Corporation's Solaris 10 operating system has a similar model (Rich 2005), as do POSIX capabilities in some versions of Linux (Solar and Mondi 2005).

In Windows, you can create an account that has just the privileges you want and have your service run under that account. Another way to solve the least-privilege problem is to run the service under a well-known account, such as Network Service, and then drop the privileges you don't need by calling *AdjustTokenPrivileges(...,SE_PRIVILEGE_REMOVED, ...)* on application startup. Windows Vista goes one step further by allowing you to define only the privileges you need by calling *ChangeServiceConfig2(...,SERVICE_CONFIG_REQUIRED_PRIVILEGES_INFO,...)*.

As for group membership, the most dangerous group is the Administrators group, and the only way to exclude this security identifier from the application token is to run the application as a non-administrator in the first place. In *nix, you can create a special group for the application and use *setgid <groupname>*.

Services and Low Privilege

Rather than running your Windows services as Local System (also referred to as SYSTEM), you should use less-risky service accounts such as Network Service or Local Service unless there is a very good reason to run under the Local System account.

Sometimes your service simply must run as the Local System account because the code performs some form of system-wide management or security-related tasks. But you can still run with lower privilege by splitting the application into more than one executable process and running only the management process with elevated privileges while the user-facing code runs with a lower privilege. Apache and IIS 6.0 use this model. In the case of Apache on *nix, the first httpd process starts up as root, and its role is to start, stop, and control other httpd process and open the HTTP ports. The spawned processes run with lower-privilege accounts such as the "nobody" or "apache" account. In the case of IIS6, the main administrative service runs as SYSTEM, but the main processes that handle user requests run as the much-lower-privilege Network Service account. The high-privilege administrator processes don't handle any user requests, and this decreases the potential threat to the high-privilege code. Figure 7-3 gives you an idea of how this pattern manifests itself.

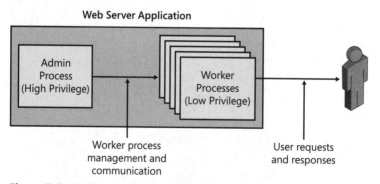

Figure 7-3   Split an application into multiple processes based on privilege. The low-privilege processes handle untrusted user requests, and the high-privilege process handles administrative tasks.

More Attack Surface Elements

Depending on the operating system or application you use, other elements of attack surface should be investigated. The following elements are some of the most important.

UDP vs. TCP

User Datagram Protocol (UDP) has a higher attack surface than TCP because the source IP address is easily spoofed. TCP performs a full three-way handshake to verify the address and port of the caller and callee, whereas UDP is a datagram "fire and forget" protocol. We're not saying you should remove UDP support from your application; the UDP protocol simply increases the attack surface of your product.

> **Note**   In Windows XP SP2 and later versions, all RPC datagram protocols are disabled by default to reduce attack surface.

Weak Permissions vs. Strong Permissions

A weak permission or ACL on an operating system object can render the computer vulnerable. In general, the default permissions on Windows objects are good enough, but you should always review the ACL your setup code explicitly sets on an object to make sure it offers appropriate defense. The same rule applies to *nix; you should review your code that sets permissions to make sure untrusted users do not have unnecessary access to the object.

An example of a weak ACL includes an ACL in a device driver that allows a normal user to overwrite the valid driver with rogue software. When the operating system loads the driver, the user's code, not the valid device driver, is loaded into kernel mode. This is an example of a local privilege-elevation bug.

.NET Code vs. ActiveX Code

The Microsoft .NET technology was designed from the ground up to support fine-grained permissions enforced by a central run-time policy engine. ActiveX controls have no such restrictions; hence, ActiveX controls have a larger attack surface. Sometimes an ActiveX control is the most appropriate solution to a problem, but not all the time. Always consider managed run-time technologies first. If they're not appropriate, consider ActiveX.

ActiveX "Safe for Scripting"

If you absolutely must create an ActiveX control, make sure it's not marked safe for scripting unless it's absolutely safe to call the control from untrusted mobile code such as JavaScript running in a Web browser. ActiveX controls that are marked safe for scripting have a larger attack surface than ActiveX controls that are not marked this way because these controls are accessible to low-trust code. One infamous example is an ActiveX control used to uninstall the XCP digital rights management (DRM) software written by First 4 Internet and distributed on some Sony BMG audio CDs. The uninstall control is marked safe for scripting and supports several potentially dangerous methods, including *RebootMachine*, *InstallUpdate*, and *IsAdministrator*.

ActiveX SiteLocked Controls

Web sites can render many forms of mobile code from HTML pages, and in many cases, mobile code that resides on a computer can be called by any Web page, including Web pages from malicious Web sites. ActiveX can limit which Web sites can call a control named *SiteLocking* (Microsoft 2002), which enables an ActiveX developer to restrict access so that the control is accessible only from a predetermined list of domains. This limits the ability of Web page authors to reuse the control for malicious purposes. You can also use the SiteLock template to make a control that behaves differently in different domains. The template consolidates domain checking into a single shared library that makes the ActiveX much more secure and much easier to fix when a problem arises.

A SiteLocked ActiveX control has a smaller attack surface than a non-SiteLocked control because the number of domains that can access the control is smaller.

Managed Code *AllowPartiallyTrustedCallers* Attribute

Strong-named assemblies marked with the *AllowPartiallyTrustedCallers* attribute (APTCA) can be called by code that is not fully trusted, such as code running from the Internet.

> **Note**   A strong name consists of the assembly's identity—its text name, version, and culture information—plus a public key and a digital signature.

You should mark your strong-named assembly with the APTCA only when your code must *categorically* be called from non-Full Trust code. Because code marked with APTCA can be called by less-trusted code, APTCA increases the attack surface of the code.

Table 7-1 lists attributes of an application that contribute to larger or smaller attack surfaces.

Table 7-1   Relative Attack Surface Rankings

Higher Attack Surface	Lower Attack Surface
Feature running by default	Feature not running by default
Open network connection	Closed network connection
Listening for UDP and TCP traffic	Listening only for TCP traffic
Anonymous access	Authenticated user access

Table 7-1   Relative Attack Surface Rankings

Higher Attack Surface	Lower Attack Surface
Authenticated user access	Administrator access (be careful not to make too much code admin-only because this can start violating the principle of least privilege)
Internet access	Subnet, link-local, or site-local access
Subnet, link-local, or site-local access	Local machine access
Code running with Administrator, Local System, or root privileges	Code running with Network Service, Local Service, or custom low-privilege account
Weak object permissions	Strong object permissions
ActiveX control	.NET code
ActiveX control marked safe for scripting	ActiveX control not marked safe for scripting
Non-SiteLocked ActiveX control	SiteLocked ActiveX control

Table 7-2 shows examples of how Microsoft has reduced the attack surface of some commonly used products.

Table 7-2   Attack Surface Reduction in Some Microsoft Products

Product	Attack Surface Reduction Step	Example of. . .
Microsoft Office 2003	Do not install various file format filters	Reducing running code
	Run by default only signed and trusted macros	Reducing Office code paths to trusted code
Microsoft Exchange Server 2003	Turn off POP, IMAP, and NNTP by default	Reducing running code
	Allow only trusted users to create root public folders	Strong permissions
	Disable many less-used RPC interfaces	Reducing running code
Microsoft Visual Studio 2005	Microsoft SQL Server Express allows only local connections by default	Reducing network accessibility
	Web server allows local connections by default	Reducing network accessibility
	ASP.NET runs as a non-admin account	Least privilege
	Web services reject HTTP GET requests	Reducing running code
	Debugging requires group membership	Strong permissions

Table 7-2   Attack Surface Reduction in Some Microsoft Products

Product	Attack Surface Reduction Step	Example of. . .
Windows XP SP2	All RPC communication must be authenticated	Strong permissions
	Turn on firewall by default	Reducing network accessibility
	Disable some services (for example, NetDDE)	Reducing running code
	No longer run some services as Local System (for example, RPC)	Least privilege
SQL Server 2005	Main SQL Server process runs as Network Service	Least privilege
	Disable xp_cmdshell	Reducing running code
	Disable .NET common language runtime	Reducing running code
	Disable COM integration	Reducing running code
	Disable ad hoc remote queries	Reducing running code

Developers have taken SQL Server 2005 one step further than most products, providing a small tool to determine which functionality is enabled or disabled by default and which networking protocols can be used. Figure 7-4 and Figure 7-5 show the SQL Server 2005 Surface Area Configuration tool.

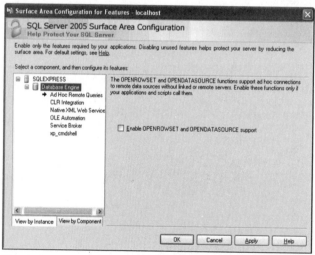

Figure 7-4   SQL Server 2005 can reduce features.

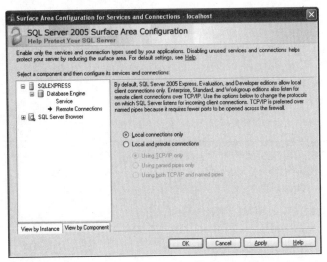

Figure 7-5   SQL Server 2005 can reduce network access.

Important   Attack Surface Reduction is as important as getting the code right because you will never get the code perfect!

Best Practices   Reduce attack surface early; do not wait until the product is nearly complete before you think about how you'll reduce the amount of code exposed by default to untrusted users.

We finish this section with a very important point. Personal firewalls, or firewalls installed on individual computers, are here to stay regardless of the operating system installed on the computer. Do not simply punch arbitrary holes in the firewall, and certainly do not tell users to turn the firewall off to run your application, even if the user's enterprise has a perimeter firewall. This is especially true for portable computers, which are often used outside the defenses offered by the corporate firewall. Build your application with an understanding that the machine on which it will run probably has a firewall installed, and that firewall should not be disabled.

Summary

In recent years, a lot of attention has been paid to secure-coding best practices and much less to secure-design principles. The SDL mandates that engineers spend time in the design phase thinking about the security of features and implementing secure designs. It's important that you learn the well-respected secure-design principles by reviewing and learning from some of the references in the following section.

Attack Surface Analysis is just as important as trying to secure the code because you will never secure the code 100 percent—you cannot predict the future, and humans make mistakes. The product you ship embodies a subset of the security best practices of the day, yet software security research continues. Document your attack surface, and aim to reduce it as much as is consistent with a usable product.

References

(Saltzer and Schroeder 1975)   Saltzer, Jerome H., and Michael D. Schroeder. "The Protection of Information in Computer Systems," *http://web.mit.edu/Saltzer/www/ publications/protection/index.html*. 1975.

(Computer Security Resource Center 2002)   "Early Computer Security Papers, Part I," *http:// csrc.nist.gov/publications/history/index.html*. June 2002.

(Yan and Randell 2005)   Yan, J., and B. Randell. "Security in Computer Games: From Pong to Online Poker," *http://www.cs.ncl.ac.uk/research/pubs/authors/byType.php?id= 408*. February 2005.

(Anderson 2001)   Anderson, Ross. *Security Engineering: A Guide to Building Dependable Distributed Systems*. New York, NY: John Wiley & Sons, 2001.

(Bishop 2002)   Bishop, Matt. *Computer Security: Art and Science*. Boston, MA: Addison-Wesley, 2002.

(Howard and LeBlanc 2003)   Howard, Michael, and David LeBlanc. *Writing Secure Code, Second Edition*. Redmond, WA: Microsoft Press, 2003.

(Rescorla and Korver 2003)   Rescorla, E., and B. Korver. "Guidelines for Writing RFC Text on Security Considerations," *ftp://ftp.rfc-editor.org/in-notes/rfc3552.txt*. RFC 3552, July 2003.

(Wikipedia 2006)   "Kerchoff's Law," *http://en.wikipedia.org/wiki/Kerchoffs_law*.

(McCabe and Watson 1994)   McCabe, Thomas J., and Arthur H. Watson. "Software Complexity," *http://www.stsc.hill.af.mil/crosstalk/1994/12/xt94d12b.asp*. Crosstalk, December 1994.

(VanDoren 2000)   VanDoren, Edmond. "Cyclomatic Complexity," *http://www.sei.cmu.edu/ str/descriptions/cyclomatic.html*. July 2000.

(VanDoren 1997)   VanDoren, Edmond. "Halstead Complexity Measures," *http:// www.sei.cmu.edu/str/descriptions/halstead.html*. January 1997.

(Microsoft 2004)   Microsoft Security Bulletin MS04-030. "Vulnerability in WebDAV XML Message Handler Could Lead to a Denial of Service," *http://www.microsoft.com/technet/ security/bulletin/ms04-030.mspx*. October 2004.

(Microsoft 2005a)   "Malicious Software Encyclopedia: Win32/Sasser," *http:// www.microsoft.com/security/encyclopedia/details.aspx?name=Win32%2fSasser*. January 2005.

(Microsoft 2005b) "Malicious Software Encyclopedia: Win32/Zotob," *http://www.microsoft.com/security/encyclopedia/details.aspx?name=Win32%2fzotob.* November 2005.

(Microsoft 2006) "Using the Checkv4.exe Utility," *http://msdn.microsoft.com/library/en-us/winsock/winsock/using_the_checkv4_exe_utility_2.asp.* MSDN, January 2006.

(Microsoft 2005c) "Privileges," *http://msdn.microsoft.com/library/en-us/secauthz/security/privileges.asp.* MSDN, December 2005.

(Rich 2005) Rich, Amy. "The Least Privilege Model in the Solaris 10 OS," *http://www.sun.com/bigadmin/features/articles/least_privilege.html.* February 2005.

(Solar and Mondi 2005) Solar, and Adam Mondi. "POSIX Capabilities," *http://www.gentoo.org/proj/en/hardened/capabilities.xml.* January 2005.

(Microsoft 2002) "SiteLock Template 1.04 for ActiveX Controls," *http://msdn.microsoft.com/archive/en-us/samples/internet/components/sitelock/default.asp.* MSDN, May 2002.

Chapter 8
Stage 3: Product Risk Assessment

Before investing a great deal of time designing and implementing software, you should understand the costs of building secure applications, especially those handling data with privacy considerations. Obviously, you want to expend as much effort as needed to create the appropriate level of protection, but not too much more. Higher risk translates into higher development and support costs. As discussed in Chapter 1, "Enough Is Enough: The Threats Have Changed," privacy and security are intricately intertwined, and understanding the impact of both on your software is an important part of performing a risk assessment required to build protections into the software.

The purpose of the product risk assessment stage is to clarify the level of effort required to fulfill Security Development Lifecycle (SDL) requirements. During this phase, you should identify

- What portions of the project will require threat models before release.

- What portions of the project will require security design reviews.

- What portions of the project will require penetration testing (possibly by a mutually agreed-upon third party).

- The scope of fuzz testing requirements.

Note The steps involved in this stage of the SDL are for guidance purposes only—it is left to the development team to estimate the actual amount of effort required to build the application. Obviously, security and privacy ramifications are important considerations in software estimation, but so are product size, product scope, level of automation, maturity of the development team, and so on. See Steve McConnell's *Software Estimation: Demystifying the Black Art* for more on estimation (McConnell 2006).

Your risk assessment should include two distinct deliverables: first, the Security Risk Assessment and, second, the Privacy Impact Rating. Let's look at each.

Security Risk Assessment

The Security Risk Assessment is used to determine the system's level of vulnerability to attack. When we first started the security engineering effort at Microsoft, one of our earliest requirements was for teams to fill out a short questionnaire, which the security team used to determine how deeply to probe various parts of the software. This questionnaire was a little like the health-related paperwork you fill out when you first visit a medical practitioner; the paperwork helps the physician know where to poke and probe to determine what might ail you.

On the CD   The disc that accompanies this book includes a version of the Security Risk Assessment document.

Some of the questions in the risk assessment are listed in the following sections.

Setup Questions

- On which operating systems is your software installed?
- Does your setup program require an Administrators password?
- Does your setup application configure access control lists (ACLs)? If yes, why are you not using the default operating system ACLs?
- Does your installer modify the Active Directory directory service schema? If yes, what are the changes?

Attack Surface Questions

- Is your feature installed by default? If yes, why?
- Does your feature run by default? If yes, why?
- Does your feature run with elevated privileges? If yes, why?
- Does your feature listen on network sockets? If yes, which port numbers does it use?
- Does your feature have any network connections that are accessible on the Internet? If yes, why are they not restricted to a smaller set of addresses?
- Does your feature set any firewall policy? If yes, what is the policy?
- Does your feature have any unauthenticated network connections? If yes, which are unauthenticated and why?

Mobile-Code Questions

- Does your feature include ActiveX controls (does it use IDispatch)? If yes, why?

- If you build one or more ActiveX controls, why are you not using technologies with fine-grained security permissions, such as .NET or Java?

- If you build one or more ActiveX controls, are they marked as safe for scripting? If yes, why?

- Does your feature include any script code? If yes, what does the code do, and what languages do you use?

Security Feature–Related Questions

- Does the application implement any security mechanisms such as authentication or authorization?

- Does the application implement or use any cryptographic mechanisms?

General Questions

- Is this a new product? If not, how big is the delta from the prior version?

- Has this product had serious security bugs in the past? If yes, what are the bug numbers?

- Has a penetration-testing engagement been performed on a previous release of this project?

- Does your application parse files?

- Does your application parse network traffic?

- Does your application query a database?

- Does your application include an Internet Server Application Programming Interface (ISAPI) application or filter?

- Does your application include sample code?

- What extensibility mechanisms do you have (for example, plug-in protocol handlers)?

- What components can download and execute code (for example, an automatic-update feature)?

- Does your application have user-mode and kernel-mode components?

- Do your application's non-administrative users interact with elevated processes such as services?

Analyzing the Questionnaire

Although there are no absolute right or wrong answers in the risk assessment questionnaire, if you can answer affirmatively to many of these questions, the security team will need to analyze your application more deeply to ensure that the development team does the best it can to shore up the application's defenses.

That being said, here are some general rules you can apply:

- Every method and property on every ActiveX control must be reviewed to determine safety.

- If this is a new product, it will require a thorough security design review.

- If the application has a networking interface, it must be threat modeled.

- If the application has kernel-mode and user-mode interaction, it must be threat modeled.

- If non-administrators interact with higher-privileged processes, the application must be threat modeled.

- If the application is a security feature, it must be threat modeled.

- Sample code must meet the same quality standards as shipping code and must therefore follow all SDL requirements.

- If an application parses files or network traffic, the application is subject to the SDL fuzzing requirements as defined in Chapter 12, "Stage 7: Secure Testing Policies."

Privacy Impact Rating

The next part of product risk assessment is to assess the Privacy Impact Rating of the project. This assessment is much simpler than the security risk analysis because it has only three policy values: privacy ranking 1, privacy ranking 2, and privacy ranking 3. Before we explain the three levels, take a look at Table 8-1 for descriptions of some important terminology used when describing the data associated with the privacy levels.

Table 8-1   Important Privacy-Related Definitions

Data Type	Description
Anonymous data	Any user data that is not unique or tied to a specific person and cannot be traced back to the person. This data might include hair color, system configuration, method by which a product was purchased (retail, online, and so on), or usage statistics distilled from a large collection of users.
	Note that if anonymous data is associated with personally identifiable information (PII), it must also be treated as PII.

Table 8-1   Important Privacy-Related Definitions

Data Type	Description
Personally identifiable information (PII)	Any user data that uniquely identifies a user such as contact information (name, address, phone number, e-mail address, and so on).
	–Or–
	Data that is commingled or correlated with the user's PII, for example, demographics stored with the user's PII or with a unique ID that can be linked to the user's PII.
	–Or–
	Data that is sensitive PII.
Sensitive PII	Any user data that identifies an individual and could facilitate identity theft or fraud. This data includes social security numbers, tax IDs, credit card numbers, and bank account numbers.
	–Or–
	Data that is commingled or correlated with PII and used as an authorization key, such as passwords and PINs (personal identification numbers), biometric information (when used to authenticate), mother's maiden name, and so on.
	–Or–
	Data that is commingled or correlated with PII and could be used to discriminate, such as sexual preference or sexual lifestyle, political or religious beliefs, ethnicity or race, or trade union membership.
	–Or–
	Data that is commingled or correlated with PII and contains medical history or health records or financial information.
	–Or–
	Data that has breadth and contents that are unknown at the time of collection and could hold sensitive PII. An example of this kind of data is a raw memory dump.

Now we'll explain the three privacy rankings. Components determined to be at the highest privacy ranking must be subjected to thorough privacy analysis, often involving privacy experts, to make sure that the application does not leak private data or violate any privacy laws or regulations.

> **Note**   Privacy rankings do not indicate the software's correctness; rather, they indicate the level of privacy thoroughness required, which translates into necessary cost, time, and effort.

Privacy Ranking 1

If any of the following statements are true of your application, it has the highest-possible privacy ranking and therefore requires the highest privacy due diligence:

- The application stores PII or transfers PII to the software developer or a third party.

- The application is targeted at children or could be deemed attractive to children, or the application includes any user experiences in which you know the user's age. Knowing that the application might be used by children is especially important in online applications because such applications must protect users under age 13 to abide by the Children's Online Privacy Protection Act (COPPA 1998), which requires adult permission to collect PII.

- The application continuously monitors the user of your application.

- The application installs new software or changes the user's file-type associations (for example, it changes the application that handles JPEG files), home page, or search page.

> **Important**   Before collecting and transferring PII, you must have compelling business value and customer value. Many customers are accustomed to making deals, but when a deal does not benefit them, they often feel cheated and might begin to distrust your company. Collect personal data only if you can clearly explain the benefit to users. If you are hesitant to any degree to tell users what you plan to do with their PII, do not collect their data.

Privacy Ranking 2

If your application transfers anonymous data to the software developer or to a third party, the application is rated at privacy ranking 2.

Privacy Ranking 3

If the application exhibits none of the behaviors in privacy rankings 1 and 2, the application is rated at privacy ranking 3.

Pulling It All Together

Once you have determined your application's level of security and privacy risk, you must allot time in the schedule to make sure the appropriate level of expertise and effort is applied to reduce the overall risk to customers. For example, if your software product has many security risks, you must evaluate and analyze each risk to make sure the correct security decisions have been made to protect customers.

> **Note** Sometimes an insecure design is necessary to support legacy environments. In that case, you should evaluate the tradeoff between risk and compatibility.

If the application handles and transfers sensitive data, identify the business and customer benefits for doing this. If there is no customer and business benefit for collecting such data, remove that feature from your application.

Summary

The product risk assessment stage is critically important because it helps you determine how best to spend resources when developing the software. Before you begin product development, your team should complete a simple questionnaire to determine the software's highest-risk components. If the questionnaire shows that you employ numerous potentially risky technologies, or if you determine that you risk privacy violations, the application must undergo much greater security and privacy scrutiny. In some cases, your potential security issues determine the level of effort you must dedicate to other parts of the SDL, such as fuzzing, security design review, and threat modeling.

References

(McConnell 2006)   McConnell, Steve. *Software Estimation: Demystifying the Black Art.* Redmond, WA: Microsoft Press, 2006.

(COPPA 1998)   Federal Trade Commission. Children's Online Privacy Protection Act of 1998, *http://www.coppa.org/*.

Chapter 9
Stage 4: Risk Analysis

If we had our hands tied behind our backs (we don't) and could do only one thing to improve software security—threat modeling, better security code reviews, or better security testing—we would do threat modeling every day of the week. The reason is simple: when performed correctly, threat modeling occurs early in the project lifecycle and can be used to find security design issues before code is committed. This can lead to significant cost savings because issues are resolved early in the development lifecycle. Derived from numerous studies and research sources, Table 9-1—from Steve McConnell's *Code Complete* (McConnell 2004)—shows the relative cost of fixing defects in code.

Table 9-1 Relative Cost of Removing Software Defects

Defect Introduction Point	Defects Found During Requirements	Defects Found During Architecture	Defects Found During Construction	Defects Found During Test	Defects Found After Release
Requirements	1	3	5–10	10	10–100
Architecture	None	1	10	15	25–100
Construction	None	None	1	10	10–25

The idea behind threat modeling is simply to understand the potential security threats to the system, determine risk, and establish appropriate mitigations. Threat modeling also helps businesses manage software risk, creates awareness of security dependencies and assumptions, and provides the ability to translate technical risk to business impact (and vice versa). Over the last two years, Microsoft has extensively researched how to improve threat modeling and has garnered feedback from the Microsoft Trustworthy Computing Academic Advisory Board (TCAAB 2003), Microsoft employees, and others in the software and security industries and academia.

> **Note**   The meaning of the word *threat* is much debated. In this book, a threat is defined as an attacker's objective. To some, the threat is the attacker or adversary; we refer to this entity as the threat agent. These definitions are used in the Common Criteria.

The threat-modeling processes documented in *Writing Secure Code, Second Edition* (Howard and LeBlanc 2003) and then explained further in *Threat Modeling* (Swiderski and Snyder 2004) have received some valid criticism; most notably, they require too much security expertise, and they're subjective (Torr 2005).

The updated method described in this chapter addresses both these issues by providing a more streamlined and coherent process. Note that threat modeling is not a static process. At Microsoft, we are constantly learning how make the technique easier, more approachable, and frankly, more beneficial.

The benefits of threat modeling are numerous. Notably, threat modeling

- Contributes to the risk management process because threats to software and infrastructure are risks to the user and environment deploying the software.

- Uncovers threats to the system before the system is committed to code.

- Revalidates the architecture and design by having the development team go over the design again.

- Forces development staff to look at the design from a different viewpoint—that of security and privacy. To understand the most at-risk components, development staff focuses on components with a high attack probability.

- Helps clarify the selection of appropriate countermeasures for the application and environment.

- Contributes to the Attack Surface Reduction (ASR) process for the software. (See Chapter 7, "Stage 2: Define and Follow Design Best Practices.")

- Helps guide the code review process.

- Guides the penetration testing process.

We'll discuss all of these throughout the rest of this chapter. But before we do, we want to explain something very important about threat models. At Microsoft, we have found that a good set of threat models is a sign of a "security healthy" team. Good threat models mean the team has thought through the security and privacy issues in depth. Contrast this with a group that has poor or incomplete threat models, and this might indicate the team has not spent enough time thinking through the threats to the system. It does not mean the code is poor quality; it might very well be rock-solid, but the team still might need help understanding the threats.

> **Best Practices**   A good set of threat models is a sign of a "security healthy" team. It indicates that the team has thought through security and privacy issues in depth. A group that has poor or incomplete threat models might not have spent enough time thinking through the threats to the system. Although the code they produced might be great, team members might need help recognizing that code threats continue to be a serious issue.

Threat-Modeling Artifacts

The main output of the threat-modeling process is a document (or documents) that describes background information about the application and defines the high-level application model, often by using data flow diagrams (DFDs); a list of assets that require protection; threats to the system ranked by risk; and, optionally, a list of mitigations. Relevant background information includes the following:

- **Use scenarios**   Deployment configurations and broad customer uses
- **External dependencies**   Products, components, or services the application or system relies on
- **Security assumptions**   Assumptions you make about the security services offered by other components
- **External security notes**   Information useful to your product's end user or administrator to operate the system securely

We'll explain these subjects in further detail shortly.

> **Note**   In the "classic" Microsoft threat-modeling process, internal security information (also called *internal security notes*) can also be tracked. Such tracking is infrequently done, so in the interests of brevity, we won't discuss internal security notes in this chapter.

Once the threat model is complete, the document should be placed under normal document control policy. At this point, the threat model is treated like any other specification or design document, and it should be revisited often and updated as needed.

> **Important**   A threat model should be updated for evolving threats perhaps every six months. A threat model that is more than a year old is probably woefully out of date because of ongoing security research. For example, in mid-September 2005, researchers at the University of California, Berkeley, found a way to analyze keyboard clicks to determine in real time what a user types (UC Berkeley 2005). To some people, this is not a big deal, but to others it might very well be a serious system threat. Prior to September 2005, this potential threat was unknown.

What to Model

Large software products are composed of smaller modules, and modeling smaller modules is often more efficient than modeling the entire product. However, this approach leads threats to the system once the system is fully composed. After all, a system can be secure at a micro level, but the interaction between two components can cause insecurity if your security assumptions about other components in the system are incorrect.

As a start, consider the trust boundaries of your application, and model all the components inside that trust boundary. Next, look outside the boundaries to determine what is really part of your application. If the answer is "nothing," you have successfully bounded the scope of your DFD. We'll discuss trust or privilege boundaries shortly.

> **Note**   This chapter uses the example of an e-commerce application named Pet Shop 4.0. Vertigo Software created Pet Shop 4.0 for Microsoft Corporation to demonstrate Microsoft .NET development best practices (Pet Shop 2006).

Building the Threat Model

A common question we hear is, "Who builds the threat model?" The threat-modeling process is owned by a person in the design group, for example, an architect, program manager, or analyst. The person who has the most security background is probably the most appropriate choice for this role. Other engineering disciplines such as software development, user education, and testing are also involved to provide important design information, but they do not drive the process; that is left to designers. Threat modeling is part of the design process, after all.

At a high level, the model-building process follows these steps:

- **Prepare**   System designers take the lead in preparing, with input from the development team, to build the DFDs. The resulting artifact is sent to other team members for review before the core threat-modeling analysis process begins.

- **Analyze**   All threats are uncovered through the analysis process and are added to the threat model document. At this stage, you include more people in the process. However, try to keep the number of attendees manageable—if you include more than ten people, you'll probably model too much. Also remember that at this stage you should discuss only threats, not mitigations.

- **Determine mitigations**   More of the product team is involved in identifying mitigations. This step is performed once the threat model is basically complete. The team considers the model to determine the appropriate remedies to the threats. No doubt there will be feedback from people not involved in the earlier analysis stage; this is to be expected.

The rest of this chapter describes the threat-modeling process in detail. We'll cover the following topics:

- The threat-modeling process
- Mitigation techniques
- Using a threat model to aid code review
- Using a threat model to aid testing

The Threat-Modeling Process

Although the high-level steps involved in creating a threat model may seem numerous, many of the elements require little security expertise and are virtually rote. The steps are as follows:

1. Define use scenarios.
2. Gather a list of external dependencies.
3. Define security assumptions.
4. Create external security notes.
5. Create one or more DFDs of the application being modeled.
6. Determine threat types.
7. Identify the threats to the system.
8. Determine risk.
9. Plan mitigations.

1. Define Use Scenarios

At this stage of the process, the team needs to determine which key threat scenarios are within scope. For example, if you create a mobile or small device, you'll probably want to cover the stolen-device scenario. However, you may determine that the device stores no sensitive data whatsoever, so the risk associated with a stolen device is low. In this situation, you should explicitly state the reasoning behind your decision. If you don't, someone years from now is bound to ask why you did not cover the stolen-device scenario! If you later decide to store sensitive data on the device, you'll need to revisit the model.

You should also consider the insider-threat scenario—should your product protect against attackers who work for your company? If so, the threats you need to consider will be quite different from those that you can expect from external threat agents. Never lose track of who you are up against.

Also include other common, but not security-related, scenarios such as the type of customer you expect to use your software. An application designed solely for administration purposes (for example, a disk analysis tool) has a different threat profile than a product that is primarily accessed by anonymous users (for example, a Web or e-mail server).

 Caution   Do not confuse use scenarios with UML Use Cases; the terms sound similar, but they are not the same.

2. Gather a List of External Dependencies

Your application is not self-sufficient: it runs on operating systems and might use a database, Web server, or high-level application framework. It's important that you document all the other code your application depends on. For example, the Internet-based pet store application, Pet Shop 4.0, might depend on the following:

- A Web-based client using Microsoft Internet Explorer 6.0 or later and FireFox 1.5 or later.
- Microsoft Windows Server 2003 and Solaris 10 servers
- On the server only, Microsoft SQL Server 2005 (on Windows Server 2003) and Oracle 10g (on Solaris 10)
- On the server only, Microsoft Message Queue 2.0
- Microsoft .NET Framework 2.0 and common language runtime 2.0 (server only)

You should also consider the default system-hardening configuration. For example, in the case of Windows Server 2003, you might require only the default hardened version of the operating system to run. Or perhaps you might need to loosen some of the security settings in the system. If you do this, you must inform your users.

3. Define Security Assumptions

This is a critically important section because if you make inaccurate security assumptions about the environment in which the application resides, your application might be rendered utterly insecure. For example, if your application stores encryption keys, a design requirement might be that you rely on the underlying operating system to protect the keys, so the assumption is that the operating system will protect the keys correctly. Let's analyze this assumption: in the case of Microsoft Windows XP and later, this might be true if you store the keys using the data protection API (DPAPI). However, in the case of Linux (as of the 2.6 kernel), there is no such service, so the assumption is incorrect, and you shouldn't store encryption keys in plaintext unless you have other viable defenses. For the record, most files holding sensitive data are stored in Linux by using a permission that allows access to only the most trusted user, the root account. But this storage option might not be enough; you might want to allow only a specific user access to his or her sensitive data, not the administrator and not the root account.

But trying to restrict access to only valid users and not administrators is interesting; we have defined some external security notes about the role of the root account.

4. Create External Security Notes

Users and other application designers who interact with your product can use external security notes to understand your application's security boundaries and how they can maintain security when using your application.

The prior section mentions that sensitive files in Linux are often protected by a permission that allows only root to access them. This means that root, like the administrator and SYSTEM accounts in Windows, is all-powerful and can usually read or manipulate any file or setting in the operating system. Your users should know this.

In some scenarios, this might not be the case if you are using SELinux, which can enforce mandatory access control or, in the case of tampering rather than disclosure, Microsoft Windows Vista with its mandatory integrity control might suffice. These are both examples of security technologies and dependencies that you assume behave as advertised.

As you can see, there is a tight relationship among external security notes, security assumptions, and dependencies. The following Pet Shop example shows how external dependencies, security assumptions, and external security information might relate.

Pet Shop 4.0 External Dependencies

We expect and rely on the following components within the system. You should also outline specific version numbers.

- Client
    - Clients running Internet Explorer 6.0 or later or FireFox 1.5 or later.
- Servers
    - Windows Server 2003 SP1
    - Microsoft Internet Information Services (IIS) 6.0 (Web server computers)
    - Microsoft ASP.NET 2.0 and .NET Framework 2.0 (Web server computers)
    - Microsoft SQL Server 2000, Microsoft SQL Server 2005, or Oracle 10g (database server computers)
    - Windows Server 2003 Terminal Services (all servers)
    - Microsoft Message Queue 2.0 (Web server computers)
    - Microsoft Distributed Transaction Coordinator (MSDTC) (all computers)

Pet Shop 4.0 Security Assumptions

Security assumptions are the guarantees you expect from the external dependencies:

- No sensitive data is deliberately persisted on the client, but sensitive data is sent over SSL/TLS connections, and some browsers might locally cache data sent over these connections.

■ DPAPI is used on the server to protect sensitive connection strings and encryption keys for non-administrators.

■ The database server holds authentication information.

■ The database server adequately protects authentication data by using database server authorization technology and, potentially, encryption.

■ IIS 6.0 and ASP.NET enforce authentication correctly.

■ Web service security configuration is held in Web.config files and can be manipulated only by valid administrators. This rule is enforced through operating system access control lists (ACLs).

■ The server application setup program correctly configures the ACL for the Web.config file.

■ Only valid admins administer any server by using Terminal Services or physically accessing the server when needed.

■ Only valid admins have physical access to the Web and database servers.

■ Browsing the Internet, reading e-mail messages, and using peer-to-peer or instant messaging applications on the servers is expressly prohibited.

■ Databases are configured to use their native authentication protocols rather than operating system authentication protocols. For example, SQL Server uses Standard authentication and not Windows authentication. This is done for two main reasons. First, most users are Internet-based users, not Windows users. The second reason is performance—native authentication schemes are faster.

■ The connection information for each database is stored in the application's Web.config file and protected by using the Protected Configuration option, which uses DPAPI.

Pet Shop 4.0 External Security Information

The threat model must explain security-relevant information that end users could employ to secure their systems or, in some cases, understand the security ramifications of enabling certain functionality. Here's the list of external security information for our running example:

■ Admins can change any setting in the system, including the Web service.

■ The only ports open are TCP/3389 (for administration accessible only to other administration computers), TCP/80 (for HTTP traffic accessible from the Internet), TCP/443 (for HTTPS traffic accessible from the Internet), TCP/1433 and TCP/1521 (for database access that is accessible only by the Web server and by administration computers), and TCP/3372 (for MSDTC, which is accessible by all computers involved in order-processing transactions—these are usually just the Web server computers and database server computers).

The network diagram in Figure 9-1 shows the port relationship among computers in the application.

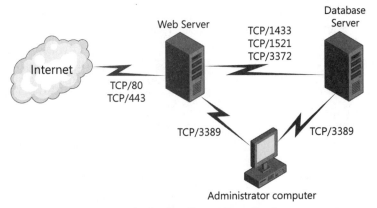

Figure 9-1   Port usage in the Pet Shop 4.0 application.

What Is Modeled and What Do You Depend On?

What follows is a best practice that can help uncover the boundary between something you control and can threat-model and something you can't control but depend on, which might have security assumptions. This will probably be iterative because you need to understand where to interface with components you don't control. Let's say you're building a Web application that sits on top of some Web class helper libraries you wrote, which in turn use a framework library, which sits on top of a Web server, which sits on top of a TCP/IP stack, which sits on top of a network driver, which sits on top of a network card. Figure 9-2 schematically represents this scenario. When you put a line just below whatever you control, everything above the line should be in your threat model, and everything below it is something you depend on.

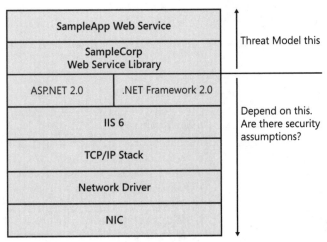

Figure 9-2   Drawing the line between what you threat-model and what you depend on.

5. Create One or More DFDs of the Application Being Modeled

The next stage is creating DFDs for the application. It's critical that you get this right because if the DFD is wrong, the rest of the threat-modeling process is wrong. We won't explain the DFD process in great detail here because there is plenty of good literature available on the subject (Kozar 1997, Sauter 2002, Drewry 2005, Ambler 2006, DFD 2006, Yourdon 2006). However, we'll cover enough to give you a good overview of the process.

The highest-level DFD is the context diagram, which shows the system under development at the center and the external entities that interact with the system. The context diagram helps you understand who interacts with your code. Figure 9-3 shows a context diagram for Pet Shop 4.0.

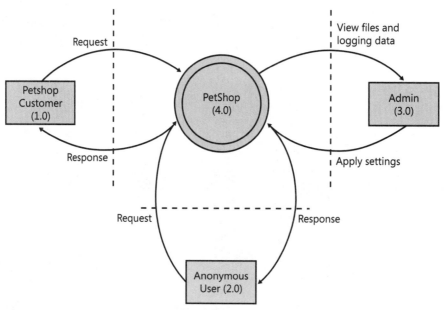

Figure 9-3   Context diagram for Pet Shop 4.0.

The shapes listed in Table 9-2 are used when building DFDs.

Table 9-2   DFD Element Types

Shape	DFD Element Type	Description
<double circle>	Complex process (also called a multiprocess)	A logical representation of a process that performs many distinct operations. Examples include a service or daemon, an assembly, a Win32 .exe file that hosts many dynamic-link libraries (DLLs).
<circle>	Process	A logical representation of a process that performs one discrete task. Some DFD references use a rounded rectangle to represent a process.

Table 9-2   DFD Element Types

Shape	DFD Element Type	Description
<rectangle>	External entity (also interactor)	Someone or something that drives your application but that your application cannot control. Examples include system users, asynchronous events, and external processes.
<parallel lines>	Data store	Persistent data storage such as files and databases; could also include cached information. Some DFD references use an open-ended rectangle to represent a data store.
<arrowed line>	Data flow	Means by which data moves around the system. Examples include networking communications, shared memory, and function calls.
<dotted line>	Privilege boundary (also trust boundary)	Specific to threat modeling, privilege boundaries delineate data moving from low to high trust and vice versa. Examples are machine-to-machine boundaries, process boundaries (where, for example, a low-privilege user communicates with a high-privilege process), and the line between kernel-mode and user-mode code.

As you can see in the context diagram in Figure 9-3, one central complex process is the entire Pet Shop 4.0 application itself. The only external entry points are to anonymous users, Pet Shop customers, and administrators.

Value of Privilege or Trust Boundaries

Trust boundaries are demarcation points in the application that show where data moves from lower privilege to higher privilege. These boundaries can help pinpoint areas in the application where data must be analyzed for correctness, but they can also be the site of sensitive data leaks. For example, an anonymous user creates a request that is sent to a higher-privilege process for consumption. Because the data moves from low privilege to a higher privilege, the request must be vetted for correctness. Any code on a boundary like this must be human-reviewed for correctness. This is especially true if the trust delta is large. For example, an anonymous user interacting with code running as admin, root, or system constitutes a very large privilege delta, whereas an administrator interacting with the same code constitutes a substantially lower privilege delta.

But there is more to this. Because data moving from high to low privilege must not leak sensitive, private, or confidential data, you must analyze the data traveling from the high-privilege process to make sure error messages and the like do not leak enough to aid an attacker.

Notice how all the components of the context diagram in Figure 9-3 are numbered, and each data flow is associated with a verb or verb/noun. Adding verbs and possibly nouns to a data flow helps provide context for the tasks you expect the user to perform. For some data flows, you can use create, read, update, and delete (CRUD) nomenclature. This nomenclature is fine for most data flows, but it's not very descriptive because you often need to include a noun to describe what is being manipulated.

The next step is to look at the context diagram, drill down into the complex processes, and create the next diagram, which is called the level-0 DFD. The context diagram for Pet Shop 4.0 has only one complex process: element 4.0. Figure 9-4 shows the level-0 DFD—the view of the application when you drill inside the Pet Shop 4.0 complex process.

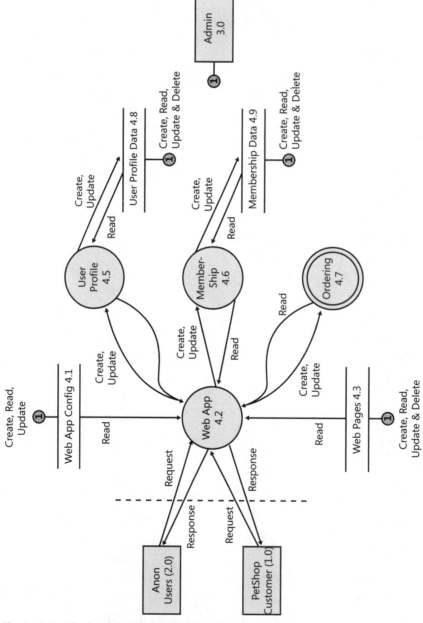

Figure 9-4   The level-0 DFD for Pet Shop 4.0.

As you can see, it's a little more complex when you drill down. You'll also notice one more complex process in the level-0 DFD: the order-processing process (4.7). We need to drill down into that, too, until there are no complex processes left. In the interests of clarity, we reduce the number of data flows from the administrator to the various data stores she manages. Figure 9-5 shows the level-1 DFD for order processing.

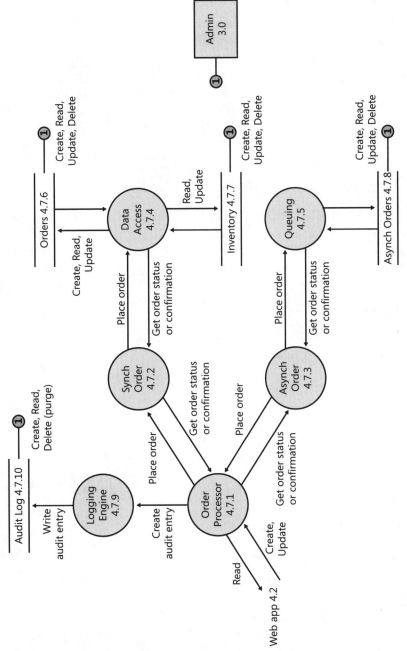

Figure 9-5   The level-1 DFD for order processing within Pet Shop 4.0.

At this level, we can see that the Pet Shop 4.0 application handles both synchronous and asynchronous requests. Asynchronous orders generally allow for greater application throughput. In this application, throughput increases by up to 30 percent. In the Pet Shop 4.0 application, asynchronous orders are not fulfilled immediately; rather, they are fulfilled by an external application that is not covered by this threat model.

Note that the numbering system for each of the DFD elements is a hierarchical dotted notation. Element 4.0 in the original context diagram (Figure 9-3) contains elements 4.1 through 4.9 in the level-0 DFD, and element 4.7 contains elements 4.7.1 through 4.7.10.

> **Important**   The original Pet Shop 4.0 application did not include an audit-log facility; we added it (4.7.9 and 4.7.10) and made a design-change request to the Pet Shop authors. Programs such as online e-commerce applications *need* auditing facilities beyond those offered by the Web server and the database engines because many of the ordering semantics are lost to the Web and database servers that see only HTTP requests and database queries.

6. Determine Threat Types

Microsoft uses a threat taxonomy called STRIDE to identify various threat types. STRIDE considers threats from the attacker's perspective. Another common taxonomy is CIA, described below, which defines desirable security properties. STRIDE is more complete than CIA in that CIA does not address common security issues today, such as authentication. The properties of CIA are as follows:

- **Confidentiality**   Ensures that information is not accessed by unauthorized users
- **Integrity**   Ensures that information is not altered by unauthorized users in a way that is undetectable by authorized users
- **Availability**   Ensures that principals (users or computers) have appropriate access to resources

The following sections describe the components of STRIDE.

Spoofing Identity

Spoofing threats allow an attacker to pose as something or somebody else, such as another user pretending to be Bill Gates, a server pretending to be Microsoft.com, or even code posing as Ntdll.dll.

Tampering

Tampering threats involve malicious modification of data or code. The data or code being manipulated could be at rest or ephemeral "on-the-wire" data.

Repudiation

An attacker makes a repudiation threat by denying to have performed an action that other parties can neither confirm nor contradict. For example, a user makes a repudiation threat when he performs an illegal operation in a system that can't trace the prohibited operation.

Non-repudiation is a system's ability to counter repudiation threats. For example, in a commercial system, if a user signs for a purchased item upon receipt, the vendor can later use the signed receipt as evidence that the user received the item. As you can imagine, non-repudiation is important for e-commerce applications.

An important caveat you should understand about repudiation is that only humans repudiate (Ellison 2000). However, computers and software can gather evidence that can be used to counter the claims of the repudiating party.

Information Disclosure

Information disclosure threats involve the exposure of information to individuals who are not supposed to have access to it. Examples of this type of threat include a user's ability to read a file that she was not granted access to and an intruder's ability to read data in transit between computers.

 Caution   Information disclosure threats, if left unmitigated, can become privacy violations if the disclosed data is confidential or personally identifiable information (PII).

Denial of Service

Denial-of-service (DoS) attacks deny or degrade service to valid users—for example, by making a Web server temporarily unavailable or unusable. You must protect against certain types of DoS threats simply to improve system availability and reliability.

Elevation of Privilege

Elevation-of-privilege (EoP) threats often occur when a user gains increased capability, often as an anonymous user who takes advantage of a coding bug to gain admin or root capability. One of the many examples of this threat is a series of defects in the open-source version-control software—Concurrent Versions System, or CVS—on Linux (CERT 2003), which led to a compromise of the kernel source code (Silicon 2003).

EoP is more subtle than as previously described because it does not apply only to anonymous or low-trust users. For example, the ability to go from an anonymous to a valid user is an EoP, as is moving from user to admin.

EoP threats also exist in code; for example, if a flaw in the Java or .NET runtime grants a unit of code more permission than normal, that too is an EoP threat. Java Web Start Untrusted Application Privilege Escalation (CVE-2005-1974) is an example of this threat. Likewise, running mobile code in a Web browser with more capability than the code should have is an EoP. Firefox/Mozilla Chrome UI DOM Property Override Privilege Escalation (CVE-2005-1160) is an example of this kind of EoP, as is the URL Decoding Zone Spoofing Vulnerability in Internet Explorer (CVE-2005-0054).

7. Identify Threats to the System

Once the DFD is done, you need to list all the DFD elements (also often referred to as assets) because you need to protect these elements from attack. Table 9-3 lists all the elements in the preceding DFD diagrams. Note that you don't include complex processes; rather, you include the processes, data stores, and data flows inside the complex process. However, you do model data flows in and out of a complex process.

Table 9-3   DFD Elements Within the Pet Shop 4.0 Application

DFD Element Type	DFD Item Numbers
External Entities	Pet Shop customer (1.0)
	Anonymous user (2.0)
	Administrator (3.0)
Processes	Web application (4.2)
	User profile (4.5)
	Membership (4.6)
	Order processor (4.7.1)
	Synchronous order processor (4.7.2)
	Asynchronous order processor (4.7.3)
	Data access component (4.7.4)
	Queuing component (4.7.5)
	Auditing engine (4.7.9)
Data Stores	Web application configuration data (4.1)
	Web pages (4.3)
	User profile data (4.8)
	Membership data (4.9)
	Orders data (4.7.6)
	Inventory data (4.7.7)
	Asynch orders data (4.7.8)
	Audit-log data (4.7.10)

Table 9-3   DFD Elements Within the Pet Shop 4.0 Application

DFD Element Type	DFD Item Numbers
Data Flows (partial list for brevity)	Anonymous user request (2.0→4.2)
	Anonymous user response (4.2→2.0)
	Pet Shop customer request (1.0→4.2)
	Pet Shop customer response (4.2→1.0)
	Web application reading configuration data (4.1→4.2)
	Web pages read by Web application (4.3→4.2)
	Admin creating or updating Web application configuration data (3.0→4.1)
	Admin reading Web application configuration data (4.1→3.0)
	Admin creating, updating, or deleting Web pages (3.0→4.3)
	Admin reading Web pages (4.3→3.0)
	Web application creating or updating an order (4.2→4.7.1)
	Web application reading an order (4.7.1→4.2)

Now we have a list of all the DFD elements or assets within the application. Note that nearly all of the data flows are bidirectional. You should think of them as being separate for the time being.

You can apply a process called *reduction* to reduce the number of entities you will analyze. In short, if you have two or more DFD elements of the same type (for example, two or more processes) behind the same trust boundary, you can model the elements as one entity, as long as the elements were written in or are using the same technology and are handling similar data. In other words, when you analyze the threats to one of the elements, that same analysis applies to the other element also. You can see the biggest benefit of this process when you reduce data flows, which tend to be numerous. The first consideration is whether to reduce the bidirectional flows. For example, the anonymous user request and response (2.0→4.2 and 4.2→2.0) can be collapsed because:

■ The data flows use the same technology (HTTP over TCP).

■ They share the same process and external entity (2.0 and 4.2).

■ The data content in either direction is public and anonymous.

The same reduction process applies to a Pet Shop customer request and response (1.0→4.2 and 4.2→1.0). The only difference is that the data flows carry authentication information, too, and the user can place orders and look up order information. You can also reduce the Web pages used for configuration (4.3→3.0 and 3.0→4.3), Web application configuration data (4.1→3.0 and 3.0→4.1), and Web application reading or manipulating order information (4.2→4.7.1 and 4.7.1→4.2).

The synchronous and asynchronous order-processing processes, 4.7.2 and 4.7.3, can also be reduced because they handle exactly the same data types, are within the same trust boundary, and are written in the same language (C#). The same applies to the data-access (4.7.4) and queuing (4.7.5) components and the orders (4.7.6) and asynchronous orders (4.7.8) data stores.

So now, after reduction, the abbreviated list of DFD elements looks like that in Table 9-4.

Table 9-4   Reduced DFD Elements Within Pet Shop 4.0

DFD Element Type	DFD Item Number
External Entities	Pet Shop customer (1.0)
	Anonymous user (2.0)
	Administrator (3.0)
Processes	Web application (4.2)
	User profile (4.5)
	Membership (4.6)
	Order processor (4.7.1)
	Sync/Async order processors (4.7.2 and 4.7.3)
	Data-access or queuing components (4.7.4 and 4.7.5)
	Auditing engine (4.7.9)
Data Stores	Web application configuration data (4.1)
	Web pages (4.3)
	Use profile data (4.8)
	Membership data (4.9)
	Order and async orders data (4.7.6 and 4.7.8)
	Inventory data (4.7.7)
	Audit-log data (4.7.10)
Data Flows (partial list)	Web application reading configuration data (4.1→4.2)
	Web pages read by Web application (4.3→4.2)
	Anonymous user request/response (2.0→4.2→2.0)
	Pet Shop customer request/response (1.0→4.2→1.0)
	Admin reading, creating, updating Web application configuration data (3.0→4.1→3.0)
	Admin reading, creating, updating, deleting Web pages (3.0→4.3→3.0)
	Web application reading, creating, updating an order (4.2→4.7.1→4.2)

> **Note**   We have already defined STRIDE, but to save you time, here's what the acronym means: spoofing, tampering, repudiation, information disclosure, DoS, and EoP. Remember, STRIDE looks at threats from an attacker's perspective.

Once the list of DFD elements is complete, you can apply STRIDE to each of the elements in the list by following the mapping of STRIDE categories to DFD element types in Table 9-5.

Table 9-5   Mapping STRIDE to DFD Element Types

DFD Element Type	S	T	R	I	D	E
External Entity	X		X			
Data Flow		X		X	X	
Data Store		X	†	X	X	
Process	X	X	X	X	X	X

In essence, everything in the DFD is subject to attack, and the nature of the potential attack is determined by the DFD element type. For example, a data flow is subject to tampering, information disclosure, and DoS attacks.

> **Note**   Most, but not all, DoS attacks against data stores and data flows are against a process at one end of the data flow or the process serving the data store.

Note the dagger mark (†) at the intersection of the data store row and the repudiation column. If the data store contains logging or audit data, repudiation is a potential threat because if the data is maliciously manipulated in any way, an attacker could cover his or her tracks, or a criminal could renege on a transaction. Of all the data stores in the DFDs, only one, the audit data store (4.7.10), is of concern from a repudiation perspective. The audit data store is important because it holds process-ordering audit information such as the following:

- Transaction date and time

- Pet Shop customer ID

- Pet Shop customer IP address

- Order transaction ID

The order transaction ID can then be used to cross-reference with the actual order in the ordering system.

The term *spoofing* is often misused in the context of security; many spoofing threats are in fact tampering threats. Replacing a file with a bogus file or changing bytes in a file is tampering. A real example of process spoofing would be spoofing a Web server. Ordinarily, the attacker does not have direct access to the Web server software serving Web pages for say, Microsoft.com, but the attacker might be able to spoof the site, perhaps using cache or Domain Name System (DNS) poisoning. However, one could argue that these attacks are really tampering threats against a data store (the user's cache, a proxy's cache, or the DNS server records.) The security of the appropriate caches and servers could be treated as a security assumption—you are assuming that all the appropriate caches and infrastructure servers (DNS, DHCP, and so on) are performing correctly.

A variant of spoofing is *typosquatting*, in which an attacker creates a valid domain name, such as Micros0ft.com (note the zero instead of the letter *o*) and then builds a Web page that looks like valid Microsoft content. This is a very low-tech attack.

> **Important**   Sometimes a perceived threat might in fact be a security assumption violation. For example, a spoofed Web site could manifest itself as a corrupted or tampered-with hosts file on a user's computer.

In Table 9-6, we combine the list of DFD elements with the STRIDE mappings to arrive at a list of threats to the system being modeled. To do this, we gather the elements from Table 9-4 and then determine the threats to which each is susceptible by using Table 9-5.

Table 9-6   Determining Threats for DFD Elements Within Pet Shop 4.0

DFD Element Type	Threat Types (STRIDE)	DFD Item Numbers
External entities	SR	(1.0), (2.0), (3.0)
Processes	STRIDE	(4.2), (4.5), (4.6), (4.7.1), (4.7.2 and 4.7.3), (4.7.4 and 4.7.5), (4.7.9)
Data stores	T(R)ID	(4.1), (4.3), (4.8), (4.9), (4.7.6 and 4.7.8), (4.7.7), (4.7.10 repudiation)
Data flows (partial list for brevity)	TID	(4.1→4.2), (4.3→4.2), (2.0→4.2→2.0), (1.0→4.2→1.0), (3.0→4.1→3.0), (3.0→4.3→3.0), (4.2→4.7.1→4.2)

Notice the parentheses around the letter *R* in the data stores row; a data store might be subject to repudiation threats if the data held in the store is logging or auditing data. In our Pet Shop example, data store 4.7.10 is subject to repudiation threats because it stores auditing data.

Table 9-7 gives us a complete list of potential threats to the system by showing the information from Table 9-6 a different way.

Table 9-7   Threats to the System

Threat Type (STRIDE)	DFD Item Numbers
Spoofing	External entities: (1.0), (2.0), (3.0)
	Processes: (4.2), (4.5), (4.6), (4.7.1), (4.7.2 and 4.7.3), (4.7.4 and 4.7.5), (4.7.9)
Tampering	Processes: (4.2), (4.5), (4.6), (4.7.1), (4.7.2 and 4.7.3), (4.7.4 and 4.7.5), (4.7.9)
	Data stores: (4.1), (4.3), (4.8), (4.9), (4.7.6 and 4.7.8), (4.7.7), (4.7.10)
	Data flows: (4.1→4.2), (4.3→4.2), (2.0→4.2→2.0), (1.0→4.2→1.0), (3.0→4.1→3.0), (3.0→4.3→3.0), (4.2→4.7.1→4.2)
Repudiation	External entities: (1.0), (2.0), (3.0)
	Data flow: (4.7.10)
Information disclosure	Processes: (4.2), (4.5), (4.6), (4.7.1), (4.7.2 and 4.7.3), (4.7.4 and 4.7.5), (4.7.9)
	Data stores: (4.1), (4.3), (4.8), (4.9), (4.7.6 and 4.7.8), (4.7.7), (4.7.10)
	Data flows: (4.1→4.2), (4.3→4.2), (2.0→4.2→2.0), (1.0→4.2→1.0), (3.0→4.1→3.0), (3.0→4.3→3.0), (4.2→4.7.1→4.2)

Table 9-7 **Threats to the System**

Threat Type (STRIDE)	DFD Item Numbers
DoS	Processes: (4.2), (4.5), (4.6), (4.7.1), (4.7.2 and 4.7.3), (4.7.4 and 4.7.5), (4.7.9)
	Data stores: (4.1), (4.3), (4.8), (4.9), (4.7.6 and 4.7.8), (4.7.7), (4.7.10)
	Data flows: (4.1→4.2), (4.3→4.2), (2.0→4.2→2.0), (1.0→4.2→1.0), (3.0→4.1→3.0), (3.0→4.3→3.0), (4.2→4.7.1→4.2)
EoP	Processes: (4.2), (4.5), (4.6), (4.7.1), (4.7.2 and 4.7.3), (4.7.4 and 4.7.5), (4.7.9)

Now that we have this list, it's time to look at the potential risk of each threat.

8. Determine Risk

Historically, security specialists have used numeric calculations to determine risk. The problem with using numbers is they can be very subjective. For example, Microsoft often used DREAD ratings (Damage potential, Reproducibility, Exploitability, Affected users, Discoverability) to calculate risk, and sometimes people used a calculation like this one:

Risk = Chance of Attack × Damage Potential

Simply put, the problem is determining the chance of attack. You can't predict the future, so you have no idea, other than a guess, what the chance of attack really is. We're not saying security risk calculation using numbers is useless—it's not—but it's very hard to be consistent and accurate (especially as team members move around), so use numeric calculations with caution.

Microsoft has created a *bug bar* that defines the characteristics of a threat and, thereby, the level of risk. Rather than use numbers, the risk rankings are derived in part from the Microsoft Security Response Center (MSRC) security bulletin rankings. We will use the term "risk level" to indicate overall risk; risk level 1 is highest and risk level 4 is the lowest. The characteristics of a threat include:

- Server application (for example, an e-mail server) versus client application (for example, a word processor).
- Local versus remote accessibility.
- Accessibility to anonymous versus authenticated users.
- Accessibility to authenticated users versus administrators.
- On by default versus off by default.
- The degree of user interaction required.
- In the case of an information disclosure threat, whether the data is personally identifiable information (PII) or is sensitive data.
- In the case of a DoS attack, whether the application continues service or is nonfunctional once an attack stops.

Figures 9-6 through 9-10 illustrate an abbreviated set of trees outlining the core elements of the Security Development Lifecycle (SDL) bug bar document.

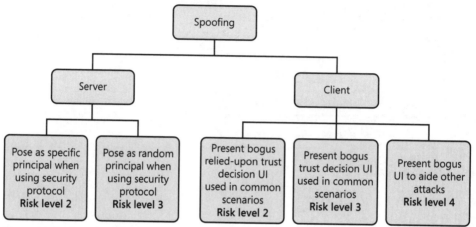

Figure 9-6   Spoofing threats risk ranking.

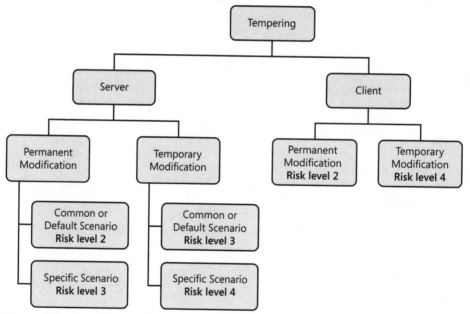

Figure 9-7   Tampering threats risk ranking.

In Figure 9-8, *target* means the ability to disclose selected data. An example of an untargeted attack is one that perhaps yields random heap data.

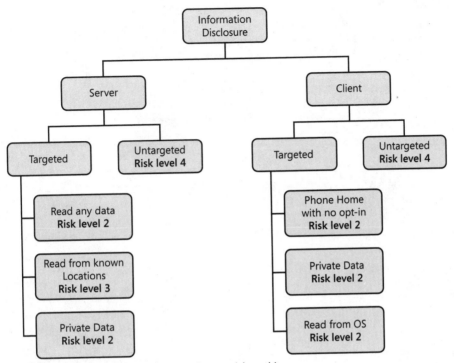

Figure 9-8   Information disclosure threats risk ranking.

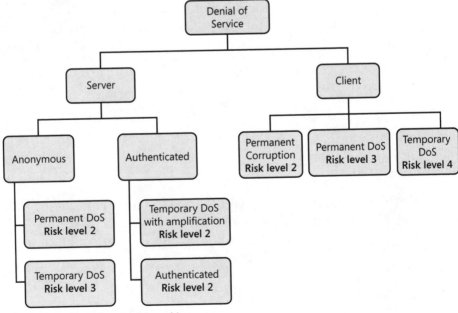

Figure 9-9   DoS threats risk ranking.

In Figure 9-9, *with amplification* means the attack leads to an increase in denied service. For example, an attacked computer begins to attack all computers on the subnet, as in the TCP/IP *smurf* attack.

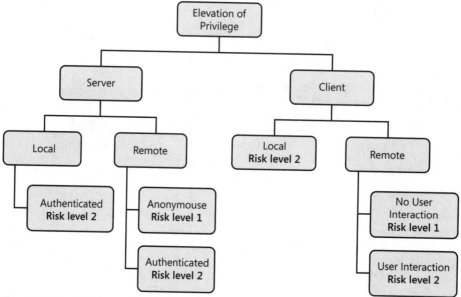

Figure 9-10   EoP threats risk ranking.

Note that there are no risk rankings for repudiation threats. The threats remain unranked for various reasons—most notably because Microsoft has issued no security bulletins relating to repudiation. In general, the feeling is that any such errors follow the tampering risk rankings.

By the end of the risk-identification stage, you should have ranked your threats by risk, from high to low. Obviously, you should address the highest-risk items first. Risk level 1 or 2 threats must always be remedied during the development phase. Risk level 3 threats should be fixed before the product becomes a release candidate, and risk level 4 threats should be fixed if time permits.

9. Plan Mitigations

Often referred to as countermeasures or defenses, mitigations reduce or eliminate the risk of a threat. You have only a small set of mitigation strategies available to you:

- Do nothing.
- Remove the feature.
- Turn off the feature.
- Warn the user.
- Counter the threat with technology.

Let's look at each option in detail.

Do Nothing

For low-risk threats, doing nothing could be a valid strategy. However, you might find it worthwhile to update your external-security notes to reflect such threats.

Remove the Feature

Removing a feature is the only way to reduce the risk to zero. We have done this numerous times at Microsoft when threat models indicate that the risk is too great or the mitigations are untenable. In those cases, the best course of action is to not build the feature in the first place. Obviously, this is a balancing act between user features and potential security risks.

Turn Off the Feature

Turning off a feature is less drastic than removing a feature and should be used only to reduce risk further. Building a threat-ridden feature and then simply turning it off by default is unacceptable. Consider this only as a defense-in-depth strategy.

Warn the User

For some threats, you should warn the user. However, be aware that most users, especially non-technical users, make poor trust decisions. Beware of threat models that are rife with user-warning mitigations.

Counter the Threat with Technology

Countering threats with technology is the most common mitigation strategy. Use a technology such as authentication or encryption to solve specific issues. To determine what mitigations to use, consider threat types. Table 9-8 outlines high-level mitigation strategies by threat type.

Table 9-8   Mitigation Techniques Based on STRIDE Threat Type

Threat Type	Mitigation Technique
Spoofing	Authentication
Tampering	Integrity
Repudiation	Non-repudiation services
Information disclosure	Confidentiality
DoS	Availability
EoP	Authorization

For each of the mitigation techniques, you can use one or more technologies. Table 9-9 gives some examples.

Table 9-9   Mitigation Technologies

Mitigation Technique	Mitigation Technology
Authentication	Authenticate principals:
	■ Basic authentication
	■ Digest authentication
	■ Cookie authentication
	■ Windows authentication (NTLM)
	■ Kerberos authentication
	■ PKI systems such as SSL/TLS and certificates
	■ IPSec
	■ Digitally signed packets
	Authenticate code or data:
	■ Digital signatures
	■ Message authentication codes
	■ Hashes
Integrity	■ Windows Vista Mandatory Integrity Controls
	■ ACLs
	■ Digital signatures
	■ Message authentication codes
Non-repudiation services	■ Strong authentication
	■ Secure auditing and logging
	■ Digital signatures
	■ Secure time-stamps
	■ Trusted third parties
Confidentiality	■ ACLs
	■ Encryption
Availability	■ ACLs
	■ Filtering
	■ Quota
	■ Authorization
Authorization	■ ACLs
	■ Group or role membership
	■ Privilege ownership
	■ Permissions

A complete list of mitigation mechanisms and best practices for choosing the appropriate mitigation is beyond the scope of this book, but much literature on the topic exists (Viega and McGraw 2001, Ferguson and Schneier 2003, Howard and LeBlanc 2003).

The next step in countering threats is to take all the threats from the threat model, look up the mitigation techniques, and then determine an appropriate mitigation technology.

Table 9-10 provides a list of some "interesting" assets from the Pet Shop 4.0 example. The list is highly abbreviated and is intended only to give an example of the final stages of the threat-modeling process.

Table 9-10   Abbreviated List of Interesting Threats to Pet Shop 4.0

Example Asset	Asset Type	Threat Type Susceptibility	Example Threat
(1.0→4.2→1.0)	Data flow from Pet Shop user to Web application and back	TID	I
4.7.10	Audit log data store	T(R)ID	T
4.7.1	Order processor process	TRIDE	STRIDE

Now let's look at the potential mitigations.

(1.0→4.2→1.0) Data Flow from Pet Shop User to Web Application and Back

Data flows are subject to tampering, information disclosure, and DoS attacks. We'll focus on the information disclosure threat because the data flow from the Pet Shop user to the Web application and back could contain potentially sensitive data such as the user name and password and credit card information. The mitigation technique for such threats is confidentiality, and in this case, we can use SSL/TLS because

- High-level protocols are always a preferred way to mitigate threats because they are well proven and easy to implement.
- SSL/TLS solves the confidentiality problem through encryption.
- SSL/TLS solves the tampering threat by using Message Authentication Codes (MACs).
- SSL/TLS solves the spoofing threat to the Web application (4.2) by providing authentication services.

(4.7.10) Audit Log Data Store

Data stores are subject to tampering, information disclosure, DoS, and, potentially, repudiation attacks. In this audit log example, we're going to look at the tampering threat because this could lead to repudiation issues. If an attacker can tamper with the data log store, he can cover his tracks or repudiate his transactions.

Tampering threats are mitigated with integrity technologies such as ACLs, hashes, digital signatures, or MACs. You should use a good ACL on the log file that allows only the logging process and trusted users to manipulate the file. Then you should use a signature or message authentication code on the file as well, depending on your business requirements.

(4.7.1) Order Processor Process

Finally, processes are susceptible to spoofing, tampering, information disclosure, DoS, and EoP attacks. The tampering threat for the processor process can be mitigated in the same way the tampering threat is mitigated for the audit log file: use an ACL and a MAC or digital signature. In the case of a process, you'll probably use a signature; these are commonly used to protect code. The two mitigations for the EoP threat are first to authorize only valid users to access the code, and second to always run the code by using the lowest-possible privilege.

We finally have a list of mitigations we can build into the design of the Pet Shop 4.0 application. Table 9-11 summarizes our defenses.

Table 9-11   Defenses Used in Portions of Pet Shop 4.0

Asset	Asset Type	Example Threat	Example Mitigation
(1.0→4.2→1.0)	Data flow from Pet Shop user to Web application and back	I	SSL/TLS (also mitigates the tampering threat)
4.7.10	Audit log data store	T	ACL and MAC
4.7.1	Order processor process	T and E	ACL, MAC, and reduced process privilege

Role of Threat Trees

If you are familiar with other texts that cover threat modeling, you may notice that threat trees are not covered in this chapter. This is by design. Threat trees, although very useful, require a lot of security expertise to build and use correctly. One of the most frequent criticisms we face about the earlier threat-modeling process is the level of security expertise required to build a good threat model. Analysis revealed that the key weakness was building the threat trees. So rather than expecting non–security experts to build accurate and consistent trees, we have removed them and replaced them with threat tree patterns. These trees illustrate common attack patterns and allow the application designers to think about other conditions in the system. You'll find a complete list of threat trees in Chapter 22, "Threat Tree Patterns."

After you build your threat model, you can consult the trees to determine other conditions to consider. For example, if you have a spoofing threat against a user, you can consult the "Spoofing Threats Against External Entities and Processes" tree and look at the leaf nodes. These will prompt you to ask other relevant questions about the design of the system.

Using a Threat Model to Aid Code Review

One of the deliverables from the threat-modeling process is a list of entry points to the system. This is really what the context diagram shows. If you look at the context diagram for Pet Shop 4.0, shown earlier in Figure 9-3 (on page 110), you see three main entry points to the system: points accessible to anonymous users, points accessible to Pet Shop customers, and points accessible to administrators. When it comes to reviewing the Pet Shop code for security bugs, it's imperative that you review all code that is remotely and anonymously accessible before reviewing other code. Simply look at the data flow diagram to determine which elements are accessible in this manner.

Using a Threat Model to Aid Testing

As we have mentioned, specific threat types (spoofing and tampering, for example) have specific mitigation techniques. These techniques can also be attacked. Determine how best to build attacks or perform penetration testing by looking at the relevant threats' tree patterns, defined in Chapter 22, and considering the leaf nodes of each tree. These leaf nodes can give you not only design insight but also attack insight. Refer to Chapter 22 for more information.

Key Success Factors and Metrics

What makes a good threat model? For quite some time at Microsoft, we struggled with this question because determining a good threat model is rather subjective. The conundrum was a little like judge Potter Stewart's famous comment about the definition of pornography (Stewart 1964): "But I know it when I see it." Eventually, during the development of Windows Vista, we had so many threat models to evaluate that we started to use metrics to separate the good from the not-so-good threat models. We eventually adopted the version of the metrics shown in Table 9-12.

At a minimum, threat models should be rated "OK" and components that are to be penetration tested should be "Good" or better.

Table 9-12   Threat-Model Quality Guidelines

Rating	Comments
No threat model (0)	■ No threat model is in place—this is simply not acceptable because it indicates that no threats are being considered.

Not acceptable (1)	■ Threat model is clearly out of date if:
	  ❑ Current design is significantly different from that defined in the threat model.
	■ –Or–
	  ❑ Date in document shows that it is older than 12 months.

OK (2)	■ A data flow diagram or a list of the following exists:
	  ❑ Assets (processes, data stores, data flows, external entities)
	  ❑ Users
	  ❑ Trust boundaries (machine to machine, user to kernel and vice versa, high privilege to low privilege and vice versa)
	■ At least one threat is detailed for each software asset.
	■ Mitigations are provided for all risk level 1, 2, and 3 threats.
	■ Model is current.

Table 9-12   Threat-Model Quality Guidelines

Rating	Comments
Good (3)	■ Threat model meets all definitions of "OK" threat models.
	■ Anonymous, authenticated, local, and remote users are all shown on the DFD.
	■ All S, T, I, and E threats have been identified and classified as either mitigated or accepted.
Excellent (4)	■ Threat model meets all definitions of "Good" threat models.
	■ All STRIDE threats have been identified and have mitigations, external security notes, or dependencies acknowledged.
	■ Mitigations have been identified for each threat.
	■ External security notes include a plan to create customer-facing documents (from the external security notes) that explain how to use the technology safely and what the tradeoffs are.

Summary

Threat modeling is critically important to helping build secure software because it is the cornerstone to understanding how your product could be attacked and how to defend it. The process is also a great way to determine the overall security health of a software development team because security-savvy teams are more in tune with the threats to their code and, therefore, tend to build better threat models.

By following the updated threat-modeling process, you can systematically uncover threats to the application, rank the risk of each threat, and determine appropriate mitigations. Threat modeling can also help you perform code reviews and build penetration tests.

References

(McConnell 2004)   McConnell, Steve. *Code Complete*, 2d ed. Redmond, WA: Microsoft Press, 2004.

(TCAAB 2003)   Microsoft Corporation. "Microsoft Convenes Trustworthy Computing Academic Advisory Board," *http://www.microsoft.com/presspass/press/2003/Feb03/02-20TWCAABPR.mspx*. February 2003.

(Howard and LeBlanc 2003)   Howard, Michael, and David LeBlanc. *Writing Secure Code*, 2nd ed. Redmond, WA: Microsoft Press, 2003.

(Swiderski and Snyder 2004)   Swiderski, Frank, and Window Snyder. *Threat Modeling*. Redmond, WA: Microsoft Press, 2004.

(Torr 2005)   Torr, Peter. "Guerrilla Threat Modelling (or 'Threat Modeling' if you're American)," *http://blogs.msdn.com/ptorr/archive/2005/02/22/GuerillaThreatModelling.aspx*. February 2005.

(UC Berkeley 2005)   Yang, Sarah, University of California, Berkeley. "Researchers recover typed text using audio recording of keystrokes," *http://www.berkeley.edu/news/media/ releases/2005/09/14_key.shtml.* September 2005.

(Pet Shop 2006)   Leake, Gregory, Microsoft Corporation. "Microsoft .NET Pet Shop 4: Migrating an ASP.NET 1.1 Application to 2.0," *http://msdn.microsoft.com/library/ default.asp?url=/library/en-us/dnbda/html/bdasamppet4.asp.* MSDN, February 2006.

(Kozar 1997)   Kozar, Kenneth A. "The Technique of Data Flow Diagramming," *http://spot.colorado.edu/~kozar/DFDtechnique.html.* 1997.

(Sauter 2002)   Sauter, Vicki, University of Missouri, St. Louis. "Data Flow Diagrams," *http://www.umsl.edu/~sauter/analysis/dfd/dfd_intro.html.* September 2002.

(Drewry 2005)   Drewry, Tony. "Data Flow Diagrams," *http://www.cems.uwe.ac.uk/~tdrewry/ dfds.htm.* October 2005.

(Ambler 2006)   Ambler, Scott W. "Data Flow Diagrams (DFDs)," *http://www.agilemodeling .com/artifacts/dataFlowDiagram.htm.* April 2006.

(DFD 2006)   "Data Flow Diagrams - Free Online Tutorial & Download," *http:// www.data-flow-diagrams.com/.*

(Yourdon 2006)   Yourdon, Ed. *Just Enough Structured Analysis* project. Chapter 9, "Data Flow Diagrams," *http://www.yourdon.com/strucanalysis/chapters/ch9.html.*

(Ellison 2000)   Ellison, Carl. "Non-repudiation," *http://world.std.com/~cme/ non-repudiation.htm.*

(CERT 2003)   Carnegie Mellon Software Engineering Institute, CERT Coordination Center. "CERT Advisory CA-2003-02 Double-Free Bug in CVS Server," *http://www.cert.org/ advisories/CA-2003-02.html.* January 2003.

(Silicon 2003)   Lemos, Robert. "Linux kernel suffers Trojan horse hack," *http://software .silicon.com/os/0,39024651,39116796,00.htm.* November 2003.

(CVE-2005-1974)   Common Vulnerabilities and Exposures. Java Web Start Untrusted Application Privilege Escalation, *http://cve.mitre.org/cgi-bin/cvename.cgi?name= CVE-2005-1974.*

(CVE-2005-1160)   Common Vulnerabilities and Exposures. Firefox/Mozilla Chrome UI DOM Property Override Privilege Escalation, *http://cve.mitre.org/cgi-bin/cvename.cgi?name= CVE-2005-1160.*

(CVE-2005-0054)   Common Vulnerabilities and Exposures. URL Decoding Zone Spoofing Vulnerability in Internet Explorer, *http://cve.mitre.org/cgi-bin/cvename.cgi?name= CVE-2005-0054.*

(Viega and McGraw 2001)   Viega, John, and Gary McGraw. *Building Secure Software: How to Avoid Security Problems the Right Way.* Reading, MA: Addison-Wesley Publishing Co., 2001.

(Ferguson and Schneier 2003)   Ferguson, Niels, and Bruce Schneier. *Practical Cryptography.* New York, NY: John Wiley & Sons, 2003.

(Howard and LeBlanc 2003)   Howard, Michael, and David LeBlanc. *Writing Secure Code,* 2nd ed. Redmond, WA: Microsoft Press, 2003.

(Stewart 1964)   Stewart, Potter. *http://en.wikiquote.org/wiki/Potter_Stewart.*

Chapter 10

Stage 5: Creating Security Documents, Tools, and Best Practices for Customers

In mid-2005, one of us (Howard) had a conversation with a Fortune 100 customer about an interesting trend in compromised Web servers. After the CodeRed and Nimda worms (CERT 2001a; CERT 2001b) struck in July and September 2001, respectively, affecting Microsoft Web servers, Microsoft Internet Information Services (IIS) 4 and IIS 5 became the most compromised Web servers on the Internet. This led Gartner Vice-President John Pescatore to advise Gartner clients to seriously consider not using either Web server (Gartner 2001) and to use other Web servers instead that were perceived at the time to be more secure than IIS. The customer wanted to know what had happened around late 2003 because the trend had changed. IIS on Microsoft Windows was no longer the most compromised Web server platform—Apache on Linux had taken this dubious honor—and it has been this way ever since (Zone-H 2006). The reason, the client was told, was simple: an important part of the Security Development Lifecycle (SDL) is the production of *easy-to-use* security tools and *prescriptive* security best practices.

We had produced such deliverables around late 2001 for IIS 4 on Microsoft Windows NT 4.0, IIS 5 on Windows 2000, and IIS 5.1 on Windows XP. We also had the IIS Lockdown Wizard (Microsoft 2001a), the URLScan Security Tool (Microsoft 2001b), and the IIS Security Checklist for IIS 4 (Microsoft 2001c) and IIS 5 and IIS 5.1 (Microsoft 2001d). The tools appealed to unsophisticated users because they could run the tools easily to set a more secure default configuration or to audit their configurations. Figure 10-1 shows the IIS Lockdown tool.

The checklists appealed to a more technical audience because these more sophisticated users want to know what knob to turn and which lever to pull; they like the feeling of being in control, and the checklists give them that control. It was this guidance and these tools that enabled IIS administrators to lock down their servers more securely, and this is what led to a dramatic reduction in compromised IIS servers. No code was changed, and no bugs were fixed. All we did was give administrators help in controlling their systems. This is key. There is no single silver bullet for fixing security ills. Many security practitioners believe that getting the code and designs right is the path to security nirvana, and it is in large part, but that path is strewn with human error and determined attackers, so you must recognize that you will *never* get the design and code 100% correct and that you have to employ other security strategies to compensate for such errors.

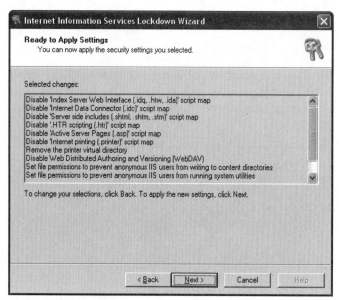

Figure 10-1   The IIS Lockdown tool about to lock down ("harden") an IIS 5.1 server on Windows XP Service Pack 2 (SP2).

The Value of Automated Updates

As this chapter was being written (February 17, 2006), its author was returning from the RSA Security Conference in San Jose. At a panel discussion on software development processes, one panelist commented that Microsoft Windows was obviously no more secure than it was five years ago because Microsoft had to make it easier to deploy security updates through Windows and Microsoft Update. This is an example of "security expert myopia." There will always be security bugs in every piece of software, and enabling easy updates offers one massive benefit that the panelist missed—having an easy and automated updating process protects customers from being *compromised*. This point was proven when the famed Windows Meta File (WMF) flaw was uncovered in late 2005 (Microsoft 2006); there was very little damage. In fact, it was a bit of a non-event because updates were applied rapidly to the vast majority of computers, thereby making the systems secure from attack quickly.

> An always-on computer with automatic updates enabled will be secure from attack between one hour and two days after the update is available on the Microsoft download servers. But the most important statistic is the number of machines that pick up the update. For Windows XP SP2, it's a staggering 95 percent of computers that take the updates. We see the effect of automatic updates through Windows Error Reporting (WER) statistics; once the updates start trickling to computers, we see a *precipitous* decline in WER reports associated with the bug being fixed. Microsoft has a complete feedback cycle that lets us gauge the effectiveness of the patching process.

Earlier, we used the words "being in control," and we want to focus on this. Controlling the computers under your management—or, more specifically, managing the software on those computers—is paramount. Poorly maintained systems are the number one cause of compromise, according to Gartner. In fact, mismanagement has a larger impact than the sum of all other conditions, including new and old vulnerabilities and zero-day attacks (Gartner 2004).

The only way you can make sure that your customers stay in control is to provide prescriptive security guidance and tools to help them. And this is what the rest of this chapter discusses.

Why Documentation and Tools?

When adopting SDL, you will spend time making the designs more secure, building more secure code with fewer security bugs, and building tools to help confirm that the software product is more secure. After you have completed all these tasks, you turn the software over to customers to help them perform the tasks for which they procured the software. Customers will use products in different ways, and not all customers will use a product in its default, secure configuration. It is important to provide detailed security information to customers so that they can make informed decisions on how to securely deploy a product and so that they can understand the security implications of the configurations decisions they have made. Because security and usability may conflict, it is important to educate customers on both the threats that exist and the tradeoffs between risk and product functionality involved in making decisions on how to operate and deploy products.

Now let's look at the recommendations for building documentation and tools.

Creating Prescriptive Security Best Practice Documentation

First, we want to point out that this chapter is not a lesson in how to write documentation for your customers. Rather, it outlines what security best practice information you should add to the documentation.

The first step is to inventory what sort of documentation you have. From there, you can determine what security information you need to add. The following sections discuss the various forms of documentation and offer ideas for what you should add.

Setup Documentation

It is critical that setup documentation outline the best practices that should be adhered to when installing your application. The setup document should not be a replacement for a secure, reduced attack surface default, however. For example, adding text such as ". . . and make sure you change the application's admin password to something strong" is bad, because the setup application should enforce this.

Setup documentation is where you should add any information of use to firewall administrators. What ports do you open, and which protocols do you use and why? Are there any best practices that administrators should use at the firewall, for example setting a firewall access control policy that restricts access to your application to only a small set of trusted hosts or to a trusted subnet?

You should also note in this document any backward compatibility issues that cannot be addressed in the setup application.

Are there any risks that people should know about the setup process? For example, in Windows setup on a virgin install, there is no way to hide sensitive data through encryption because the cryptographic services are not available, and even if they were, where would you store the encryption key? So the documentation reflects this fact. It's a relatively low-risk threat, but it's worthwhile letting administrators know this.

Next, does your application work in a more secure manner when used with other security technologies, such as IPSec? If your application uses SSL/TLS, you should instruct users on how to acquire a certificate and private key. Again, this could be part of the setup application, but sometimes you don't know all the appropriate information at setup time, and the setup documentation is, therefore, the correct place to include such information.

Be wary of upgrade scenarios. Usually on upgrades from an older version of your software, you can't go changing a customer's configuration. It is important to document the security implications of the upgrade process.

Finally, consider including instructions to lock down ("harden") the software more securely than the default configuration. This text will probably be focused on specific scenarios rather than on general product use. Better yet, provide tools or scripts to help customers lock down the software. We'll discuss this issue later.

Mainline Product Use Documentation

For this critical piece of work—the user manual—you should have the most security-savvy person read through drafts of the document and comment on areas that may constitute insecure practice. For example, text recommending that users grant themselves a dangerous privilege or reduce the effectiveness of an access control, such as an access control list (ACL) in Windows or a permission in Linux, is clearly insecure. If there is no other way to complete the task than to perform an insecure operation, it is critically important that the text be updated to reflect the security impact and risk associated with the action. Also, you should inform the reader that it's a good idea to set the insecure setting back to a secure state once the task is complete.

Egregiously insecure advice should not be tolerated and must be removed as soon as possible. Better yet, it should not be written in the first place.

An example of really bad advice includes instructing users to add their accounts to the local administrator's group to achieve a specific task when the development team could have remedied the issue correctly during the application design.

End-user documentation should also include sidebars or security notes that point out the security ramifications of enabling other features beyond those included in the default installation. For example, if your application has a baseline functionality, but a user wants to install an optional component that is implemented as, say, a Windows service, make sure the user knows that for this component to work correctly, you must open port TCP/1234 at the firewall and that it's recommended that the user restrict access to the port to only the local subnet. In this example, you've not only told the user what resource is required (a TCP socket), but also a best practice for reducing the threat of attack.

Good documentation should extend beyond just simple security best practice. For example, if you have an application that requires specific privileges to operate, but the privileges are required only when specific functionality is used, you must inform the user of this situation. In fact, it's best to tell users that they can disable that privilege, and thereby reduce risk, if they don't use the scenario for which the privilege is required. In our experience, technical users love this level of information because it helps demonstrate to them that they are in control of the system.

You should also set security expectations in your documentation. Don't be afraid to tell your customers where your security boundaries lie and that your product might have weaknesses when used in specific situations. A great example is the Microsoft Fingerprint Reader. In early 2006, Mikko Kiviharju presented an interesting paper at BlackHat Amsterdam outlining weaknesses in the hardware (Kiviharju 2006). However, Microsoft indicates in the documentation that accompanies the hardware (Microsoft 2004a) that the device should not be considered a security device, but a convenience tool, and should not be used to protect sensitive data:

> ***Security Disclaimer:*** *The fingerprint reader is not a security feature and is intended to be used for convenience only. It should not be used to access corporate networks or to protect sensitive data, such as financial information. Instead, you should protect your sensitive data with another method, such as a strong password that you either memorize or store in a physically secure place. For more information, see the Security Information topic in the on-screen Help file installed with DigitalPersona Password Manager software.*

Backward compatibility and older protocols are often less secure than present functionality, but they may still be supported, and customers must be informed of the security implications raised by enabling such older functionality. Documentation should inform customers of these tradeoffs and how and when to turn off older compatibility modes to achieve the best possible security.

You should also add a single "security best practice" section to the base documentation. We have found that customers find it useful to have a single location where they can find the core security best practices. This best practice text can also form the basis for a security best practice checklist and, in some cases, a security tool. More on this later.

If your application is big or complex, you should also consider a single document that contains the security information about the product. This document would cover the security architecture of the product as well as best practices for setup, use, development, and maintenance. Microsoft has many such examples (Microsoft 2005a), including checklists, guides, and how-to articles for securing Windows Server 2003 (Microsoft 2005b), ISA Server 2004 (Microsoft 2004b), Exchange Server 2000 (Microsoft 2004c), and SQL Server 2000 (Microsoft 2003).

Finally, you should talk to your support personnel to determine what security challenges people have encountered when using prior versions of the product. Is there something you can add to the documentation to alleviate the number of support calls made by customers?

Help Documentation

Help documentation tends to be more task-oriented than general documentation; a user presses F1 to get help and up pops task-sensitive help. Because help is task-sensitive, you should tailor the help to include the security best practice for each task. This allows you to be very specific about the advice you give.

Developer Documentation

If you provide an API or set of classes or objects that developers can use to build applications on your platform, you should include security information and best practice for each applicable function or method call. For example, this is something that Microsoft has done extensively in the Microsoft Developer Network (MSDN). Figure 10-2 shows an example of the documentation in MSDN (in this case, within Microsoft Visual Studio 2005, but the same document is also available online) of the venerable (and vulnerable) *strncpy* function.

MSDN also includes programming language–specific security guidance for developers as well as an online portal for security-relevant developer information (MSDN 2006). Developers like "one-stop shopping" for all classes of technology, including security.

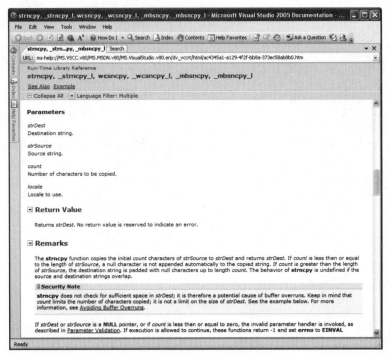

Figure 10-2   Developer documentation for the C runtime *strncpy* function, drawing the developer's attention to security issues when using the function.

Creating Tools

Security tools are paramount for helping users set a secure configuration and audit against a secure baseline. Such tools can range from simple scripts or templates all the way to complex configuration software. The best advice we can give is to build tools based on real customer issues. This is how the IIS4 and IIS5 checklists evolved, and then Microsoft took those checklists and built the IIS Lockdown tool.

Another tool example is the easy-to-use Security Configuration Wizard (SCW) in Windows Server 2003 SP1. SCW determines the minimum functionality required for a server's role or roles and disables functionality that is not required. Specifically, SCW

- Disables unneeded services.
- Blocks unused ports.
- Allows further address or security restrictions for ports that are left open.
- Prohibits unnecessary Internet Information Services (IIS) Web extensions, if applicable.
- Reduces protocol exposure to server message block (SMB), LanMan, and Lightweight Directory Access Protocol (LDAP).
- Defines an appropriate audit policy.

Summary

Security documentation is important for your users because they need to know the security implications of their actions and configurations. You should include guidance about locking down the system beyond the default install, the implications of an upgrade from an older product version, or, perhaps, the implications of an upgrade from a competitor's application. Your application is more secure than the competitor's, after all!

When creating this documentation and building configuration tools, make sure that you understand the needs of the user. Don't simply build geeky tools that only a security expert can understand and appreciate. The goal of this collateral is to help customers install, maintain, and use secure software. Never lose sight of that.

References

(CERT 2001a)   Carnegie Mellon Software Engineering Institute, CERT Coordination Center. "CERT Advisory CA-2001-19 'Code Red' Worm Exploiting Buffer Overflow in IIS Indexing Service DLL," *http://www.cert.org/advisories/CA-2001-19.html*. July 2001.

(CERT 2001b)   Carnegie Mellon Software Engineering Institute, CERT Coordination Center. "CERT Advisory CA-2001-26 Nimda Worm," *http://www.cert.org/advisories/CA-2001-26.html*. September 2001.

(Gartner 2001)   Pescatore, John. "Nimda Worm Shows You Can't Always Patch Fast Enough," *http://www.gartner.com/DisplayDocument?doc_cd=101034*. September 2001.

(Zone-H 2006)   Zone-H, The Internet Thermometer. *www.zone-h.org*.

(Microsoft 2001a)   "IIS Lockdown Tool 2.1," *http://www.microsoft.com/downloads/details.aspx?displaylang=en&FamilyID=DDE9EFC0-BB30-47EB-9A61-FD755D23CDEC*.

(Microsoft 2001b)   URLScan Security Tool 2.0, *http://www.microsoft.com/windows2000/downloads/recommended/urlscan/default.asp*. November 2001.

(Microsoft 2001c)   "Microsoft Internet Information Server 4.0 Security Checklist," *http://www.microsoft.com/technet/archive/security/chklist/iischk.mspx*. July 2001.

(Microsoft 2001d)   "IIS 5.0 Baseline Security Checklist," *http://www.microsoft.com/technet/archive/security/chklist/iis5cl.mspx*.

(Microsoft 2006)   Microsoft Security Bulletin MS06-001. "Vulnerability in Graphics Rendering Engine Could Allow Remote Code Execution," *http://www.microsoft.com/technet/security/bulletin/ms06-001.mspx*. January 2006.

(Gartner 2004)   Pescatore, John. "Stay Ahead of Changing Software Vulnerabilities," *http://www.gartner.com*. April 2004.

(Kiviharju 2006)   Kiviharju, Mikko. Black Hat 2006, "Hacking Fingerprint Scanners," *http://www.blackhat.com/presentations/bh-europe-06/bh-eu-06-Kiviharju/bh-eu-06-kiviarju.pdf*. January 2006.

(Microsoft 2004a)   "Getting Started: Microsoft Fingerprint Reader," *http://download .microsoft.com/download/1/3/9/139a8c30-34cc-4453-a449-7a1c586a3ae5/ Fingerprint_Reader.pdf.* April 2004.

(Microsoft 2005a)   "Server Security," *http://www.microsoft.com/technet/security/topics/ serversecurity.mspx.*

(Microsoft 2005b)   "Windows Server 2003 Security Guide," *http://www.microsoft.com/ technet/security/prodtech/windowsserver2003/W2003HG/SGCH00.mspx.* December 2005.

(Microsoft 2004b)   "ISA Server 2004 Security Hardening Guide," *http://www.microsoft.com/ technet/prodtechnol/isa/2004/plan/securityhardeningguide.mspx.* December 2004.

(Microsoft 2004c)   "Securing Exchange 2000 Servers Based on Role," *http:// www.microsoft.com/technet/security/prodtech/exchangeserver/secmod43.mspx.* February 2004.

(Microsoft 2003)   "SQL Server 2000 SP3 Security Features and Best Practices," *http:// www.microsoft.com/technet/prodtechnol/sql/2000/maintain/sp3sec00.mspx.*

(MSDN 2006)   Microsoft Corporation. MSDN, Microsoft Security Developer Center, *http:// msdn.microsoft.com/security.*

Chapter 11
Stage 6: Secure Coding Policies

As we mentioned in Chapter 7, "Stage 2: Define and Follow Design Best Practices," the software industry is replete with security software coding best practices—of which very few are followed. The Security Development Lifecycle (SDL) mandates specific coding practices and backs up many of the practices with tests to verify that the policies are adhered to. This chapter outlines the high-level policy and best practices for secure coding. The chapter is purposefully high level because the low-level specifics are covered in Chapter 19, "SDL Banned Function Calls," Chapter 20, "SDL Minimum Cryptographic Standards," and Chapter 21, "SDL Required Tools and Compiler Options."

The following coding best practices must be adhered to for new code and actively analyzed for legacy code:

- Use the latest compiler and supporting tool versions.
- Use defenses added by the compiler.
- Use source-code analysis tools.
- Do not use banned functions.
- Reduce potentially exploitable coding or design constructs.
- Use a secure coding checklist.

Let's look at each of these best practices in detail.

Use the Latest Compiler and Supporting Tool Versions

Ultimately, code written by a developer is compiled to a format that is executed by the computer, and the generated code can include defenses added by the compiler. We'll cover this process in more detail in the next section. You should also define which compiler and tool flags you'll use.

These include optimization flags, linker options, and so on. For example, it is advised that for new code, you compile with the highest possible warning level (*/W4* in Microsoft Visual C++, *-Wall* in GNU C Compiler [GCC], and *-w* in Borland C++) and compile "cleanly," with no warnings or errors. You must compile cleanly with -W3 if you are using Visual C++.

Use Defenses Added by the Compiler

The newer Microsoft compilers add defenses to compiled code. This defensive code is added automatically by the compiler, not by the developer. The major defensive options are the following:

- Buffer security check: */GS*
- Safe exception handling: */SAFESEH*
- Compatibility with Data Execution Prevention: */NXCOMPAT*

Buffer Security Check: */GS*

The */GS* flag is a great example of defensive code added by the compiler—the compiler injects code into the application to help detect some kinds of buffer overruns at run time. The latest Microsoft implementation of this defense in Microsoft Visual Studio 2005—it was first available in Visual Studio .NET 2002—performs the following steps when compiling native Win32 C/C++ code:

- A random "cookie" is placed on the stack before the return address. The cookie value is checked before the function returns to the caller. If the cookie has changed, the application aborts.

- The compiler rearranges the stack frame so that stack-based buffers are placed in higher memory addresses than other potentially attackable stack-based variables such as function pointers. This process reduces the chance that these other constructs will be overwritten by a buffer overrun.

- Code is added to protect against vulnerable parameters passed into a function. A vulnerable parameter is a pointer, C++ reference, or C structure that contains a pointer, string buffer, or C++ reference.

> **Best Practices**   You must compile all C/C++ code with */GS*.

Safe Exception Handling: */SAFESEH*

The */SAFESEH* linker option adds only safe exceptions to the executable image. It does this by adding extra exception-handler information that is verified by the operating system at run time to make sure the code is calling a valid exception handler and not a hijacked (overwritten) exception handler.

> **Best Practices**   You must link your code with */SAFESEH*.

Compatibility with Data Execution Prevention: */NXCOMPAT*

The */NXCOMPAT* linker option indicates that the executable file was tested to be compatible with the Data Execution Protection (DEP) feature in Microsoft Windows (Microsoft 2005).

> **Best Practices**   You must test your application on a computer that uses a CPU that supports DEP, and you must link your code with */NXCOMPAT*.

The Microsoft Interface Definition Language (MIDL) compiler, used for building remote procedure call (RPC) and Component Object Model (COM) code, also adds stricter argument checking to the compiled code when you use the /robust switch.

As you can see, the extra defenses are cheap because the compiler automatically adds them. Also note that the execution time and code size overhead is tiny. In our analyses, the potential code size or performance degradation is balanced out by better compiler optimizations.

> **Best Practices**   If your compiler does not add extra defenses to the code, you should consider upgrading the compiler to one that does. This is especially true for C/C++ compilers.

> **Important**   Defenses added by a compiler do not fix security bugs; they are added purely as a speed bump to make attackers' work harder. Defenses are no replacement for good-quality code.

Use Source-Code Analysis Tools

You must understand that, by themselves, source-code analysis tools do not make software secure. Analysis tools are incredibly useful, but they are no replacement for human beings performing manual code reviews. No tool will replace humans. Make no mistake, we are big fans of source-code analysis tools, but people who use these tools can fall into the traps explained in the following section.

Source-Code Analysis Tool Traps

People fall prey to the first source-code analysis tool trap when they think of source tools as a "silver bullet." There is no such thing as a secure-code silver bullet; you have to do many things to make code more secure, and tools are just one part of the mix. Thinking that you can run tools to find all bugs of a certain type is a false and dangerous premise.

The next trap is mistaking *false positives* (also called *noise*) for real bugs. For example, some common tools report the following code excerpt as defective because it uses the "dangerous function" *strcpy*:

```
void function(char *sz) {
    char buff[32];
    strcpy(buff,sz);
}

void main() {
    function("Hello, World!");
}
```

This code section is not defective in any way because the source buffer is a constant and is not controlled by an attacker. Another common tool, ITS4 (Cigital 2000; Azario 2002), reports the following:

```
C:\its4>its4 test.cpp
test.cpp:5:(Very Risky) strcpy
This function is high risk for buffer overflows
Use strncpy instead.
```

Too many false positives such as this frustrate developers because they must spend a lot of time chasing down non-bugs. The net effect of too many false positives is that developers eventually stop using the tool at all.

The next issue is that many tools miss real bugs. To reduce the amount of noise created by a tool, developers of source-code analysis tools add heuristics to determine bug probability. The problem with this practice is that the tool might miss real but subtle code bugs.

Next, source-code analysis tools tend to focus on a subset of programming languages. For example, the Microsoft PREfast technology in Visual Studio 2005 analyzes C and C++ code only, and Watchfire's AppScan is Web specific. So if your solution uses multiple languages, you may have to invest in multiple source-code analysis tools.

The final issue is that most tools find only source-code bugs, not design errors. For example, Coverity ran its source-code analysis tool on the MySQL database and claimed to have found only 97 bugs (Lemos 2005). Yet many of the security bugs in MySQL are design or installation issues, such as "MySQL ALTER TABLE/RENAME Forces Old Permission Checks" (OSVDB 2004).

Of course, source-code analysis tools do have many benefits when used correctly. Let's look at some.

Benefits of Source-Code Analysis Tools

Source-code analysis tools offer two major benefits: first, they help scale the code review process, and second, tools can help enforce secure-coding policies. At Microsoft, when we find an "interesting" bug class, we create a tool or add capabilities to an existing tool to help find the bug. Then we use the tools to query an entire code base rapidly. Make no mistake—at this point, we don't think the interesting bug type has been removed from the code; this is just the start. If the tools find a large number of potential bugs in the code, we update educational programs and, in some cases the SDL process, to provide prescriptive remedies for the bug type.

Take as an example the coding bug in Windows RPC/DCOM that the Blaster worm took advantage of (Microsoft 2003). The defective code looks like this:

```
HRESULT GetMachineName(WCHAR *pwszPath) {
    WCHAR wszMachineName[N + 1]);
    ...
    LPWSTR pwszServerName = wszMachineName;
    while (*pwszPath != L'\\')
        *pwszServerName++ = *pwszPath++;
    ...
```

In this code, the attacker controls the *pwszPath* argument so that she can overflow the *wszMachineName* buffer. This code bug was not picked up by any tools available within Microsoft, so a Perl script was rapidly written to search for the core construct within the RPC runtime:

```
use strict;
use File::Find;

my $RECURSE = 1;
my $VERBOSE = 0;

################################################################
foreach(@ARGV) {
  next if /^-./;
  if ($RECURSE) {
      finddepth(\&processFile,$_);
  } else {
      find(\&processFile,$_);
  }
}

################################################################
sub processFile {
  my $FILE;
  my $filename = $_;

  if (!$RECURSE && ($File::Find::topdir ne $File::Find::dir)) {
    # Recurse is not set, and we are in a different directory
    $File::Find::prune = 1;
    return;
  }

  # only accept .cxx, .cpp, .c and .cc and header extensions
  return if (!(/\.cpp$|\.c$|\.cxx$|\.cc$|\.hpp$|\.h$|\.hxx$/i));

  print "Checking $filename\n" if $VERBOSE;
```

```
warn "$!\n" unless open FILE, "<" . $filename;

# reset line number in case the same file is parsed twice (duh!)
$. = 0;

while (<FILE>) {
  # Find the core coding construct (++p = ++q or p++ = q++)
  if (/\*\+\+\w+\s*=\s*\*\+\+\w+/ ||
      /\*\w+\+\+\s*=\s*\*\w+\+\+/) {

    s/^\s+//;
    s/\s+$//;

    print $File::Find::name . " (" . $. . ")\n\t" . $_ . "\n";
  }
 }
}
```

Because of this bug, education was also updated to include the defective code and direction on how to fix the code. Microsoft Research started working on a less noisy source-code analysis tool, which is now part of the normal round of tools run on code as it's written. As you can see from this example, Microsoft created a "quick and dirty" tool to find potentially defective code, but the purpose was to understand how many problematic coding constructs existed in the Windows code base so that we could determine how bad the problem might be. With this information in hand, we could move resources around to get more developers hand-reviewing code.

The second use for source-code analysis tools is to enforce coding policy. Good tools are the best way to enforce policies such as a ban on certain functions or constructs. We do this at Microsoft at code check-in time. A battery of tools runs just before a developer's check-in, and any bugs found by the tools are flagged and triaged for repairs. Again, these tools are no replacement for good developers; they simply augment the code-review and code-quality process and act as a backstop, just in case a developer makes a mistake.

The two major source-code analysis tools from Microsoft are PREfast and FxCop. In Chapter 21, you can find a list of the warnings from these tools that must be triaged and fixed.

Best Practices   You should augment your software development process with good source-code analysis tools. Used alone, source-code analysis tools will not solve your source-code security issues. They are a defensive backstop.

Do Not Use Banned Functions

The subject of banned functions is covered in great detail in Chapter 19. For our purposes here, all you need to know is that there is a population of functions that, although fine 20 years ago, is simply not secure enough in light of today's threats. You can find banned functions by using header files, code-scanning tools, or updated compilers. An example header file named banned.h is included on the disc accompanying this book. The latest version of the Visual C/C++ compiler from Microsoft deprecates many functions, and the developer is warned during code compilation.

Reduce Potentially Exploitable Coding Constructs or Designs

This section may seem like a broader version of the two prior sections, but it's quite different. Some commonly used coding constructs or designs are not secure. For example, in Windows, it's possible to create an object with a NULL DACL—in other words, an object with an empty access control list (ACL), which means the object has no protection. Obviously, this is insecure. Tools such as Application Verifier—discussed in Chapter 12, "Stage 7: Secure Testing Policies"—can detect these weak ACLs at run time, and the PREfast source-code analysis technology built into Visual Studio 2005 will also detect this at compile time. Therefore, code such as this:

```
SetSecurityDescriptorDacl(&sd, TRUE, NULL, FALSE);
```

will result in this compiler warning:

```
c:\Code\testDACL\testDACL.cpp(21) : warning C6248: Setting a SECURITY_DESCRIPTOR's DACL to
NULL will result in an unprotected object
```

The *SetSecurityDescriptorDacl* function is not insecure, but it can be called in a way that would render a system insecure.

Other examples of potentially vulnerable constructs in Windows include shared writable segments and executable pages. We're not going to explain these in detail because they are discussed in other texts (Howard and LeBlanc 2003). On *nix systems, examples of bad design constructs include symbolic-link errors (Wheeler 2002; OSVDB 2006).

In C# code, you should consider wrapping networking-facing code that performs arithmetic and array bounds lookup with the *checked* operator:

```
UInt32 i = GetFromNetwork();
try {
    checked {
        UInt32 offset = i * 2;
        // Do array lookup
    }
}
catch (OverflowException ex) {
    // Handle exception
}
```

Failing this, you could perform the integer arithmetic overflow check to avoid the overhead of a potential exception (Howard, LeBlanc, and Viega 2005).

Use a Secure Coding Checklist

Create a secure coding checklist that describes all the minimal requirements for any code that is checked in to the software product. It's useful to have a checklist to follow to make sure the code meets a minimum-security bar. Although checklists are useful, you can't write secure code simply by following a checklist. But doing so is a reasonable start, and it's useful for new employees.

Summary

In recent years, a great deal of attention has been paid to secure-coding best practices, but although much material is available, alarmingly few developers adhere to, or are even aware of, such best practices. The SDL mandates that coding best practices be adhered to. These are taught during standard yearly education for all developers, and they are enforced through the use of source-code analysis tools. Such tools are very useful and can help find security bugs, but they are not a silver bullet; do not rely on any source-code analysis tool to replace a developer's skills. Also, the SDL has banned certain function calls and cryptographic algorithms that have led to security vulnerabilities in the past. You must not simply ban dangerous functionality—you must also provide prescriptive replacements. In our experience, developers have no problem adhering to security requirements as long as you give them good guidance and tools verify adherence.

References

(Microsoft 2005)   Microsoft Corporation. "Data Execution Protection," *http://msdn.microsoft .com/library/en-us/memory/base/data_execution_prevention.asp*. MSDN, December 2005.

(Cigital 2000)   Cigital, Inc. "ITS4: Software Security Tool," *http://www.cigital.com/its4/*. February 2000.

(Azario 2002)   Azario, Jos. "Source Code Scanners for Better Code," *http://www.linuxjournal .com/article/5673*. Linux Journal, January 2002.

(Lemos 2005)   Lemos, Robert. "Study: Few bugs in MySQL database," *http://news.com.com/ Study+Few+bugs+in+MySQL+database/2100-1002_3-5563918.html*. CNET News.com, February 2005.

(OSVDB 2004)   Open Source Vulnerability Database. "MySQL ALTER TABLE/RENAME Forces Old Permission Checks," *http://www.osvdb.org/displayvuln.php?osvdb_id=10660*. October 2004.

(Microsoft 2003)   Microsoft Corporation. Microsoft Security Bulletin MS03-026. "Buffer Overrun in RPC Interface Could Allow Code Execution," *http://www.microsoft.com/technet/ security/Bulletin/MS03-026.mspx*. TechNet, July 2003.

(Howard and LeBlanc 2003)   Howard, Michael, and David LeBlanc. *Writing Secure Code, Second Edition*. Redmond, WA: Microsoft Press, 2003. Chapter 23, "General Good Practices."

(Wheeler 2002)   Wheeler, David A. *Secure Programming for Linux and Unix HOWTO – Creating Secure Software*, published online. Chapter 7, "Structure Program Internals and Approach," *http://www.dwheeler.com/secure-programs/Secure-Programs-HOWTO/avoid-race.html#TEMPORARY-FILES*. Last updated June 3, 2002.

(OSVDB 2006)   Open Source Vulnerability Database. Symlink Vulnerabilites, *http://www.osvdb.org/searchdb.php?vuln_title=symlink*. Last updated January 31, 2006.

(Howard, LeBlanc, and Viega 2005)   Howard, Michael, David LeBlanc, and John Viega. *19 Deadly Sins of Software Security*. New York, NY: McGraw-Hill, 2005. Chapter 3, "Integer Overflows."

Chapter 12
Stage 7: Secure Testing Policies

You can't test quality into a product, and you also can't test security into it. If the product is written in an insecure manner, uses many insecure coding practices, or has a large attack surface, no amount of testing is going to make the product secure.

That said, you should provide a testing "sanity check" of the code before release. Testing is, of course, a necessary task, and anecdotal evidence indicates that as product groups at Microsoft release a subsequent product version covered by Security Development Lifecycle (SDL), engineers tend to spend less time testing for security bugs because the design and coding is more secure in the first place. (At the time of this writing, we have no hard data to back up the claim, however.) This observation does not trivialize the need for the methods we will discuss; it simply shows that to build secure software, you must get as much right as early as possible, and testing must be what it is supposed to be: verification. Again, you cannot test security into a product.

The testing phase requires the following steps:

1. Fuzz testing

2. Penetration testing

3. Run-time verification

4. Re-reviewing threat models

5. Reevaluating the attack surface

Let's look at each task in detail.

Fuzz Testing

Originally developed to find reliability bugs (Miller, Fredriksen, and So 1990; Miller et al. 1995; Miller 2005; Gallagher, Jeffries, and Landauer 2006), fuzz testing is an effective way to find certain classes of security bugs, too.

Fuzzing means creating malformed data and having the application under test consume the data to see how the application reacts. If the application fails unexpectedly, a bug has been found. The bug is a reliability bug and, possibly, also a security bug.

> **Note** At Microsoft, about 20 to 25 percent of security bugs are found through fuzzing a product before it is shipped. The vast majority of bugs are in old, pre-SDL code, however.

Fuzzing is aimed at exercising code that analyzes data structures, loosely referred to as parsers. There are three broad classes of parsers:

- **File format parsers** Examples include code that manipulates graphic images (JPEG, BMP, WMF, TIFF) or document and executable files (DOC, PDF, ELF, PE, SWF).

- **Network protocol parsers** Examples include SMB, TCP/IP, NFS, SSL/TLS, RPC, and AppleTalk. You can also fuzz the order of network operations—for example, by performing a response before a request.

- **APIs and miscellaneous parsers** Examples include browser-pluggable protocol handlers (such as callto:).

Let's focus on each parser type in more detail.

Fuzzing File Formats

Fuzzing file formats means building malformed files to be consumed by your application. For example, if your application parses and displays TIFF files, you could build a malformed TIFF and have the application read the file. Of course, you don't create just one malformed file; SDL mandates that you create and test at least 100,000 malformed files for every file format and every parser you support.

> **Important** SDL requires that you test 100,000 malformed files for each file format your application supports. If you find a bug, the count resets to zero, and you must run 100,000 more iterations by using a different random seed so that you create different malformed files.

A generic file-fuzzing process The process for fuzzing files is simple. It consists of the following steps:

1. Identify all the file formats your application supports.

2. Collect a library of valid files your application supports.

3. Malform (fuzz) a file.

4. Have the application consume the malformed file, and then observe the application.

The following paragraphs address each of these steps in detail.

Identify all valid file formats   The first step in the file-fuzzing process is to identify all file formats your application reads and handles. It's important to identify the formats your code handles. If the file data is handed off to a platform API—such as Microsoft Windows BitBlt or Graphics::DrawImage (Microsoft 2006a) or the open-source LibTIFF library (Still 2002)—and the fuzzed file causes the application to fail, the bug is probably not in your code but rather in code developed by other parties. On failure, a stack trace will confirm this.

> **Tip**   A useful list of extensions is the MIME-handler list file extension list. A MIME-handler is an application invoked when a file is double-clicked by a user. Such handlers must be fuzzed because they are a common social-engineering attack vector.

Your application should fail gracefully if faced with a file format it simply does not render or understand. Similarly, any component you have developed should fail gracefully and, just as important, bubble errors up to the next level of code.

Collect a library of valid files   You should gather as many valid files from as many trusted sources as possible, and the files should represent a broad spectrum of content. Aim for at least 100 files of each supported file type to get reasonable coverage. For example, if you manufacture digital photography equipment, you need representative files from every camera and scanner you build. Another way to look at this is to select a broad range of files likely to give you good code coverage.

Note that some file types are hard to fuzz—for example, files that are encrypted or have a digital signature associated with them. You should test with the signature checking—you do check the signature, right?—in your code enabled and disabled during fuzzing. In some cases, the procedure can be more complex than this if there are layers of code below your code that require decrypted data or a signature check before your code accesses the bits.

You should continue to build on this library over time as you define new formats or new format variants.

Malform a file   The work really starts when you begin malforming a file. You need to build or use a tool that chooses a file at random, malforms the file, and then passes the file to the software under test (van Sprundel 2005, Sutton and Greene 2005, Oehlert 2005).

The two broad classes of file fuzzing are smart fuzzing and dumb fuzzing. *Smart fuzzing* is when you know the data structure of the file format and you change specific values within the file. *Dumb fuzzing* is when you change the data at random. For example, PNG files start with a well-known signature followed by a series of blocks, named chunks (Milano 1999). The signature is 8 bytes long and must have the following value:

0x89 0x50 0x4E 0x47 0x0D 0x0A 0x1A 0x0A

Each chunk has the following format:

- **4-byte length**   The number of bytes in the data field
- **4-byte type**   The name of the chunk (such as IHDR or IDAT)
- **n-byte data**   The data, the format of which depends on the chunk type
- **4-byte CRC (cyclical redundancy check)**   A CRC-32 calculated from the data

The IHDR chunk type always follows the signature, specifies image dimensions and color information, and has the following format:

- **4-byte width**   Image width in pixels
- **4-byte height**   Image height in pixels
- **1-byte bit depth**   1, 2, 4, 8, or 16 bits per pixel
- **1-byte color type**   0 for grayscale, 2 for RGB, 3 for palette, 4 for gray with alpha channel, and 6 for RGB and alpha
- **1-byte compression mode**   Always zero
- **1-byte filter mode**   Always zero
- **1-byte interlace mode**   0 for none and 1 for Adam-7 format

It's important to know also that PNG files structure multibyte integers with the most significant byte first. This structure is also called *big endian* (Cobas 2003).

Knowing the basic PNG format and the IHDR chunk type, you can be very specific about how you corrupt a PNG file. We'll give file-corruption examples a little later.

Dumb fuzzing is a shotgun approach: you take a valid file and randomly corrupt it. It really is that simple.

On the CD   We have included on the companion disc a simple file fuzzer named MiniFuzz (written in C++), which demonstrates the malforming process. This application outlines in code the steps required to fuzz a file by using dumb fuzzing and, to a lesser extent, smart fuzzing.

You can smart fuzz or dumb fuzz a file in many ways, including these:

- Making the file smaller than normal
- Filling the entire file with random data
- Filling portions of the file with random data
- Searching for null-terminated strings (in ASCII and Unicode) and setting the trailing null to nonnull
- Setting numeric data types to negative values

- Exchanging adjacent bytes

- Setting numeric data types to zero

- Toggling, setting, or clearing high bits (0x80, 0x8000, and so on)

- Doing an exclusive OR (XOR) operation on all bits in a byte, one bit at a time

- Setting numeric data types to 2^N +/- 1

Looking back at the PNG format, you could be very specific and smart fuzz a file by using the following techniques:

- Set the chunk length to a bogus value.

- Create random chunk names. (They are case sensitive, and the case has specific meaning.)

- Build a file with no IHDR chunk.

- Build a file with more than one IHDR chunk.

- Set the width, height, or color depth to invalid values (0, negative values, 2^N +/- 1, little endian, and so on).

- Set invalid compression, filter, or interlace modes.

- Set an invalid color type.

In the PNG example, you would also need to build a valid CRC for each malformed file; otherwise, a CRC failure would prevent most of the parsing code from being exercised.

For some file formats, you should also consider locking files, escaping data (for example, HTML encoding), and so on.

Consume the file and observe the application   Finally, have the application consume the file—for example, simply via a command-line argument that includes the file name. As the application runs, monitor for failures such as access violations or core dumps, and watch for spiked CPU usage. In Microsoft Windows, you can control a process and monitor it as it executes, by using job objects (Microsoft 2006b). Or you can set the fuzzing tool to be a mini-debugger by using debugging APIs (Robbins 2003), and then you can write failure information to a log file. The sample fuzzer, MiniFuzz, shows how to do this.

> **Best Practices**   You must refuzz your application every time you update the product or parser.

If the application fails, perhaps because of a buffer overrun or a null-pointer dereference, you can reload the malformed file at any point and run the application under a debugger if you are not already doing so. When the application fails, determine the source of the failure and fix the code. This strategy assumes the application does not store state between invocations.

> **Best Practices** Keep all malformed files that cause your application to fail. They will be needed to reproduce the bug. You can also use them later to verify that code regressions have not reintroduced the bug.
>
> If any security bug is found in your product, keep the test cases that verify the existence and removal of the bug, and rerun these tests every time you rebuild the product to verify the bug has not reentered the code base. You should also consider using publicly known exploit code as a test case. Obviously, you should run such code on computers that are not connected to your production network.

You should also watch for increased memory usage over time; this might indicate a memory leak. This leads to an important point: you should always run the application that you are testing under a debugger or similar tool. At Microsoft, we usually use a debugger such as cdb, or we run the code under Application Verifier (AppVerif) (Howard 2003). AppVerif is a test tool that is part of the Application Compatibility Toolset, which helps developers find bugs at run time. For example, AppVerif will catch the following classes of errors:

- Heap-based memory leaks and overwrites
- Uninitialized variables (dirty stacks)
- Dangerous APIs
- Thread local storage issues
- Lock usage

When fuzz testing an application, you must enable heap checking. It is recommended that you enable first-chance exceptions and handle checking, as shown in Figure 12-1.

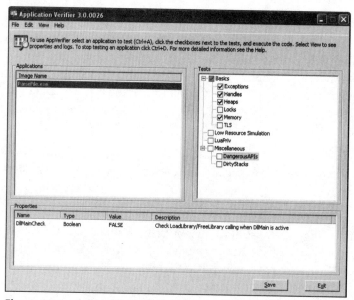

Figure 12-1 AppVerif set to use the SDL required and recommended fuzz-testing settings.

> **Note**   AppVerif is a tool for unmanaged Microsoft Win32 code, not managed .NET code.

You inform AppVerif that your application is to be monitored, by using the following command line:

```
Appverif /verify myapp.exe
```

The /verify command-line argument will enable the following checks:

- HANDLE_CHECKS
- RPC_CHECKS
- COM_CHECKS
- LOCK_CHECKS
- FIRST_CHANCE_EXCEPTION_CHECKS
- FULL_PAGE_HEAP

Once the tests are complete, use the following command line to stop AppVerif from monitoring your application:

```
Appverif -disable * -for myapp.exe
```

Next, you can read the log files by first exporting them from their native binary form to text, by using this:

```
Appverif -export log -for myapp.exe -with to=c:\logs\myapp.log.txt
```

It is recommended that you also run the application using fault injection:

```
Appverif /verify myapp.exe /faults
```

There is a good chance that this option will exercise different code paths within the application as it runs.

> **Note**   The fault injection option mimics certain common functions failing—for example, file I/O, memory allocations, and registry access.

Note that AppVerif does not test the application; it simply intercepts function calls from the application to the operating system when you run your test suite.

> **Best Practices**   When fuzz testing an application, run the application under AppVerif to detect faults earlier.

Fuzzing Network Protocols

Fuzzing network connections is both similar to and different from fuzzing file formats. It is similar in that you use an application to create malformed data. But rather than creating files, you drop malformed packets on the network to attack a process listening on a network port such as a TCP (Transmission Control Protocol) or UDP (User Datagram Protocol) socket (Nuwere and Varpiola 2005), an RPC endpoint, or a pipe. You should perform network fuzzing on a private subnet because otherwise you could accidentally attack production servers.

> **Note**   The more message sequences a protocol uses, and hence the more state it stores or updates, the harder it is to reach the "deep" parts of the protocol.

There are three effective ways to fuzz network traffic:

- Create bogus packets.
- Record-fuzz-replay packets.
- Malform packets just before they are placed on the network or right after they are read from the network.

We'll look at each method in the following sections.

Create bogus packets   To create bogus packets, you must have a good understanding of the network protocol format because you build malformed packets based on the format. Let's look at an example. Microsoft SQL Server 2000 can listen on two ports: TCP/1433 and UDP/1434. The latter port is used by SQL Server to help determine which instances of SQL Server 2000 are available on a computer. A serious bug in the code listening on this port led to the Slammer worm (Boutin 2003). The data format is pretty straightforward—it's a one-byte "verb" followed by a short null-terminated string. The value of the first byte can be only 1 through 9.

The following code excerpt, written in Perl, shows how you can create bogus UDP packets and send them to a remote computer. The first byte is a random value from 1 through 9, and the string is just a series of random bytes from 1 to 2,048 bytes long.

```
use Strict;
use Socket;

die "Usage: <host> [port]\n" if !$ARGV[0];

my $server = $ARGV[0];
my $port = 1434;
print "Connecting to $server:$port\n";

srand 31337; # to make it easy to repro tests
```

```
while (1) {
    # create socket
    my $sock;
    socket(sock, PF_INET, SOCK_DGRAM, getprotobyname('udp')) || die "$!";
    my $iaddr = gethostbyname($server);
    my $sin = sockaddr_in($port, $iaddr);

    # build packets
    # format of packet is 1-byte verb (1..9) and n-byte string
    my $packetsize = int(rand(2048));
    my @chars= ('a'..'z','A'..'Z',0..9,qw(! @ # $ % ^ & * - _ = +));
    my $junk = join("",@chars[map{rand @chars} (1 .. $packetsize)]);
    my $verb = 1 + int(rand(9));
    $junk = pack("ca" . $packetsize,$verb,$junk);

    # lob the grenade
    print "Sending $packetsize bytes, verb $verb\r";
    send(sock, $junk, 0, $sin);
}
```

This code will crash a computer running an unpatched SQL Server 2000 in an average of three seconds. Obviously, some data formats are more complex than this format used by SQL Server 2000, but building fuzzers for complex protocols is more important than building fuzzers for simple protocols because complex protocols are potentially more buggy.

Record-fuzz-replay packets   In this testing scenario, you capture valid network packets using a network packet sniffer, fuzz the packets of interest to you, and then replay them. For example, you would perform the following steps if you wanted to test a Web application:

1. Enable a packet sniffer on the subnet.

2. Collect a few thousand (or more) HTTP packets.

3. Fuzz the HTTP packets in the recorded file.

4. Replay the fuzzed HTTP packets.

Tools such as Cenzic's Hailstorm can automate much of this process (Cenzic 2006).

Malforming packets on the fly   Another effective technique for fuzzing network traffic is to tweak packets within the application before sending the packets to the destination computer. This is a classic man-in-the-middle attack. To do this, you can place stub code in your network code to tweak the data at random. The following example is from a WinSock client application:

```
int SendData(SOCKET socket, const char *pBuf, size_t cbBuf) {
    ...
    int nRet = send(socket,
                    pBuf,
                    cbBuf,
                    0);
```

As you can see, this code simply sends string data to another socket. But with a small change, the code could be turned into fuzz code designed to stress-test the destination application code.

```
#ifdef __FUZZ__
void Fuzz(char *pBuf, size_t *pcbBuf) {
    const size_t FUZZ_THRESHOLD = 2; // corrupt 2% of packets
    if (rand() % 100 <= FUZZ_THRESHOLD) {
        // Fuzz data
    }
}
#endif // __FUZZ__

int SendData(SOCKET socket, char *pBuf, size_t cbBuf) {
    ...

#ifdef __FUZZ__
Fuzz(pBuf,&cbBuf);
#endif // __FUZZ__

    int nRet = send(socket,
                    pBuf,
                    cbBuf,
                    0);
```

Of course, make sure you disable the fuzzing code before you ship your software to customers.

As we mentioned before, you can fuzz the data in numerous ways, such as by flipping high bits, writing random data, truncating the data stream, setting null-terminators or other sentinel characters to invalid characters, and so on.

> **Best Practices**   When performing network fuzz testing, don't fuzz only data that goes from the client to the server; build a rogue server to fuzz data going from the server to the client.

Some formats require that you be methodical while fuzzing. Take HTTP as an example—you should fuzz all the subcomponents of a valid HTTP payload. For example, you could:

- Add invalid headers (headers that are too long or too short or that have invalid characters or names, and so on).
- Change header fields (delete them, make them too long or too short, tweak characters, or add invalid characters—such as by setting the Content-Length header to a negative value [SecurityTracker 2006]).

> **Tip**   Setting a value to –1 is often a very effective way to change header fields because many server implementations add 1 to this value to accommodate for a trailing null. Server implementations then use this value to allocate heap memory.

- Duplicate valid headers.

- Remove or tweak sentinel characters such as the CR/LF combinations.

- Change the HTML content (fill it with random data, randomly truncate it, tweak bytes at random, and so on).

Be wary when fuzzing XML payloads, such as SOAP traffic, because you might end up testing the XML library's schema validation code and not your code. The same caveat applies to RPC code.

One of the advantages of file and network fuzzing is that once the test harness is constructed and operational, little human effort is required to keep the process running. Code reviews, on the other hand, require constant and expensive human attention. Of course, fuzzing does not replace code reviews, but it does effectively augment the security process.

Miscellaneous Fuzzing

Any code that consumes, manipulates, or analyzes data structure that comes from untrusted sources must be parsed. Good examples are arguments to ActiveX controls or any mobile code such as Java, Macromedia Flash, or .NET code that could be hosted in a browser. Identify all methods and properties to the code, and fuzz them all systematically. A simple way to do this is to build an HTML page that instantiates the mobile code, and then use JavaScript to fuzz all the methods and properties owned by the mobile code. Even the URL that hosts the mobile control can be fuzzed. For example, make the hosting URL very long (longer than 1,000 characters) and see if the mobile code can handle that if it checks to see which URL it was loaded from.

Fixing Bugs Found Through Fuzz Testing

Table 12-1 and Table 12-2 outline conservative triage bars for bugs found through fuzz testing. These outlines are likely to evolve as new bug classes are discovered, so please treat them as *minimum* bars and err on the side of caution.

Table 12-1   Client Code Bug Bar

Category	Errors
Must Fix	■ Write Access Violation
	■ Read Access Violation on extended instruction pointer (EIP) register
Must Investigate (Fix is probably needed.)	■ Large memory allocations
	■ Integer Overflow
	■ Custom Exceptions
	■ Other system-level exceptions that could lead to an exploitable crash
	■ Read Access Violation using a REP (repeat string operation) instruction where ECX is large (on Intel CPUs)
	■ Read Access Violation using a MOV (Move) where ESI, EDI, and ECX registers are later used in a REP instruction (on Intel CPUs)

Table 12-1   Client Code Bug Bar

Category	Errors
Security issues unlikely (Investigate and resolve as a potential reliability issue according to your own triage process.)	■ Other Read Access Violations not covered by other code areas ■ Stack Overflow exception (This is stack-space exhaustion, not a stack-based buffer overrun.) ■ DivideByZero ■ Null dereference

Table 12-2   Server Code Bug Bar

Category	Errors
Must Fix	■ All errors leading to an elevation of privilege (EoP) or a significant denial of service (DoS). This is generally everything in all sections of the client fix bar, with the exception of large memory allocations (potentially).
Must Investigate (Fix is probably needed.)	■ Large memory allocations.
Security issues unlikely (Investigate and resolve as potential reliability issue according to your own triage process.)	■ None.

It is important to understand that every crash or unexpected error is an indication of an implementation issue, so you should always investigate such abnormalities. After you understand the problem, draw security-related conclusions. *Never* underestimate your enemy—if you don't test your code, somebody else will do it for you and with harsher consequences.

If you hit a large number of bugs in the code by fuzz testing, stop what you're doing and start a deep code review. Code reviewing and fuzzing work very well together. If you find no bugs even after 100,000 iterations, we recommend that you make sure your fuzzing tool is creating invalid files. If you have access to code coverage tools, verify that the fuzzing is exercising large code areas. If all looks well, congratulations are in order!

Finally, never lose sight of the value a small number of computers has to fuzz testing. Iterating 100,000 or more files can be time consuming, so dedicating a small number of machines to the fuzzing process is beneficial.

Let's now turn our attention to other forms of security testing required by SDL.

Penetration Testing

Penetration testing (pentesting) is a testing process designed to find vulnerabilities in information systems. You should start to plan your pentest work during the testing phase of the product development.

Best Practices   Technically speaking, you can start pentesting any time there is enough code to make a pentest cost effective. Don't start it any later than the product-testing stage; if you start it too late, you might not have time to fix serious issues, or you might delay product shipment.

Historically, such testing has been used to test networks, host operating system configurations, and patch levels (Corsaire 2004). But if you are building a complex software product, you should consider running a pentest prior to shipping the product to customers.

Consider using a third-party company to perform the pentest if you do not have the appropriate skills in-house. Because you probably don't know how good your own pentest skills are, you should initially engage a respected security company to pentest your application. Make sure you choose a trustworthy company that has expertise in the programming languages you use and the technologies you are building.

A description of what is required to perform a pentest is beyond the scope of this book.

Best Practices   Every time you find a security vulnerability in your application, build a small test plan to verify the existence of the bug, and then later reuse the test to verify that the code is fixed. Build on this series of tests as new vulnerabilities are found, and rerun all the tests on an ongoing basis.

Run-Time Verification

The final testing method is run-time verification testing using tools such as AppVerif to detect certain kinds of bugs in the code as it executes. AppVerif has been discussed earlier in the chapter as part of the fuzz-testing process. However, its usefulness extends beyond fuzz testing; it can also be used to find serious security flaws during normal testing or analysis. Hence, you should run the application regularly by using AppVerif, and you should review the log files to make sure there are no issues that require fixing.

Microsoft Windows includes a tool called Driver Verifier (Verifier.exe) to perform similar tests on device drivers (Microsoft 2005).

Reviewing and Updating Threat Models if Needed

Threat models are invaluable documents to use during security testing. Sometimes functionality and implementation change after the design phase of a project. Threat models should be reviewed to ensure that they are still accurate and comprehensively cover all functionality delivered by the software. Threat models should be used to drive and inform security testing plans. Also, the riskiest portions of an application—usually those with the largest attack surface and the threats that are the highest risks—must be tested the most thoroughly.

Reevaluating the Attack Surface of the Software

Attack surface is described in Chapter 7, "Stage 2: Define and Follow Design Best Practices." Software development teams should carefully reevaluate the attack surface of their product during the testing stage of the SDL. Measuring the attack surface will allow teams to understand which components have direct exposure to attack and, hence, have the highest risk of damage if a vulnerability occurs in those components. Assessing the attack surface will enable the team to focus testing and code-review efforts on high-risk areas and to take appropriate corrective actions. Such actions might include deciding not to ship a component until it is corrected, disabling a component by default, or modifying development practices to reduce the likelihood that vulnerabilities will be introduced by future modifications or new developments. After the attack surface has been reevaluated, the attack surface should be documented to reflect the rationale for the attack surface.

Summary

Security testing is often considered a subject known only to a few. This might be factual, but non-security experts can perform a lot of effective security testing, most notably fuzz testing. You must fuzz test all file formats your application consumes, and if your code has more than one parser per format, each parser must be tested separately. SDL mandates an absolute minimum of 100,000 fuzzed files per format and parser. You should also fuzz test your network protocols by using man-in-the-middle techniques discussed in this chapter.

For critical products, you should also consider starting an external penetration-testing program. Do not perform this testing in-house if you do not have a dedicated and experienced penetration-testing team. Amateurs will find few, if any, security bugs of merit.

Finally, you must re-review the product threat models and use the results of this review as part of the attack surface evaluation. For commercial software, you should constantly strive to reduce the attack surface over time.

References

(Miller, Fredriksen, and So 1990)   Miller, Barton P., Lars Fredriksen, and Bryan So. "An Empirical Study of the Reliability of UNIX Utilities," *http://citeseer.ist.psu.edu/ miller90empirical.html*.

(Miller et al. 1995)   Miller, Barton P., David Koski, Cjin Pheow Lee, Vivekananda Maganty, Ravi Murthy, Ajitkumar Natarajan, and Jeff Steidl. "Fuzz Revisited: A Re-examination of the Reliability of UNIX Utilities and Services," *http://citeseer.ist.psu.edu/ miller95fuzz.html*.

(Miller 2005)   Miller, Barton P. "Fuzz Testing of Application Reliability," *http://www.cs .wisc.edu/~bart/fuzz/fuzz.html*. December, 2005.

(Gallagher, Jeffries, and Landauer 2006) Gallagher, Tom, Bryan Jeffries, and Lawrence Landauer. *Finding Security Bugs*. Redmond, WA: Microsoft Press, 2006.

(Microsoft 2006a) Microsoft Corporation. "GDI+," *http://msdn.microsoft.com/library/en-us/ gdicpp/gdiplus/gdiplus.asp*. MSDN, 2006.

(Still 2002) Still, Michael, IBM Corporation. "Graphics programming with libtiff," *http:// www-128.ibm.com/developerworks/linux/library/l-libtiff/*. developerWorks, 2002.

(van Sprundel 2005) van Sprundelm Ilja. "Fuzzing," *http://static.23.nu/md/Pictures/ FUZZING.PDF*.

(Sutton and Greene 2005) Sutton, Michael, and Adam Greene, iDEFENSE Labs. Black Hat 2005, "The Art of File Format Fuzzing," *http://www.blackhat.com/presentations/ bh-jp-05/bh-jp-05-sutton-greene.pdf*. July 2005.

(Oehlert 2005) Oehlert, Peter. "Violating Assumptions with Fuzzing," IEEE Security and Privacy, March/April 2005.

(Milano 1999) Milano, John. *Compressed Image File Formats*. Boston, MA: Addison-Wesley, 1999.

(Cobas 2003) Cobas, Juan Carlos. "The Basics of Endianness," *http://www.codeproject.com/ cpp/endianness.asp*. The Code Project, 2003.

(Microsoft 2006b) Microsoft Corporation. Platform SDK: DLLs, Processes, and Threads, "Job Objects," *http://msdn.microsoft.com/library/en-us/dllproc/base/job_objects.asp*. MSDN, 2006.

(Robbins 2003) Robbins, John. *Debugging Applications for Microsoft .NET and Microsoft Windows*. Redmond, WA: Microsoft Press, 2003.

(Howard 2003) Howard, Michael, Microsoft Corporation. "Analyzing Your Applications with Windows Application Verifier," *http://msdn.microsoft.com/library/en-us/dncode/html/ secure12112003.asp*. MSDN, December 2003.

(Nuwere and Varpiola 2005) Nuwere, Ejovi, and Mikko Varpiola, SecurityLab Technologies, Inc. Black Hat 2005, "The Art of SIP Fuzzing and Vulnerabilities Found in VoIP," *http://www.blackhat.com/presentations/bh-jp-05/bh-jp-05-nuwere.pdf*. July 2005.

(Boutin 2003) Boutin, Paul. "Slammed!" *http://www.wired.com/wired/archive/11.07/ slammer.html*. Wired, July 2003.

(Cenzic 2006) Cenzic Hailstorm, *www.cenzic.com*.

(SecurityTracker 2006) SecurityTracker. "Novell Remote Manager for SUSE Linux Content-Length Heap Overflow Lets Remote Users Execute Arbitrary Code," *http:// www.securitytracker.com/alerts/2006/Jan/1015487.html*. January 2006.

(Corsaire 2004) Corsaire Limited. "Penetrating Testing Guide," *http://www.penetration-testing.com/*. 2004.

(Microsoft 2005) Microsoft Help and Support. "How to Use Driver Verifier to Troubleshoot Windows Drivers," *http://support.microsoft.com/default.aspx?scid=kb;en-us;244617*. Last Review: January 2005.

Chapter 13
Stage 8: The Security Push

When Microsoft first embarked on the journey called Trustworthy Computing in 2002, the first major foray into changing the software development process was the security push. The goal of the push was simple: to hunt for security bugs, triage them, and fix them once the push was complete. The problem with doing security this way is that security pushes are not a sustainable way to produce secure software because a push misses the point of building secure systems. Building secure software requires you to reduce the chance that security bugs are created in the first place, and hunting for bugs late in the process is anathema to "getting it right" early in the process. Just after Bill Gates announced Trustworthy Computing, all major Microsoft products went through a security push. The products included Microsoft Windows Server, Exchange Server, SQL Server 2000, and Office.

But the security push has a place in the Software Development Lifecycle (SDL), which requires that teams use the push primarily to focus on legacy code—in other words, code created before the current development cycle. However, a security push is not a "quick fix" for insecure code. Do not for one moment think you can put off security until the security push.

 Important Do not put off focusing on security until the security push. Doing so is an egregious violation of the SDL.

A security push occurs after a product has entered the verification stage and has reached code and feature complete (often around the beta time frame). Because the results of the security push might alter the default configuration and behavior of a product, a final beta test release should be planned after the security push is complete and all bugs and changes required based on the push have been resolved.

> **Note**   Anecdotally, product team members have told us the push is hard work but that it gives the team a valuable chance to focus on "nothing but security."

All software that is not brand-new uses some form of legacy code. Invariably, this code was written when less was known about building secure software or, in many cases, when security was not a main project objective. The push targets mainly this older code. We expect the need for security pushes to dwindle over time as old code is removed or upgraded to the quality of newly created code. Eventually, the need for a security push will diminish because new and earlier code is more secure. In fact, the authors believe the push might eventually be no longer needed.

> **Important**   The goal of a security push is to find bugs, not to fix them. Fixing is done after the push.

The security push is not restricted to code. The main tasks during the push are as follows:

- Training
- Code reviews
- Threat-model updates
- Security testing
- Documentation scrub

We'll look at each of these in detail shortly, but first we want to outline the preparation process for a successful security push.

Preparing for the Security Push

A successful push requires plenty of planning, and time for the push must be built into the schedule from the outset. If you tack the security push onto the schedule at a late date or as a "surprise event," you'll lose the benefits of the push. The person responsible for security of the product should drive the push, which includes setting up the push leadership team. In our experience, this team includes a small number of people representing all product design and development disciplines, such as development, testing, documentation, design, and project management, as well as one or more people from the team that owns the schedule and ultimately delivers the software to customers. At Microsoft, this team is usually the release management team, with assistance from a lead program manager.

At the outset, you should set up a security push Web site with push details, including the goals of the push, expected time frames, and a list of tasks per engineering discipline. The rest of this chapter outlines the recommended tasks.

Also, the Web site should have links to bug databases, incoming bug counts, and other up-to-date information. Make sure to keep this site current.

On the subject of bug databases, we've found that it's useful to store security-push bug information in a separate bug-tracking database, if possible, owing to the possible high bug count. At the end of the push, this separate database is triaged for bugs that should be included in the main project bug-tracking database. If it's infeasible to maintain a separate bug database, make sure you mark all push-related security bugs as "HowFound = Security Push".

Push Duration

The push is complete when the required tasks are complete, not when some arbitrary amount of time elapses. Common exit criteria follow:

- All personnel are up to date on security training.
- All high-priority (Pri1) source code has been reviewed and signed off.
- All Pri1 executable code has been signed off by the test owners.
- All threat models have been reevaluated and updated (or, for very old components or products, threat models have been created for all components).
- The attack surface has been reanalyzed, and the appropriateness of the default attack surface has been confirmed.
- All documentation has been reviewed for correct security guidance.

> **Best Practices**   Make the exit criteria crisp and actionable, and then broadly communicate the criteria to the team.

Obviously, you can save time spent on the push by making sure the threat models and documentation are up to date. Also, as the quality of older code improves over time, the push duration will diminish.

For large products at Microsoft such as Microsoft Windows, Office, and SQL Server, a push typically lasts no less than six weeks. For smaller products, the duration is typically no less than three weeks.

Training

At an absolute minimum, the software development team will need training on what to expect during the security push as well as on push logistics. Some employees might also need to attend technical security-related training, so holding extra technical classes is worthwhile. These technical classes are especially useful if a high percentage of the team members are approaching their training anniversary.

Best Practices   Our group performs a good deal of security training for teams about to start a security push. We usually fine-tune existing class material so that it's completely relevant to the team being trained.

The push logistics explanation should start with a short (perhaps 15-minute) introduction by a senior and well-respected individual, who emphasizes the importance of the security push.

Note   During the famed Windows Security Push of 2002, we provided a series of training events for each development discipline, and each training event was launched by a vice president. This provided a great deal of much-needed gravitas and emphasized Microsoft's commitment in the early days of Trustworthy Computing.

Code Reviews

No one really likes to review code for bugs, especially code written 10 or more years ago. Given the opportunity to review old code or work on a new, cool feature, developers will lean toward the latter. It's just human nature. Reviewing code is slow, tedious, and mind-numbingly boring. Unfortunately, all code that runs on computers and is used as part of your software must be reviewed, regardless of age. Attackers don't target only new functionality; they target *all* functionality. Make no mistake: the attackers will attack code regardless of its age. In fact, in some cases, it's worth the attacker's time finding bugs in older code because more people will have older versions of the software installed. The situation is compounded if the code is common to multiple versions of the product.

Important   Attackers attack all code, so waiting to make the code more secure in the next version of the product is not a good solution for protecting customers. You must secure the currently supported versions, too.

The first step in security code review is to build a database of all the files and assign an owner to each source code file. At this stage, don't exclude any code from the review; include everything. Many source-code repositories don't store the source code file "owner." In this case, you can usually use the name of the last person who updated the file. Create a table in a database with the following fields:

- **File name**   The name of the file, including the directory where it's stored.
- **File owner**   The name of the file owner.
- **Priority**   The priority for reviewing the code. Ratings range from 1 to 3, with 1 being the highest priority.

- **Reviewed by**   The name of the person who will review the code. If you plan to have multiple people review the code, you might want to make this a separate table.

- **Reviewed**   A field with only three possible values: Yes, No, and Partial.

- **Comments**   Any comments about the file that might be of interest to people reviewing the code.

Populate the table with the file and owner information. Of course, you should use a tool to do this; don't do it manually. If you are using Microsoft Visual Studio 2005 Team Foundation Server, you can query the source code repository from within the system itself or create a Microsoft Office Excel PivotTable of the data you want. If you are more development-inclined, you can access the source code database programmatically.

The next step is to determine review priority. Much of this identification should be driven by the threat model. The highest-risk components that the threat model identifies are the high-priority code segments for review. That said, you can follow some simple rules to help determine priority:

- Code running by default, listening on the Internet, or connecting to the Internet is Pri1.

- Code with numerous prior vulnerabilities is Pri1.

- Code executing with high privilege (for example, SYSTEM, administrator, root) is Pri1.

- Security-related code (for example, authentication, authorization, cryptographic, and firewall code) is Pri1.

- For .NET code, unverifiable code is Pri1. You can use the PEVerify tool (Microsoft 2006) to determine whether Microsoft intermediate language code is verifiable.

- Code that parses data structures from potentially untrusted sources is Pri1.

- Optionally installed code that runs with user privilege, or code that is installed by default that doesn't meet any Pri1 criteria, is Pri2.

- Setup code is generally Pri3 except for the code portions that set access controls or handle encryption keys or passwords. Consider these latter components Pri1 because of the sensitivity of the data and the possibility of getting default permissions settings wrong or leaving a password that's supplied at installation time in the wrong place. (We've been surprised at how many times we have seen this in the past [Secunia 2004].)

- The Q/A or test lead, not the development team, must agree with the priority list.

Code reviews should also cover sample code you make available to others who build on your code. Prioritizing sample code is a little harder than shipping code, but a good approach is to consider how your users will apply the sample code. If it is template code that requires minor modification to use in production environments, and it fits any of the Pri1 criteria noted in the previous list, the sample code is Pri1.

More Info   For more information on the tasks involved in performing a code review, refer to Appendix D, "A Developer's Security Checklist," in *Writing Secure Code, Second Edition*, as a minimum checklist of security issues to be aware of during code reviews (Howard and LeBlanc 2003). Also, *19 Deadly Sins of Software Security* (Howard, LeBlanc, and Viega 2005) and "Expert Tips for Finding Security Defects in Your Code" (Howard 2003) provide guidelines for reviewing code for security bugs.

Note that the owner does not review the code but, rather, nominates someone else to review the code. One best practice is to simply have two owners swap their source code files and then review each other's code. You might sometimes need to balance the workload equitably among code reviewers. If a reviewer finishes her assigned code, she should help others review their assigned code. But again, a reviewer should not review her own code.

Executable-File Owners

Finally, you must build a list of all the executable files (.exe files, dynamic-link libraries, COM objects, assemblies, script files, and so on) that make up the product, and you must assign a test owner to each component. Again, create a table with the following columns:

- **Executable file name**   The full path of the executable file
- **Test owner**   The name of the test or Q/A person in charge of testing this component
- **Priority**   Priority for reviewing the component, on a scale of 1 to 3, with 1 being the highest priority
- **Signed Off**   Yes or No
- **Comments**   Any comments about the component or the sign-off procedure

The goal of this task is to have the test people sign off on all high-risk executable components within the product. A successful sign-off means that the test team has agreed with the following:

- The code that makes up that component has been reviewed.
- The component has all appropriate security tests in place.
- The component's threat models are up to date and accurate.
- The component's attack-surface documentation is up to date and accurate.

Make no mistake, assigning executable-file owners is a very important substep in the SDL process and should not be taken lightly.

Threat Model Updates

The architects and program managers need to review the threat models one more time. We know that it might seem like there has been a great deal of focus on threat models, but they are very important. As we write this chapter, Windows Vista starts its verification phase, in which threat models are reviewed to make sure that they are complete and correct. The beauty of doing this is that you can ascertain which areas the various component groups might have missed, if indeed they have missed anything. The critical portions of the threat model to look at are described in Chapter 9, "Stage 4: Risk Analysis." To recap, here are some of the authors' favorite things to look for in a threat model during the security push:

- Determine whether the data flow diagram (DFD) needs to be changed since its last review. Software design changes that happen between the design phase and verification phase should be reflected in the DFD and, hence, the threat model as a whole.

- Make sure all DFD elements are mapped to appropriate STRIDE threat categories.

- Look at all the entry points into the system. Make sure the list is complete and has not changed since the last review.

- Look at all the anonymous network-facing interfaces to the system. Should they be authenticated or restricted to a local subnet or list of trusted Internet Protocol (IP) addresses?

- Make sure all the sensitive data stores are correctly protected. This protection often includes an access control list (ACL) review.

- Make sure all data flows carrying security-sensitive data are adequately protected. This includes protection from disclosure (using encryption) and tamper detection (using message authentication codes or digital signatures).

Security Testing

You might be thinking, "Didn't the prior chapter discuss security testing?" The answer is a resounding yes, but security-push testing has a slightly different focus. You can still employ many of the testing techniques discussed in the previous chapter, but testing during the push focuses on the highest-risk components only. It's also good to do one last validation to make sure that you have a list of all file formats parsed by your code and that fuzz tests are in place for all of those file formats.

Attack-Surface Scrub

Program management drives the task of reevaluating your attack surface during the security push, providing two major benefits. The first is general "good security hygiene": is your product exposing just the right amount of functionality to the correct users without putting them unnecessarily at risk? The simple list that follows will help you drive your attack-surface scrub:

- Count all the open ports, sockets, SOAP interfaces, remote procedure call (RPC) end points, and pipes. Are they all needed by default?

- Verify that all unauthenticated network entry points are needed. Can they be authenticated by default?

- Verify that all network entry points are restricted to the correct subnet or set of trusted source addresses.

- Verify that every process you run uses the right level of privilege to get the tasks done. Can you shed some privileges to protect customers?

- Verify that the ACL is correct for every object you create. If you inherit base operating system ACLs in Windows, your code is probably correct because the operating system ACLs are likely to be good.

- If you use datagram protocols, must your code listen on datagram protocols by default? Can you use stream protocols by default and allow users to opt in to datagram support if they need it and understand the risks?

The second benefit of reanalyzing the product's attack surface is that it helps drive the priority ranking for the code review task. A review of attack surface will allow teams to understand which components have direct exposure to attack and, hence, the highest risk of damage if a vulnerability occurs in those components. Obviously, the highest-risk code must be reviewed the most thoroughly.

After the attack surface has been reevaluated, the attack-surface document should be updated as appropriate. The attack-surface document explains your attack-surface rationale by asking questions such as Just why is that port open? and Why is a specific ACL set this way?

 On the CD   You will find an attack-surface rationale document on the book's companion disc.

Documentation Scrub

Finally, the writers and editors involved in building the end-user documentation should review all their draft documentation to verify that the security best practices are correct and that the documentation does not recommend potentially bad practices. If the documentation provides code examples, they should show secure coding practices.

Seriously consider adding "Security Best Practice" and "Security Alert" sections to each topic outlined in the documentation if this has not already been done. Better yet, add a security icon to highlight such sections.

Your users should be informed of the security ramifications when enabling or changing functionality, but never lose sight of who the customer is. For example, if your product is used by network administrators and a setting is changed, the security ramifications of that change should be made known to the network administrators. You might include text like this:

Security Issue: Enabling this functionality opens port TCP/1067 to anonymous and authenticated users on the local subnet.

An Important Note About Communications

Constant communication to the software development team about the progress of the security push is absolutely critical to the push success. Communication could include the following:

- Regular e-mail messages from push leadership to the development team to outline progress

- An intranet site with live statistics

These two forms of communication should include the following:

- Number of bugs found.

- Number of new bugs opened in the last 24 hours.

- Number of files and amount of code reviewed, threat models reviewed, tests executed, and so on. A chart should be provided to show progress and the glide-path down to push completion. A glide-path shows how the progress statistics trend toward a finish date.

- The names of the top bug hunters. Include information such as who has found the most bugs so far and who has found the most bugs in the oldest code.

- Funny stories or anecdotes. Although a security push is serious business, adding a human touch makes it a little less austere.

Note   We often add a little levity to the security push by having competitions and spot prizes. One of the bigger prizes is awarded to the person who finds a bug written by the most senior person. The prize is even more valuable if the senior person is currently a vice president or even more senior!

Are We Done Yet?

We have already touched on this topic a little in this chapter, but it's worth repeating: The security push is finished when the approved security push tasks are complete.

The amount of time and energy and the degree of teamwide focus required for a security push will differ for individual teams based on the state of the code base and the team's attention to security during the development process. Teams that have performed the following tasks will have a shorter security push:

- Rigorously kept all threat models up to date

- Actively and completely tested the threat model through penetrations testing

- Accurately tracked and documented attack surfaces and any changes made to them during the development process

- Completed security code reviews for all high-priority code identified and documented development and testing contacts for all code released with the product

- Adhered to stringent coding standards

- Rigorously brought all earlier code in the project up to current security standards

- Validated the security documentation plan

The amount of time needed to complete the requirements of a security push is most influenced by the size and complexity of the product, coupled with how much effort has gone into creating the exit criteria requirements earlier in the development process.

There is no easy way to predict the duration of a security push. The push duration is ultimately determined by the amount of code that needs to be reviewed for security because all pushes to date have been gated by code quantity. Teams are strongly encouraged to conduct security code reviews throughout the development process, once the code is fairly stable, because the quality of code reviews will suffer if too many code reviews are condensed into too short of a time period during the push.

Again, the push is finished when the tasks are complete, not when an arbitrary date arrives.

Summary

The focus of a security push is primarily code-review of legacy code, but it also includes updating threat models and attack-surface documentation as well as pointed security testing and an end-user documentation scrub. The push allows the team to focus on nothing but security, and the length of time needed to complete a security push is task driven, not date driven: the security push is finished when the exit criteria have been met.

Make sure that time is built into the master schedule for the security push. It's a relatively lengthy process, but we see these push durations diminishing over time as the older code is brought up to the quality dictated by current threats. If your threat models and attack-surface documentation are up to date before you enter the push and the amount of unreviewed former code is small, the security push duration will also be short.

The threat models and attack surface help drive the code-review priority. All code in the source-code tree should be assigned an owner. Then all high-priority code should be reviewed by someone other than the code owner. Bugs should be filed but not fixed at this point; fixing bugs is done after the push.

References

(Microsoft 2006)   Microsoft Corporation. .NET Framework Tools, "PEVerify Tool (Peverify.exe)," *http://msdn.microsoft.com/library/en-us/cptools/html/ cpgrfPEVerifyToolPeverifyexe.asp*. MSDN, 2006.

(Secunia 2004)   Secunia Advisories. "Novell NetWare Admin/Install Password Disclosure," *http://secunia.com/advisories/11188*. March 2004.

(Howard and LeBlanc 2003)   Howard, Michael, and David LeBlanc. *Writing Secure Code*, 2d ed. Redmond, WA: Microsoft Press, 2003.

(Howard, LeBlanc, and Viega 2005)   Howard, Michael, David LeBlanc, and John Viega. *19 Deadly Sins of Software Development*. New York, NY: McGraw-Hill, 2005.

(Howard 2003)   Howard, Michael. "Expert Tips for Finding Security Defects in Your Code," *http://msdn.microsoft.com/msdnmag/issues/03/11/SecurityCodeReview/default.aspx*. MSDN Magazine, November 2003.

Chapter 14

Stage 9: The Final Security Review

As the product draws close to completion, an important question has to be answered: from a security and privacy perspective, is the product ready to ship to customers? The goal of the Final Security Review (FSR) is to answer this question. Performed by the central security team, the FSR is not only a critical part of the Security Development Lifecycle (SDL), it's also complex, including many important tasks.

Before a software product can ship to customers, it must successfully complete its FSR. A failed FSR must be evaluated to determine how egregious the issues are. If they cannot be resolved by the product team, senior management must make the final call on resolving the issues.

The product group does not perform its own FSR. At Microsoft, the central security team performs the FSRs for all product groups.

The FSR is a review verifying that the product group has followed the SDL correctly during the product's entire development lifecycle. The word "final" makes it sound as though this is where a good deal of security work is performed, but it really is not. Bug scrubbing should be done per bug as each one arises, threat-model reviews should be performed after implementation, and tools should be used as much as possible throughout the process by making them part of your build process. If the SDL is followed correctly, an FSR should be a short affair.

Important For a software development team that has followed the SDL correctly, there should be few surprises during the FSR.

This short chapter outlines the major tasks required when performing a final security review. The following components make up the FSR process, and we'll look at each in more detail.

- Product team coordination
- Threat models review
- Unfixed security bugs review
- Tools-use validation

Product Team Coordination

This part of the FSR is not at all technical—it's pure process, but it's process that must be performed well for the FSR to run smoothly. First, the team must fill out a questionnaire. Examples of questions follow—note that many of the answers to these questions are known well before the FSR:

- Is this product standalone or a service/management/feature/add-on pack?
- Is any part of the product network-facing?
- When was the security push, and how long did it take?
- Where is the attack surface documented?
- Where are the threat models located?
- Where is the source code located?
- Where is the bug bar documented?
- Where is a list—preferably a database query—of unfixed security bugs?
- Has the security team previously reviewed the threat models? If so, who did the review, and what was the outcome?
- Are there any SDL requirements that you know the software is not compliant with? If so, what and why?
- Did you run all analysis tools, and when was the last run of the tools?

This list is not exhaustive, but as you can see, the aim is to help the reviewers in the following FSR tasks.

Threat Models Review

Threat models—explained in detail in Chapter 9, "Stage 4: Risk Analysis"—are a cornerstone for building secure systems, and it is imperative that the models reflect reality. During the FSR, the threat models should again be reviewed to verify that they are accurate, up to date, and have appropriate mitigations in place. Refer to Table 9-12, "Threat-Model Quality Guidelines" (on page 129), to determine the threat-model relevance and quality.

Pay close attention to the last time the threat models were updated. A very old threat model is probably out of date and inaccurate. Also look at the data flow diagram. Does it look accurate and complete? If not, the entire threat model is inaccurate.

Unfixed Security Bugs Review

If developers make mistakes writing code, and authors make mistakes writing documentation, and testers make mistakes building tests, doesn't it make sense that people will make mistakes when they enter bug information in the bug tracking database? The purpose of this part of the FSR is to verify that security bugs that are marked as "Won't Fix" are appropriate to leave unfixed. All security bugs that exceed the specified threshold for the product must be fixed prior to releasing the product, so it's important that the bug severity or criticality is correct. We have found that people make mistakes every now and then in entering a bug's criticality, due to simple human error.

If you have a large number of bugs, you need to make sure that you have enough people reviewing the bugs in a timely manner. At Microsoft, we normally try to review all such bugs in less than a week, and we enroll enough security people to meet the allotted time. Don't drag this phase out, even in the face of a large number of bugs.

Also note that you should mark each bug that is reviewed as such so that you don't go back over the same bugs time after time. Assuming that you are using the bug-tracking fields defined in Chapter 6, "Stage 1: Project Inception," you should create a new field named *SecAudit* with the following possible values:

- Untriaged
- Not a security concern
- Defense in depth
- Low severity
- Medium severity
- Important severity
- Critical severity

Next, mark all unfixed security bugs (where Security/Privacy Bug Effect < > Not a Security Bug) with *SecAudit = Untriaged*.

As security people review each bug, they should set the *SecAudit* field to the appropriate value listed previously.

Once all the bugs have been reviewed, the results should be analyzed (triaged) to determine which bugs should be fixed. Invariably, there will be some unfixed bugs that are borderline; our only advice is to err on the side of fixing all security bugs that exceed the specified threshold for the product. Remember, you are protecting your customers!

Tools-Use Validation

It's important for the FSR team to verify that all appropriate tools have been used during the development of the software. A list of the required tools and versions is given in Chapter 21, "SDL Required Tools and Compiler Options." Use of appropriate security testing tools, such as file and network fuzzers, must also be reviewed and verified to ensure that they have been executed correctly.

There are many ways to do this: the first is just to look at makefiles and build scripts and verify that the appropriate flags are set. For example, in the case of the Microsoft Visual C++ tools, we make sure that the compiler command line includes */GS* and no */GS-* flag settings. We also check that the MIDL compiler uses */ROBUST* and so on.

Some settings can—and should—be validated with tools, but some tools usage can be confirmed only by asking the development team. For example, static analysis tools require the development team to affirm that they used the tools.

You must document early in the process how you are going to determine compliance with tools requirements because this will vary if you use different tools.

Any compliance failure must be treated as a security bug and triaged accordingly. Assuming that a product team is trying to execute on the SDL responsibly, you should find no surprises during the FSR when validating tools usage.

After the Final Security Review Is Completed

At the end of the FSR, the security team will either agree that the FSR is completed and the product can be released to customers or determine that there are issues requiring remediation. If issues arise, each should be looked at to determine the correct course of action.

Handling Exceptions

In some instances, a development team might reasonably be unable to comply with an SDL requirement and will ask for an exception. Often such exceptions are granted earlier than the FSR, but any exception should be looked at holistically; a single non-egregious issue—perhaps there are a small number of banned application programming interfaces (APIs) left in the code—is probably fine, but a multitude of issues or, perhaps, a banned API that is obviously vulnerable is not fine!

> **Note**   Few FSRs go 100 percent smoothly!

Handling exceptions is complex, and no easy-to-follow set of rules exists. Each exception should be decided on a case-by-case basis. However, an exception should never be granted without first conducting a thorough assessment of the impact on the product's overall security if the exception is granted.

In general, if an exception is granted, the issue or issues should be remedied in the next public version of the product. This does not mean the next full version of the product—it means a service pack or a "dot release."

When you're deciding whether to allow an exception, it should not be uncommon to involve senior executives in the decision process. The pros and cons of each alternative resolution to the issue must be laid out so that upper management can make the call. You'll need to gather all the appropriate background information to aid in making the correct decision, including:

- What is the issue being resolved?

- Why is the issue being found now? Was this unknown at a time when the issue could have been fixed?

- What are the possible ramifications, if any, of not making the fix?

- What should you tell customers about the issue? Do not rely on customers reading a readme file to stay secure.

- What is the plan if the call is made to not resolve the issue, and the issue turns out to be worse than expected—or if an attack occurs?

- What is the plan to fix the issue if it's not resolved in the current product version?

- When can customers obtain an updated version that fixes the issue?

- Are there other mitigating factors that make the issue less important?

We can't give concrete guidelines to any of these questions because there are none. Again, each exception decision must be made on a case-by-case basis.

Summary

Before a product ships, a pair of critical security eyes must validate that the software complies with the SDL security and privacy policies. An FSR can take a long time, but it's critical that it be completed to make sure that the software has achieved all the SDL requirements for secure software. Remember that the FSR is not a penetration test, and it's not the point at which you do a great deal of security work. It is a means to determine the overall ship quality and nothing more. At the end of the FSR, the product is either ready to ship, or there are issues that must be remedied. In some cases, exceptions might be granted for reasonable deviations from the SDL, but decisions to grant exceptions must not be made in haste and should be made only in light of all the possible ramifications of not fixing the deviation.

Chapter 15

Stage 10: Security Response Planning

This chapter explains why you need to be prepared to respond to the discovery of security vulnerabilities in your software. Because this entire book is dedicated to telling you about a process to help you build secure software, it might seem strange that we also talk about how to respond when you fail to build secure software. So we'll first explain why it's important that you do just that.

Once we've discussed the need to prepare to respond to the discovery of vulnerabilities in your software, we'll describe the preparations you should make during the software development phases. Early preparation for security response will save you from having to figure out your plan at a time when you need to be executing it.

Why Prepare to Respond?

As we write this chapter, we can hear you saying, "These guys have spent ten chapters telling me how to build secure software. Why are they saying now that I have to be prepared to respond to vulnerabilities? Won't following all their instructions prevent me from having to deal with security response?"

We wish we could tell you that following all the guidance in this book to the letter will save you from the pain of responding when people find vulnerabilities in your software. But sadly, it's just not so. This section tells you why.

Your Development Team Will Make Mistakes

It's a fact of software development life that your team won't achieve perfection. However, from our experience in applying the Security Development Lifecycle (SDL) at Microsoft, we're confident that if you apply the techniques we describe in this book, you'll produce software with many fewer vulnerabilities than you would if you only applied development best practices. No matter how well you apply common practices for producing reliable and bug-free software, paying attention to the errors that lead to security vulnerabilities and applying practices that eliminate or detect those errors will result in more secure code, fewer vulnerabilities, and less need for security response.

But your development team is still made up of human beings, and they will make mistakes, including mistakes with security impact. At some point during development, you'll decide that the rate of vulnerability discovery is "low enough" and that it has become very difficult to discover remaining security bugs. When that point arrives, you'll decide to ship your product. No matter how hard you and your team have tried, there will be a vulnerability or two (or maybe more) that your team should have found.

New Kinds of Vulnerabilities Will Appear

If you follow the guidance in this book, you'll build software that is as secure as you can make it at the point in time when you're doing development. You and your team will do your best, and that might be very good indeed. But we can guarantee that the security researchers will keep trying, and they will find a class of vulnerability that neither you nor we knew about, and one (or many) vulnerabilities in that class will affect your software.

Back in the 1970s and 1980s, one of us (Lipner) believed that it would be possible to apply highly structured formal specification and design methods along with formal verification of specifications and programs to produce software that would be substantially free of vulnerabilities. A few projects attempted to follow this path, but all failed. (Lipner led a project that came close to releasing an operating system intended to reach Class A1—the highest level—of the U.S. Trusted Computer Systems Evaluation Criteria, or Orange Book [Karger et al. 1991].) The obvious cause of the failures was that by the time a team had executed the highly structured development process, the system they were producing was obsolete and no one wanted to buy it. But even if those highly formal processes had been efficient enough to produce competitive products, we don't believe they would have achieved their ambitious security goals. The reason is that new classes of vulnerabilities continue to be discovered, and those vulnerabilities almost always result from errors that are below the level of detail addressed by the formal methods. To quote Earl Boebert, a security researcher whose experience goes back to the early 1970s, "Security is in the weeds." Not only do you need to get the specifications and designs right, but any error in the machine code that is actually running can undo you.

If you look at the history of vulnerability reports, you can convince yourself that new classes of vulnerabilities continue to emerge. Stack-based buffer overruns go back to the 1980s or before (Eichlin and Rochlis 1989), and the authors put tremendous effort into removing them during the Microsoft Windows Server 2003 security push. But exploitable heap-based buffer overruns and integer overflow attacks on the length calculations that attempt to prevent buffer overruns are relatively new developments. For example, the ASN.1 network protocol–parsing component of Microsoft Windows was extensively scrubbed for buffer overrun vulnerabilities during the security push (CERT 2002). A researcher subsequently pointed out that the component was vulnerable to integer overflow attacks in the code that was supposed to prevent buffer overruns. Of course, our tools, training, and processes now focus on such vulnerabilities, but at the time of that particular security threat, we had to invoke our security response process and release Microsoft Security Bulletin MS04-007 to deal with vulnerabilities in a component we thought we had gotten right (Microsoft 2004a).

Integer and heap overruns are far from the only examples of new kinds of vulnerabilities. In early 2000, researchers at Microsoft discovered cross-site scripting attacks, in which a coding error in a trusted Web site can allow a malicious site to act on a client with the privileges of the trusted site (Microsoft 2000a). We remember a Web security expert telling us that everyone knew about the class of attack at issue—and we also remember that the site for this expert's organization was itself vulnerable to cross-site scripting attacks. In the subsequent six years, the discovery of cross-site scripting vulnerabilities on Web sites—and the discovery of new variations of cross-site scripting vulnerabilities such as HTTP response splitting—has become a common occurrence (Microsoft 2005).

A final example of new kinds of vulnerabilities concerns cryptography. One of us (Howard) got some press coverage during 2005 (eWeek 2005) when he remarked that Microsoft was pursuing a campaign to remove from its products some older encryption algorithms (including the DES, RC2, and RC4 symmetric encryption algorithms and the MD4, MD5, and SHA-1 hash algorithms). The reason for the removal is simple: cryptanalytic research has advanced, and in a few years, customers won't be able to trust their sensitive data to the protection afforded by those algorithms. Removing an encryption algorithm is a process with a long lead time—you have to consider compatibility with older systems, data formats, and protocols—so it was important to start early and make a concerted effort before a crisis ensued. One aspect of removal was to consider how our security response process would react if there was a catastrophic break of one of the suspect algorithms.

Rules Will Change

Since Microsoft has had a security response process (1997), we have learned, to our occasional regret, that security is often about user and public perception, not just about technical reality. Although you'd think that you'd be "done" if you simply fixed code vulnerabilities that could lead to spoofing, tampering, repudiation, information disclosure, denial of service, and elevation of privilege, the way things work in practice is much more complicated. Five years ago, if a piece of malicious software exploited a vulnerability for which Microsoft had issued a security update, our practice was to tell customers to apply the update in such terms that many heard the message that any attack or damage was their problem. If a worm or virus exploited a legitimate product feature after the user installed or executed the virus code, our answer was in essence, "You should not have run that malicious code."

Today, we take a much more expansive view. We mobilize our security response process when viruses and worms appear, even if the malicious code is misleading gullible users rather than exploiting a vulnerability, sometimes in response to vulnerabilities or attacks related to third-party (non-Microsoft) software and, especially, if the malicious code is exploiting a vulnerability for which we've already issued an update. In the last case, we try to ensure that customers do apply the update, and we often release cleaning or removal tools to help fix the damage done by malicious code. Furthermore, we've frequently made product changes to restrict the ways in which malicious programs that users have been tricked into running can exploit legitimate product features. (The first such product change was the Microsoft Office Outlook E-Mail Security Update, which blocks the delivery of executable attachments to e-mail messages [Microsoft 2000b].)

A final factor that has made security response more important is criminals' growing interest in software and the Internet. When the Microsoft Security Response Center (MSRC) was created in 1997, viruses, worms, and malicious code were primarily a form of Internet vandalism—a nuisance that disrupted the use of widely deployed software. Today, there are frequent reports of individual criminals or organized crime releasing malicious code as part of various money-making schemes (Naraine 2004). As the security of Microsoft software continues to improve, these criminals are likely to target other vendors' products rather than simply giving up. Like the famous bank robber Willie "the Actor" Sutton, they will "go where the money is" and where it's easy to steal. If your software is used in important applications or to process sensitive data, it's likely to be a target, and that means you'll need to have a response process in place and ready to go.

The bottom line for your development team is that even if you get product security "right" with regard to eliminating exploitable vulnerabilities, you are likely to need a response process. The time to plan and organize your response process is long before you need to invoke it for the first time.

Preparing to Respond

There are actually two related components to preparing for security response. The first is establishing a security response process. At Microsoft, the MSRC deals with all externally discovered vulnerabilities in Microsoft products, no matter what the products' function or customer base might be.

We could probably write another book on security response and the lessons learned from the operations of the MSRC. In this section, we'll first summarize that unwritten book, providing an outline of the organization, issues, and functions of a security response center. We'll outline the entire response process, addressing the functions of a response center proper and the related functions of the product development team that works with the response center to address newly discovered vulnerabilities.

The second component of preparing for security response is the responsibility of each product development team. In the next section, we'll discuss the response process from the perspective of the development team, building on the overall discussion of the response process but emphasizing the preparatory steps that the product team must take to be ready when vulnerabilities are discovered and reported.

Building a Security Response Center

The role of a security response center is to coordinate your software organization's response to newly discovered vulnerabilities in products that you have shipped to customers (or deployed through Web properties or released to your internal users). The response process proper begins with awareness of a newly discovered security vulnerability, extends through investigation of the implications of the vulnerability and development of a security update or patch, and culminates with release of the update and the associated communications to get users to apply the update in a timely fashion. Once the update has been released, the response process continues to monitor and assess the impact of the update—and the vulnerability it addresses—on users of the software. This monitoring function is important because the response process is also invoked in the case of emergencies such as the release of exploit code or a worm, virus, or Trojan horse (we refer to this menagerie as *malware*), whether the exploit code or malware is exploiting a newly discovered vulnerability or one for which an update is already available, or even exploiting user fallibility, where no vulnerability at all is involved.

We describe the response process by using the terminology that would normally be used by a software vendor, and we believe that essentially every software vendor should have a security response process. But user organizations such as banks, manufacturing companies, and airlines usually have large software development staffs and significant Internet presence (for e-commerce, marketing, communications, and other purposes), and that means that they might also need a security response process. If your organization builds software for its own use (especially to process customer data) or if you release software to your customers (as a product, a service such as e-commerce, or software embedded in another product such as a medical device), you might have thought about contingencies that could result from a security bug or malicious attack. A security response center helps you handle those contingencies when (not if) they occur and do it in a fast, organized, and effective way.

Which Vulnerabilities Will You Respond To?

We want to begin by emphasizing two considerations associated with the security response center and its functions:

1. The security response center deals only with vulnerabilities in fielded software (this might include applications that are fielded on the Web to your customers or only to your in-house user community). If you become aware of a vulnerability in a product that's still under development, you just fix it. The other chapters of this book deal with why and how you do that. Of course, if you become aware of a vulnerability in a fielded product and you're also working on a new product or version that might be susceptible to the same vulnerability, you need to be sure that the vulnerability is removed from the new version before it's shipped to customers.

2. The security response process deals mainly with externally discovered vulnerabilities that are found by security researchers, customers, or malicious attackers outside of your organization. You have to fix those vulnerabilities promptly and get the fixes out to your customers before they can be harmed. In the case of vulnerabilities that are discovered by your engineering team, it's almost always a much better practice to fix them in the next update, service pack, or new release than it is to release a special update or patch.

The second consideration here is worth additional discussion: if your development team finds a vulnerability that affects shipping products, why should you delay fixing that vulnerability until you have a service pack or new release ready to go? The answer is that the decision to delay is likely to keep your customers safer. If you release a fix for a security vulnerability in a patch or update, you will inevitably highlight the presence of the vulnerability. Security researchers have become very proficient at reverse engineering security updates and very prolific at releasing exploit code that can be used against systems that exhibit the vulnerability. In particular, the researchers are much faster at releasing exploit code than users are at applying the patches or updates. So your release of an update for a previously unknown vulnerability will give the vulnerability wide visibility and might lead to attacks against users who would have been safer if you had never released the update. Release in a service pack or new version is likely to obscure the security fix by mixing it with numerous other software changes that have nothing to do with security. This will make the reverse-engineering task much harder.

The previous paragraph might sound like an argument for "security through obscurity"—and it really is. One of the hard jobs that your response center and development team will have to handle is deciding how likely it is that a newly (internally) discovered vulnerability will be found outside of your organization and exploited. If the vulnerability is really bad (the potential impact is very serious, and opportunities for exploitation appear widespread and easy to find), and if the vulnerability seems likely to be discovered even if you don't release an update, the vulnerability is a strong candidate for an exception to the rule; you should consider releasing a security update even though the vulnerability was discovered by your organization. If the vulnerability appears difficult to discover, the related security update is a strong candidate for inclusion in a later service pack. Your security response center and your development team will have to work together to evaluate the vulnerability's difficulty of discovery. If an internally discovered vulnerability is very similar to one (or more!) that has been reported by external security researchers, it isn't really an internal discovery, and you should almost certainly fix it in an update. In fact, your response process should already be finding and fixing vulnerabilities similar to those reported externally.

Note   Contrary to popular belief, software vendors commonly roll up security fixes—including fixes for internally discovered vulnerabilities—into big updates, or "dot" releases.

Where Do Vulnerability Reports Come From?

In the previous sections, we refer many times to security researchers. You might wonder who these security researchers are, what they are doing, and why they do it. There's no single answer to those questions, but the following list gives you some examples from the experience of MSRC:

- Security product vendors (especially suppliers of intrusion-detection and vulnerability-assessment products) have research departments that discover software vulnerabilities and then update their products to report vulnerable software versions or attempts to exploit the vulnerabilities.

- Independent security consultants (who might be self-employed or work for consulting firms) conduct vulnerability research as a way of establishing their credibility and competence with potential clients. Some consultants also sell vulnerability information to user organizations to help them protect their systems and networks from attack.

- Students of computer science and computer security conduct vulnerability research to improve their knowledge of software and security.

- Various malicious parties conduct vulnerability research to find ways to attack computer users. These malicious parties are rumored to range from individuals with criminal intent (or individuals who want to sell vulnerability information to those with criminal intent) to organized crime rings bent on committing financial fraud to national governments seeking to steal secrets or disrupt systems or networks.

A security response center must interact with security researchers to protect users. One of the most important functions of the response center is to encourage *responsible disclosure*. Responsible disclosure refers to the practice whereby the finder of a vulnerability reports to the software developer and allows the developer to develop and release an update or patch before publicizing the details of the vulnerability. The developer's security response center keeps the researcher apprised of the status of the response and update-development process and acknowledges the researcher's cooperation when the update is released. (We'll discuss this aspect of the process later in this chapter in "Managing the security researcher relationship.") Responsible disclosure is important to the success of the response process because it minimizes the period of time when a vulnerability is known to potential attackers while users of the software are without a practical way to protect themselves from exploitation of the vulnerability. Research from Forrester (an IT analyst firm) has documented a measure of "days of risk" to quantify the benefits of an effective security response process and of responsible disclosure of vulnerabilities (Koetzle et al. 2004).

Security Response Process

The security response process integrates steps executed by the security response center with steps executed by the development team. The following section provides an overview of both sets of steps and how they fit into the overall process as well as brief descriptions of each of the steps. Figure 15-1 presents an overview of the flow of the response process.

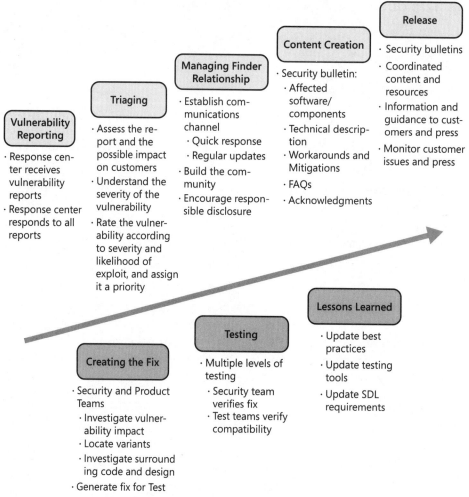

Figure 15-1 Overview of the security response process.

At a high level, the process flow is broken into two parallel tracks. On the first track, the security response center focuses on the vulnerability report, communication with the security researcher, and managing the process from report to update release. The elements of this track are shown along the upper row of blocks in the figure. Along the second track, the development team and the specialized security team focus on the technical details of the vulnerability, the fix that remedies it, and the design or implementation errors that led to the vulnerability. The elements of this track are shown along the lower row of boxes in the figure.

The following sections summarize the security response activities associated with each element of each track. As we mentioned previously, it would be easy to produce an entire book that focuses solely on the response process. But in the book you are reading, we've limited ourselves to describing the overall response process and some key details of each component in hopes of giving developers of new response processes sufficient information to get started on the right path. If you are building a response process, the information in this section will tell you what issues to focus on and what steps your new response center should expect to follow as it receives its first vulnerability reports.

Vulnerability reporting   The response process begins with receipt of a vulnerability report. Create and publicize a point of contact that security researchers can use to initiate communication with your security response center. Microsoft has accepted reports sent to *secure@microsoft.com* for more than eight years. You might wish to use another e-mail alias such as *security* or *vulnerability-report* for your response center. Regardless of your choice, it's important to make it widely known and to not change it.

> **Note**   If you believe you have found a security bug in any Microsoft product, please send an e-mail message to MSRC at *secure@microsoft.com*.

The response center must monitor the reporting alias and respond directly (with more than just a canned acknowledgement) to every e-mail message that is intended as a vulnerability report and isn't clearly spam or traffic on a mailing list. The response center should also monitor security mailing lists, such as BugTraq (SecurityFocus 2005) and Full-Disclosure (Cartwright 2002), for list traffic that might be irresponsibly disclosing a vulnerability report. Such reports increase the likelihood that a vulnerability will be exploited before your teams have developed a way for customers to protect themselves, so it's important to detect these reports quickly and act at once.

Finally, the response center needs to have a relationship with your organization's customer-support or field-service teams so that new vulnerabilities (or exploitations of vulnerabilities) reported by customers will find their way promptly into the response process. We recommend that the response center be staffed with enough "duty officers" that any report can be evaluated and acted on within a day (24 hours) of receipt, weekends and holidays included. Organizations with products that appear very unlikely to be the subject of vulnerability reports might get by with a response center that operates only during the workweek, but you accept a degree of risk (for your organization and its customers) by accepting such a limitation.

When a duty officer receives a report that isn't obviously spam or a customer question unrelated to security, she begins the response process. This will surely involve sending a personal reply to the security researcher who sent the report, perhaps with a request for more detail or clarification. If the duty officer believes that the report might be a real vulnerability (not a known issue or a nonissue), she also opens a bug in the response-center tracking database and assigns it for investigation to the product team responsible for the product in question.

Triaging   Vulnerability reports come in all varieties. At one extreme is the report that provides a code fragment, Web page content, or HTML request that causes code of the researcher's choosing to run on a vulnerable system. The report and the impact of the vulnerability are clear at once. At the other extreme is a vague hint of something that might be a vulnerability, but there are few or no specifics either because the researcher doesn't want to share full details (perhaps she wants to make the response center "work" so that the development organization will earn access to the details of the vulnerability) or because the researcher herself didn't fully understand what was happening. Unfortunately, reports of the latter kind are not uncommon, and the fact that the researcher hasn't worked out all the details definitely does not mean that the vulnerability can be ignored.

> **Important**   All incoming security vulnerabilities must be triaged.

Triage is the process of finding out enough about the reported vulnerability to assess its potential impact. The response team must reproduce the vulnerability as reported and understand what a malicious attacker might do with it. It's important to gain a full understanding of the vulnerability as reported and to find out all of its implications. The security researcher might have understood that she was reporting a vulnerability that could be used to cause a denial of service—to crash the application or the underlying operating system—whereas a more sophisticated exploit could run hostile code and allow an attacker to "own" the system. The triage team must discover the full implications of the report.

In our experience, the best organization to conduct triage combines security experts with experts in the product that is the subject of the vulnerability report. At Microsoft, the security experts are referred to as the Secure Windows Initiative Attack Team (SWIAT), and they're one component of the Secure Windows Initiative (SWI) team that manages and executes the SDL. The product experts come from the product group that built the product that is the subject of the vulnerability report; we'll talk more about their role later in this chapter in "Create Your Response Team" when we discuss product-group responsibilities for security response.

The product of the triage element of the process is an assessment that covers:

- The validity of the security researcher's report. Is the report describing a vulnerability at all?

- The severity of the reported vulnerability. Assuming that the report is valid, what kind of impact could the vulnerability have on customers' systems if exploited? Are there mitigating factors that would reduce the likelihood of successful exploit in the field? Microsoft's triage process is based on the MSRC Security Bulletin Rating System as described at *http://www.microsoft.com/technet/security/rating.mspx*.

- Any other factors that would either mitigate or amplify the need to respond to the vulnerability or the urgency of that need. For example, if the vulnerability is reported to a public e-mail list rather than directly to the response center, the potential for immediate exploitation amplifies the urgency of a response. Similarly, if the vulnerability is reported by a customer who is not pressing for an update and the vulnerability is otherwise unlikely to be discovered, the urgency of response is reduced, and it might well be appropriate to consider releasing a fix in a service pack.

When triage is complete, the response center must have a working plan for responding to the vulnerability. You should know whether an update will be released, and with what urgency, as well as about other plans such as release of public information about mitigations and workarounds for the vulnerability in advance of the release of an update.

Creating the fix   The product team works alongside the response center team in the triage of each new vulnerability report. Once triage is complete, the product team owns responsibility for developing any fix that is required to address the vulnerability. This is true whether the fix will be released in a security update or patch or in a service pack. Obviously, timing and packaging considerations differ in these two cases, but many important elements are common, and this section will discuss them.

Any fix for a reported security vulnerability has three critical aspects:

1. It must eliminate the vulnerability that was reported.

2. It must eliminate any related vulnerabilities. A related vulnerability might result either from repeating the same mistake that caused the reported vulnerability in similar code or from an underlying design flaw that leads to a pattern of vulnerabilities.

3. It must not unnecessarily "break" legitimate functions of the code that contained the vulnerability. We refer to such breakage as "causing a regression." Much of the testing element of the response process focuses on eliminating regressions, but building a regression-free fix is fundamentally a part of fix development rather than of testing. As is widely understood in software engineering, it is not possible to test quality into the end product.

Eliminating the vulnerability as reported sounds relatively simple, and it often is: you just find the code that fails to test for valid input, and you add (or correct) the test as needed. But it can be easy to make a very fundamental mistake in designing a fix. We've seen security updates (including updates released by Microsoft) that insert a test for valid input on a path leading to the vulnerable code instead of fixing the vulnerable code itself.

Figure 15-2 sketches an example of how not to fix vulnerabilities, and Figure 15-3 sketches an example of a proper fix, in which the required test is added to the underlying vulnerable code. Similar considerations apply to client-server applications or components—if the client component or code is controlled by an untrusted user, it's vital that the security check be made in the server component.

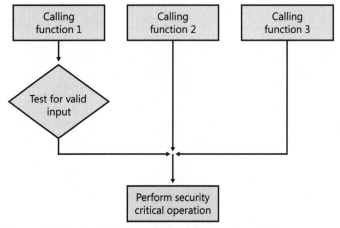

Figure 15-2   Partial fix for an underlying vulnerability.

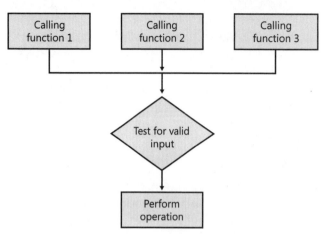

Figure 15-3   Correct fix for an underlying vulnerability.

The quest for related vulnerabilities is motivated by the fact that security researchers often look for vulnerabilities similar to one that has just been fixed. There is nothing more frustrating to response center staff than to issue one update and immediately receive a report of a new vulnerability that looks just like the last one, in the same code. It's a point of pride to MSRC and the associated product teams that in recent years they have become much more effective at finding and eliminating such related vulnerabilities.

Other factors that come into play in the response process can make the search for related vulnerabilities especially challenging. If the circumstances surrounding the vulnerability report suggest that a fix is urgent—for example, because a highly exploitable vulnerability has been made public—there might be insufficient time to do a thorough search for related vulnerabilities. If an initial review suggests that related vulnerabilities are likely to be present, the response team and product team will probably need to release multiple updates, including an immediate update to address the reported vulnerability and its most similar neighbors and a subsequent update to address the related vulnerabilities identified by a thorough search.

For an illustration of the search for related vulnerabilities, consider Microsoft Security Bulletins MS03-026, MS03-039, and MS04-012 (Microsoft 2003a, Microsoft 2003b, Microsoft 2004b), which were issued in response to an initial report of a vulnerability in the RPC/DCOM component of Windows and subsequent reports that were received after the initial update (MS03-026) was released. MSRC determined that it was important to release the initial update quickly, but a preliminary review of the affected code indicated that multiple additional vulnerabilities were present and likely to be found once security researchers saw the initial bulletin and update. So Microsoft initiated a process that involved releasing the fixes for the most urgent vulnerabilities while conducting a major review of the affected Windows components. The process culminated with the release of Microsoft Windows XP SP2 and Microsoft Windows Server 2003 SP1, in which remote anonymous access to the affected component was blocked by default, significantly reducing the attack surface to complement code-level changes that resulted from a very thorough review of the RPC/DCOM components.

> **Note**   Requiring authenticated RPC/DCOM by default protected Windows XP SP2 users from the Zotob worm.

Security fixes and regressions   The development of security fixes that do not cause regressions for legitimate users is both important and challenging. There is no single secret to the successful avoidance of regressions, but one step that Microsoft has taken in the quest for regression-free security fixes is to minimize the set of changes included in a security update or patch. Microsoft often supplies individual users (especially corporate users who have complex internal computing environments) with a non-security fix—often called a QFE (Quick-Fix Engineering)—to resolve problems with specific applications or peripheral devices. Historically, when we released a security fix for a component that had been the target of one or more QFEs, we included the QFEs as well as the security fix in the update. With the release of Windows Server 2003 and Windows XP SP2, we changed the operation of the Windows installer and the packaging of security fixes so that users who had not installed any QFEs received only the security fix when they installed a security update. Users who had installed any QFE for the component being updated received all of the QFEs as well as the security update. This change in security update packaging has reduced the rate of regressions caused by security updates, especially for corporate customers. You'll find more information on security updates and regressions in the "Testing" section later in this chapter.

Security fixes for multiple product versions and locales   One final aspect of update development concerns product versions and localization. A single vulnerability might affect multiple product versions (for example, Windows XP and Windows Server 2003). If it does, update development and testing must be synchronized so that customers using all affected versions can be protected at the same time. This practice mitigates the risk of an attacker reverse engineering the update for one software version and then exploiting the vulnerability in other versions for which the update has not yet been released. For similar reasons, if the software is available in multiple language versions (Microsoft Windows is available in 28 languages, and Microsoft Office in 35), the update must be released for all versions at the same time. It would be unseemly for the French or German language versions of a product to remain vulnerable because an attacker had reverse engineered an update released only in English.

Managing the security researcher relationship   Security response is not just about accepting vulnerability reports and issuing updates and the associated security bulletins. Rather, there is a long-term aspect to security response that involves building relationships of trust and confidence with the security researchers who find and report vulnerabilities. Such a relationship is important to the vendor because it tends to develop the conditions that allow the response center to do its job well and minimize customers' exposure to vulnerabilities for which no fix has been released.

From the response center's perspective, the best scenario is one in which researchers practice responsible disclosure—keeping their findings private until the response center has issued an update. In the best case, researchers also understand the response process well enough to see that a long time interval between report and update release is not a matter of the response center ignoring the vulnerability report or the researcher. Rather, the long interval represents the time required for the response center and product team to search for related vulnerabilities, fix them all, and release a fully tested update that has minimal regression potential.

The response center has numerous techniques at its disposal to help manage the researcher relationship effectively. The first is simple communication: it's important to keep the researcher apprised of the status of her vulnerability report (weekly updates are the norm) and to do so in a human and personal way. The MSRC used to avoid identifying the duty officer responsible for an individual report. This practice caused one researcher to conclude that the MSRC duty officer was actually a robot or artificial-intelligence program. Today, MSRC goes out of its way to identify duty officers and encourage researchers to establish a personal connection with "their" duty officers. Because researchers tend to specialize (in the browser, a spreadsheet application, or a database system), building a personal relationship between researcher and duty officer is often consistent with the efficiency of the response process because the duty officer can also be paired with one product team.

It's easy for the response center to fall into the trap of believing that security researchers are a hostile camp bent on criticizing the products that the response center is supporting, and on putting users at risk by exposing product vulnerabilities. For example, one of our colleagues in the industry has been quoted as saying, "Most [vendors] don't need threats to [fix reported vulnerabilities], and some researchers have become the problem." We refer to this attitude as a trap because a response center that takes such an attitude will inevitably make researchers into adversaries who will not practice responsible disclosure or cooperate with other aspects of the response process. In contrast, the response center that assumes security researchers share the developer's goal of making products more secure and protecting customers is likely to build a cooperative relationship with security researchers and wind up encouraging behaviors that benefit researchers, developers, and customers.

Since the late 1990s, almost all response centers have acknowledged the contribution of security researchers in the security bulletins they issue when an update is released. Such acknowledgements constitute a basic component of the cooperation between researchers and the response center. Some researchers have used public acknowledgements as indications of the quality of their work and have built healthy security research and consulting practices out of their success as researchers and vulnerability finders.

Response centers might well have options beyond acknowledgements to build more cooperative relations with researchers. Examples include offering organizations that conduct security research membership in partner programs, giving researchers early access to beta software, and offering internships or college recommendations. (MSRC has worked extensively with a very capable security researcher who is still in high school as this chapter is being written.) MSRC has also sponsored community-building events for security researchers and invited researchers with established track records to speak at in-house Microsoft security training conferences (ZDNet 2006).

Beyond keeping the security researcher apprised of the status of her report and the schedule for an update or patch, the response center might also wish to give the researcher an early copy of the update for testing and allow her to review and comment on the draft of the security bulletin. Of course, both of these options require a significant level of trust between response center and researcher, and neither is appropriate for the first report from a previously unknown researcher. But they are options for building the researcher relationship, and the response center should bear them in mind as its relationship with an individual researcher evolves over time.

Testing   Over the last 10 years, we've seen a steady reduction in the time interval between our release of a security update and the release of exploit code that shows how to take advantage of the vulnerability or even attack code that exploits the vulnerability for criminal purposes such as stealing customer information or launching distributed denial of service attacks. As a result, our advice to customers is that they apply the most critical security updates immediately, without taking a long time to test the updates for regressions or compatibility problems. We could not give such advice unless we were confident that our security updates wouldn't cause such problems, and testing is one source of that confidence. (The quality of the security fix development itself is the other source.)

Security update testing aims to accomplish two purposes:

1. To verify that the update in fact addresses the reported vulnerability and any related vulnerabilities

2. To attempt to verify that the update will not cause regressions when users install it.

Testing to verify that the update addresses the vulnerability involves more than simply trying any demonstration code that the researcher supplied to see if it still exhibits the vulnerability. The test team must review the source code for the affected component and then try variations to ensure that the fix addresses the underlying vulnerability rather than simply blocking one path to its exploitation. (See Figures 15-2 and 15-3 and the "Creating the fix" section earlier in this chapter.) The test team members must also apply their own security research skills to see that no less-obvious variations of the reported vulnerability remain. At Microsoft, the function of verifying security fixes before they are released is performed by SWIAT. In addition to applying their own skills and experience at security vulnerability research, SWIAT members stay aware of external trends in security research, including vulnerability reports against non-Microsoft products. They apply this knowledge as they test each new security update. This last fact is important; in numerous cases, we have found and fixed bugs in Microsoft products before the products were shipped by analyzing competitors' security bugs.

Although testing to ensure that the security update eliminates reported vulnerabilities is a practice unique to security, testing to detect and eliminate regressions involves more standard testing practices. Security update testing begins with execution of the regression test suites for the component being updated. It includes testing with common applications as well as with test deployments to users inside and outside of Microsoft. No user is allowed to deploy the update operationally until it is finally released and available to all customers (to ensure that all customers are protected equally). Testing by external users engages large corporate customers who are not informed of the specifics of the vulnerabilities addressed by the updates they are testing. These customers commit to special agreements to provide feedback on updates and to maintain the confidentiality of the updates they receive (because disclosure of an update could result in its being reverse engineered and exploited before Microsoft is able to release the final update and protect customers). The customers serve as proxies for other customers in their "vertical" industry segment who are likely to have similar line-of-business applications. The customer testing program has proven valuable in identifying regressions that might otherwise affect corporate line-of-business applications and in giving corporate customers confidence that they can deploy updates without unacceptable risk to the continued functioning of their applications. Although Microsoft's in-house testing against common packaged applications has proven effective at detecting potential regressions, it's difficult to anticipate all the ways in which corporate IT departments have coded the applications they develop, and it's impossible to gain access to all (or even most) such applications for testing. The customer testing program is the best way we have found to detect and eliminate potential regressions in such applications.

Content creation   The output of the response process goes beyond the security update to encompass content that provides information and guidance to customers using the affected software. MSRC produces content directed to IT professionals who work in enterprise IT departments and separate content for end users (primarily consumers who use Microsoft products at home). The end-user content is not detailed; it usually does little more than advise users that a vulnerability has been found and addressed and that they should install the update that Microsoft has released. The rationale for providing only this level of content is that most end users are unconcerned with the technical details of a security update and only want to be protected. The best and simplest way for them to be protected is to install the update. As more and more users enable the Automatic Update feature of Windows that installs new security updates without user intervention, even this content has become less relevant. However, it's important to make information available to end users who might have heard about a vulnerability and want to know what has been done in response and to users who want information about the functioning of their systems. End users who want details of the vulnerability and of Microsoft's response are referred to the content targeted at IT professionals.

Microsoft refers to content for IT professionals as *security bulletins*. Security bulletins must contain much more detail than end-user content about the vulnerability or vulnerabilities addressed by an update and the potential consequences of their exploitation. Where feasible, IT professional–oriented content should also tell system administrators about mitigations and workarounds. This information might allow administrators to determine that their particular configurations are not vulnerable to attack (even without installing the update) or tell them how they can prevent exploitation of a vulnerability without installing the update. Such information is important to organizations that need to schedule client or server downtime for update installation and that have an IT staff capable of analyzing their system environments and protecting their systems by taking administrative actions such as disabling system features or blocking network ports. At Microsoft, SWIAT develops information about mitigations and workarounds as part of the process of triaging the vulnerability report and searching for related vulnerabilities. MSRC produces the security bulletin for use by IT professionals.

Security advisories   In addition to security bulletins, Microsoft has established a practice of releasing security advisories in situations in which there is no security update. Security advisories are released when a circulating worm or virus is exploiting a vulnerability for which an update is already available or when a worm or virus is not exploiting any vulnerability. Security advisories are also released to convey information about mitigations and workarounds when information about a vulnerability becomes public before an update is ready for release.

Press outreach   One final aspect of content creation concerns preparation for press outreach. Vulnerabilities in the products of major software vendors such as Microsoft and Oracle can be newsworthy events, and the release of an update often triggers a round of coverage in the IT trade press and sometimes in the general press. MSRC prepares talking points and responses to anticipated press questions along with the other content associated with each update. MSRC personnel respond to press questions as needed when the update is released. In the case of updates that address especially serious vulnerabilities, MSRC reaches out to the press proactively to ensure wide dissemination of information about the vulnerability and its update and, thus, to encourage customers to deploy the update as rapidly as possible. Organizing for press response can help ensure that customers are not unduly confused or alarmed by the news associated with security vulnerabilities and that they get a clear picture of the risks that vulnerabilities pose and the appropriate actions to take in response.

Update release   The development and testing of a security update, the documentation of workarounds and mitigations, and the preparation of content all come together at the point of security update release. When all preparations have been completed, the updates are posted to a well-known Web site and made live for deployment through the various automatic updating facilities (Microsoft Windows Update, Automatic Update, Microsoft Update, Office Update). Security bulletins are posted to their own Web sites and an e-mail notification (and RSS feed and MSN alert) released to subscribers who have elected to be notified of the availability of new security bulletins. Microsoft's customer support and sales organizations are also notified about the release of the update. They are directed to alert customers with whom Microsoft has a direct relationship that those customers should review the bulletin and consider installing the update or taking other action to protect their IT systems.

One important aspect of update release is to maximize predictability. Originally, Microsoft released security bulletins and updates whenever they were ready on the theory that this policy would protect customers as soon as possible. Although the theory was valid as far as it went, the practice had the effect of disrupting the operations of IT staffs. And because experience showed that the release of the update was really the event that started the race to reverse engineer the update and exploit the vulnerability, it was not clear that customers benefited from a release-when-ready policy. For those reasons, Microsoft led the industry in establishing the practice of releasing security updates on a predictable schedule, initially releasing updates weekly on Wednesdays and, in recent years, releasing on the second Tuesday of each month.

A second important aspect of update release is simultaneity. We alluded to this consideration in the "Security fixes for multiple product versions and locales" section earlier in this chapter. To the maximum extent possible, updates for all affected software versions and all language versions should be released at the same time. Furthermore, no customer should receive an update before any other. We've often discussed the latter policy with Chief Information Security Officers of major customers, many of whom believe that their organizations have a critical need to receive security updates or security bulletins before other customers. They make compelling cases, but on examination, it's simply impossible to develop a consistent rationale for giving some customers access to updates before others—you find yourself on a slippery slope at whose bottom *everyone* receives the updates early. As we discussed previously, customers who receive the updates for testing are forbidden by the test agreement (and by their own best interest given that the updates they are testing are beta versions and might have unintended negative effects on customers' systems) from putting them into production and are not informed of the specific vulnerabilities addressed by the updates. Microsoft carries this policy to the point of beginning the update process for its own systems at 10:00 Pacific Time on the second Tuesday of the month—the time when updates become available to customers. (However, we would almost certainly make an exception for the case of a vulnerability in the servers used to distribute updates and security bulletins because the loss of those servers would prevent not only Microsoft but also its customers from protecting themselves.)

Emergency situations have the potential to justify exceptions to our principles of predictability and simultaneity. Simply put, if a vulnerability is being exploited widely or poses a significant threat to the safety of customers and the Internet, the need for a speedy update can overwhelm the goals of releasing on a predictable schedule and of protecting all customers at once. We would be more reluctant to abandon simultaneity than predictability because it's very hard to justify leaving some customers at risk while protecting others. (Fortunately, Microsoft's development and packaging practices make it relatively simple to release updates for all product versions and languages at the same time.) One example of a decision to abandon predictability concerned the update released with Microsoft Security Bulletin MS06-001, "Vulnerability in Graphics Rendering Engine Could Allow Remote Code Execution" (Microsoft 2006). In that case, a vulnerability in the Windows Metafile Format (WMF) was discovered to be under active exploitation during the period between Christmas 2005 and New Year's Day 2006. The MSRC team and the Windows team worked long days and nights through the New Year holiday weekend and into the following week to investigate the vulnerability, provide workaround information to customers, and build and test an update. Although the regular monthly release was planned for Tuesday, January 10, the MSRC determined that the severity of the vulnerability and the widespread customer concern would justify an out-of-band release as soon as the update had passed required testing. When that milestone was completed, the MSRC released the bulletin on Thursday, January 5, five days before the scheduled monthly release.

Once the bulletin and update are released, MSRC personnel initiate press outreach if warranted and respond to any press inquiries about the update. They also begin to monitor Internet activity for signs of the release of exploit code that would allow someone to attack customers or of worms, viruses, or other malware that exploit one of the vulnerabilities fixed by the update. Later in this chapter, the "Emergency Response Process" section discusses these situations in more detail.

Lessons learned   Although the urgent part of the response process concludes with the release of the security update and bulletin, one very important aspect remains. That is to ensure that security engineering practices, tools, testing, and training reflect the lessons to be learned from the vulnerability. At Microsoft, one staff member of the SWI team is responsible for conducting a root-cause analysis for every vulnerability fixed by a security update; for documenting the failures of design, coding, testing, training, and tools that allowed the vulnerability to make its way into the product; and for recommending changes that would prevent similar errors from occurring in the future. Updates to Microsoft's static analysis tools, PREfix and PREfast, frequently result from the "lessons learned" process, and our security training classes (especially those taught by Michael Howard) are replete with samples of vulnerable code drawn from actual security vulnerabilities and the fixes that addressed them.

We've said throughout this book that absolute security isn't achievable and that the only practical way to achieve more secure software for customers is to apply best practices and to learn from your mistakes. The "lessons learned" component of the security response process is key to learning from mistakes. It is absolutely vital that you not only recognize the specific causes and design or coding errors that lead to each security update but also use them as starting points for your own search for new kinds of vulnerabilities and ways to avoid them. In several cases at Microsoft, SWIAT investigations led to the identification of new classes of vulnerabilities related to but different from those reported by outside security researchers. The SWI team and product teams have then taken action to eliminate newly discovered vulnerabilities from product versions still under development. Most of these vulnerabilities have never been discovered by outside security researchers even though some examples remain in older product versions; if the vulnerabilities are discovered, customers who are using newer product versions that have been subject to the SDL are protected without any need to update their systems.

Emergency Response Process

The security response process described in the previous sections manages the "normal" security vulnerability cycle that begins with an external report of a vulnerability and culminates with the release of a security update and an update of development processes to reflect lessons learned. Although not exactly routine, this cycle has a relatively predictable flow and usually allows the product developer time to develop and test a security update and the associated communications.

There is an alternative vulnerability cycle that we at Microsoft refer to as the incident response or emergency response process. This cycle begins with some event—the irresponsible disclosure of a vulnerability or the launching of a worm, virus, or other piece of malware that might pose a significant and near-term threat to users of the affected software. At Microsoft, if the MSRC determines that the event in question could pose such a threat, it initiates what we refer to as the Software Security Incident Response Process (SSIRP).

The objective of the SSIRP is to mobilize Microsoft resources quickly to assess the potential threat and take action to minimize its impact on Microsoft customers. Each SSIRP incident is managed in a sequence of phases as shown in Figure 15-4. During the earlier phases, the process assembles a response team, identifies the scope and impact of the (real or potential) problem, and identifies a potential course of action toward its resolution. In the later phases, the process provides customers with information, tools, and updates as required to resolve the problem and reverse its impact to the extent feasible.

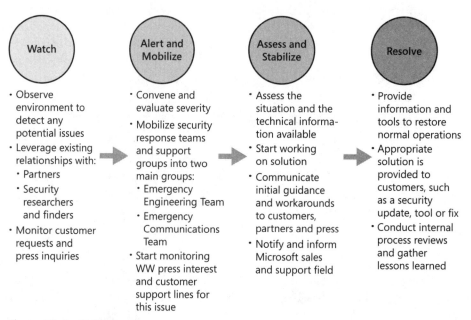

Figure 15-4   SSIRP flow.

The SSIRP is managed and executed by a cross-functional team of people drawn from MSRC, SWIAT, the customer support organization, and the Microsoft IT security organization. Each incident is assigned an emergency lead (overall manager for that incident), an engineering lead (focused on the technical aspects of the incident), and a communications lead (focused on customer impact and external communications). Engineers and managers from the product group (or groups) responsible for any affected product join the SSIRP team as required. The following sections describe the SSIRP's phases.

Watch phase   The Watch phase begins immediately after MSRC or any other team recognizes an unusual event. MSRC often initiates the Watch phase, but other teams, including customer service and the Microsoft IT groups, might also initiate Watch. Outside parties, including security vendors, customers, the press, and CERTs or government agencies, might also provide reports that lead to the initiation of the Watch phase. The Watch phase is executed by a small group of "first responders" whose objective is limited to confirming that an incident is under way. Once confirmation is complete, the process moves to the next phase.

Alert and Mobilize phase   During the Alert and Mobilize phase, a full SSIRP team is assembled, and an emergency lead, engineering lead, and communications lead are designated. The product team (or teams) responsible for the affected product (or products) mobilize during this phase. They work with SWIAT to begin determining the technical realities underlying the incident. The customer service and communications teams evaluate the incident's impact on customers and its visibility in the press. These two factors play a major role in evaluating the significance of an incident, along with the technical assessment of severity and potential impact. If an incident affects a large number of customers or affects customers in a major way, it is significant; if an incident attracts media attention, it is significant because customers will become concerned about the safety of their systems regardless of the realities of the threat. Technical considerations can also make an incident significant. For example, the irresponsible disclosure of a vulnerability that could be exploited to do significant harm to customers almost inevitably leads to a SSIRP mobilization because the exploit could occur before an update is available to protect customers. Because the release of security updates is regularly followed by reverse engineering of the updates, publication of exploit code, and release of malware that exploits a vulnerability fixed by an update, MSRC enters the Alert and Mobilize phase as a matter of course as part of the process of releasing updates on the second Tuesday of the month. This process ensures that the response and product teams are assembled and prepared to respond as quickly as possible if exploit code is released or a malicious attack is launched.

Assess and Stabilize phase   The objective of the Assess and Stabilize phase is to provide sufficient information and assistance to customers so that the threat of harm can be significantly mitigated. This objective implies that SWIAT and the product team must gain sufficient understanding of the incident to make a recommendation—either that customers apply an existing update or that they deploy some measure that mitigates the effects of a vulnerability or the potential for a successful attack. For many incidents, this sort of recommendation might be sufficient to keep the attack from causing significant harm if the attack is not damaging or widespread and if MSRC can alert customers to apply an existing update. Similarly, if an attack is not exploiting a vulnerability at all, a recommendation for user action might be sufficient.

If an incident does involve the exploitation of a new vulnerability for which no update has been developed, the identification and communication of mitigations and workarounds becomes critically important. The Assess and Stabilize phase aims to produce mitigations and workarounds as rapidly as possible and to disseminate them broadly to stop an attack or incident before it can cause significant harm. During both the Alert and Mobilize phase and the Assess and Stabilize phase, MSRC and SWIAT work with partners such as antivirus and intrusion-detection vendors to share information and to ensure that the partners provide updated signatures that can protect customers. This work with partners is especially vital when an attack is under way and no update is available or when the attack is not exploiting a vulnerability.

Resolve phase   The Resolve phase brings the incident to a close by releasing whatever tools, updates, or information is required to assist customers in recovering from the effects of an attack and protecting themselves from further attacks. If the incident involves a vulnerability for which no update is available, an update must be released before the Resolve phase can be closed. If the incident involves an attack that damages customers' systems, customer support must have the information necessary to help customers recover to the maximum extent possible. Depending on the scope of the attack, a malicious-code cleaning tool might also be released.

Cooperation with antivirus and intrusion-detection vendors continues into the Resolve phase. Customer and press communication also continues until customers are aware of the workarounds, mitigations, updates, and tools released in response to the incident.

At the conclusion of the SSIRP for a given incident, the team conducts a postmortem to identify lessons learned and potential improvements for the SSIRP process. This postmortem goes beyond the normal security response "lessons learned" process because it covers the teams involved in customer recovery and a broader range of communications activities, in addition to covering a software vulnerability and the steps needed to prevent similar vulnerabilities in the future.

Security Response and the Development Team

In the previous section, we presented an overview of the functions and organization of a security response center, drawing heavily on our experience with the Microsoft Security Response Center and the way it handles both normal vulnerability reports and security incidents that range up to the seriousness of full-blown Internet emergencies. That overview referred to the role of the product team responsible for the affected product in each of the stages of response, from triage, through update development and testing, to release. This section focuses on the aspects of preparation for security response that our experience has shown to be necessary if a product team is to execute its part of the response process effectively. The two guiding principles to this section are first, that the time to prepare for security response is *before* a vulnerability has been reported, and second (as we point out repeatedly in this book), that every team that ships software needs to be ready for security response.

Create Your Response Team

Our discussion of the security response process addressed at length the role of the response center as well as how the product team deals with a vulnerability report or security incident. That discussion assumed that the product team had people in place to execute their part of the response process and that the response center staff knew how to reach them. The times are long past when MSRC had to scramble to find the team responsible for a product or component after a vulnerability had been reported.

Today, the rule is simple: when you ship a piece of software, whether it's a revenue product or a free release, you must identify the people who will respond to externally discovered vulnerabilities in that software and must provide their contact information to the response center. You should identify enough people that the response center can always find someone despite vacations and holidays. When someone in a response role leaves the product team, you must replace her. If the contact process breaks down, response center staff normally start contacting individuals higher in the management chain until they find someone who has the authority to get the response moving. At Microsoft, MSRC maintains emergency contact information for every product team's management up to the vice president level as a backup for the contact lists of the people who are supposed to respond. All individuals on the contact lists provide information so that they can be contacted 24 hours a day and seven days a week.

The question of who plays the response-contact role is pretty well settled at Microsoft—almost all product teams designate program managers to drive their response process. The response program manager is expected to find testers to work with SWIAT to produce the vulnerability report. This program manager should also bring in the developers who are responsible for the offending code and can diagnose the root cause and make the fix as needed. Individual product groups organize the specifics of this process differently. Some have a dedicated, sustained engineering team with developers and testers who can build and test fixes whereas others assign sustained engineering program managers to coordinate the process but use developers and testers from the core development team. In every case, the response process can call on the developer who "owns" the code that exhibits the vulnerability to ensure clear understanding of the problem and the development of a correct fix.

Beyond merely creating the response team, you will need to be able to respond to vulnerabilities as long as the product is supported. For Microsoft products, this period is usually 10 years. As a result, we occasionally have to consider how we'll support the security of a product long after we've stopped new development and reassigned most of the team originally responsible for the code. There's no single solution to this problem, although the usual answer is that support responsibility goes to the team that develops the closest successor product. You'll always have to be aware of continuing security response support, especially when you stop new development on a product or version.

Support Your Entire Product

The less-formal way of stating the requirement to support your entire product is to say, "If you ship it, you need to understand how to update it." In large software organizations such as Microsoft, sharing and reuse of code and software components are common. (We've referred to those components as *giblets,* after the plastic bag of assorted innards that comes inside a frozen turkey.) The practice of reusing and sharing components has benefits for efficiency and consistency, but it does carry with it the risk that a vulnerability in giblet A will be manifest in product B, whose development team didn't create giblet A and might not have the capability to update it.

The recommended response to this problem is simply, "Don't do that." If at all possible, rely on platform services that can be updated once as part of the operating system to protect users of all applications when a vulnerability is discovered. If you ship a component that was developed by another team, you must have a service-level agreement with the developing team so that they will respond when vulnerabilities are found and will work with you to develop, test, and package the necessary updates. If you can't get such an agreement, take ownership of the source code and be prepared to respond on your own. If you can't get ownership of the source code, develop your own component so you can support it correctly.

In the case of a widely shared component such as an image parser, class, component, or library, it's especially important that the team that develops the component provide a plan for security response. Occasionally, after a vulnerability is reported to a team that shipped a component, the response center and the "shipping" team discover that the report actually affects a reused component. At that point, ideally, the response center brings in the team that developed the vulnerable component, and that team diagnoses the problem, develops a fix, and ensures that the fix is released by all of the "shipping" teams that have used the vulnerable component. Getting to this ideal state requires that the team that develops the component know which teams ship it and that there be a way to update the component wherever it's used. Meeting the first requirement means that the developing team needs to have an authoritative list of "shipping" teams. Meeting the second requirement means that the installation and updating tools have to be robust enough to detect the vulnerable versions and apply the fix where needed. None of this is rocket science, but it can get very complicated in the case of a widely used component in which different "shipping" products might install different component versions and in which some of the teams involved fail to think about the need to update. At Microsoft, we're still working to improve our processes in this area.

Support All Your Customers

It's probably obvious that you'll need to respond to vulnerabilities in all supported versions of your product, but we want to stress the point anyway. Our discussion of the response process emphasized the need to provide simultaneous updates for all supported versions, service packs, and local-language versions. Meeting this need means that your source control and testing systems need to be organized to produce and test the necessary updates for all supported versions (not just the most recent). Your customers do not want to be forced to upgrade to a new version, or even to a new service pack, to protect themselves from exploitation of a security vulnerability.

Support for local languages is another aspect of the development team's role. Ideally, the local language support in your product will be designed well enough to allow you to build a single fix that applies to all language versions. However, some aspects of the fix or update might differ, depending on the language version. In that case, you should be prepared to do the necessary development and testing to release the fix for all languages at the same time. At Microsoft, our work to improve localization support for products has reduced the localization burden for updates so that only a few messages from the update installer package vary with local language. Furthermore, our processes now ensure that the localization work is completed rapidly enough so that updates for all supported languages ship at the same time. If you support an international market, it's important to get the localization and internationalization support right in the first place because it will make security updating—as well as product enhancements in general—simpler for both your customers and your development teams.

To give you an idea of the level of effort required to support all your customers, we'll cite the example of the Microsoft Internet Explorer browser component. At one time, before they could ship an update, the Internet Explorer team had to ensure the availability and testing of about 425 different packages, driven by the numbers of supported versions, operating system platforms, and local languages. Few products or technologies are as widely used or supported as Internet Explorer, but it's still very important to consider the total number of versions you'll need to support and to factor that number into your plans.

Make Your Product Updatable

Once you've produced an update and released it, your customers aren't protected until they've installed it. This section is about the work that the product team does to ensure that customers can actually install the update. At Microsoft, we've found that improvements to update deployment and installation have been one of the most significant factors in improving our security response processes—and our customers' security. Even if your users are technology-savvy, they'll benefit from easy update deployment and installation.

There are a wide range of techniques for installing security updates. The least-effective technique is to ship your customers a package of updated product files and a readme file that tells them where on their system to copy the files. At the other extreme, you can build a tool into your product that detects the availability of a new update, copies it over the Web, and installs it for the customer with no manual intervention (assuming, of course, that the customer has consented to having his system updated in this manner). At Microsoft, we've sought to implement the latter approach. The reason is simple: more customers will actually deploy the updates, and fewer customers will be affected by malicious code and hostile attacks.

Achieving a consistent updating experience is easiest if you pick one and use it for all your products. At Microsoft, we started with eight individual installers that had been developed or adopted by product teams over the years. We were rightly criticized by customers and analysts for having such a confusing set of updating tools, so we initiated a multi-year transition to two installers (one for operating system components and the other for applications) to ease the burden on customers. Even those two installers use identical installer flags for various options, such as silent installation, to ease the system administrator's task. Similarly, we are moving from a variety of ways of getting to the updates on the Web—Windows Update, Office Update, the Microsoft Download Center Web site, and individual product download Web sites—to a single Microsoft Update Web site that supports automatic updating plus a consistent family of enterprise updating tools for use by administrators who must update large numbers of computers.

Our objective in making the transition to a consistent updating approach is to reduce the difficulty of updating for customers and, thus, to help them install updates more rapidly. We'd like to see all home users install updates automatically as soon as they're released (because they are unlikely to have complex custom applications in which compatibility with an update becomes an issue), and we'd like to see businesses install updates very rapidly with little or no delay attributable to the difficulty of packaging and deploying updates. We still see a few software suppliers releasing updates in a form in which the administrator has to copy individual files into the appropriate directories on the system. We believe that such a manual and error-prone approach inevitably delays update deployment and thus increases risk to customers. Your organization is not likely to have as many products or versions to contend with as Microsoft does, but it's still very desirable to make a common choice of updating technology and then apply it for all of the products you release.

The last component of making your product updatable involves ensuring that updates are delivered securely. We still see individuals and some organizations that post updates to the Web without giving their users any way of confirming either the source of the update or the integrity (freedom from alteration) of the content. Installing any code whose origin and integrity you can't confirm is risky, and that statement is even more pertinent for a security update. You should ensure that your updating mechanism includes provisions for digitally signing the update content, for confirming that the signer is in fact the organization that claims to have authored the update, and for verifying that the signed content has not been tampered with. All of Microsoft's updating mechanisms incorporate these attributes, and in the case of the automatic updating mechanisms (Windows Update, Office Update, Microsoft Update), signature and integrity verification are performed by the update client as part of the download and installation process. Finally, have a plan to deal with the compromise of the key that you use to sign your updates. Although we've never had to deal with this problem, in 2001 we did have to deal with a situation in which a commercial certification authority certified two fraudulently acquired code-signing digital certificates that claimed to belong to Microsoft (Microsoft 2001). We revoked the certificates, and to the best of our knowledge, they were never used. The experience reinforced our commitment to being able to deal with such a contingency.

Find the Vulnerabilities Before the Researchers Do

The final but most important response-related task for the product team is to use vulnerability reports as a learning experience and to fix as many vulnerabilities as possible with as few updates as possible. To do this, the team must develop an in-depth understanding of each reported vulnerability and then determine whether the vulnerability represents an instance of some recurring pattern. If it does, the team must try to find the other instances and correct them all. In previous sections in this chapter, we discussed the three Microsoft updates, beginning with MS03-026, that addressed RPC/DCOM vulnerabilities. After the initial vulnerability report, MSRC, SWIAT, and the DCOM team quickly realized that the issue was just one instance of a pattern of vulnerabilities that they needed to address. In addressing the underlying problem, they conducted a series of code reviews and tests that lasted for several months. Ideally, they would have been able to release a single update to resolve all of the vulnerabilities at once, but receipt of new reports and concern over customers' safety caused them to decide to release a series of three updates that eliminated progressively more vulnerabilities.

Some customers were upset over the fact that Microsoft released a succession of three updates to address the RPC/DCOM vulnerabilities; we would have preferred to release only one. But consider the alternatives: if we had simply fixed vulnerabilities as they were reported, we might well have issued 20 or more updates over a period of months or years, each addressing "the next" vulnerability. If we had waited until all of the vulnerabilities were eliminated before releasing any update, the odds were high that at least one of the vulnerabilities would have leaked out and been exploited while customers were still defenseless. We think we made the right choice to protect our customers.

Learning from security vulnerabilities involves two separate cycles. The shorter cycle is the security response cycle: the product team takes an external report, investigates it, and develops and releases an update that addresses the reported vulnerability and related vulnerabilities. The longer cycle reaches into the product-development process. The product team and the central security team update processes, training, tools, and standards to attempt to ensure that new product versions are not affected by the vulnerability or anything like it. This longer cycle is critically important, and it's why we view security response as an integral component of SDL.

Summary

In the real world, products do not achieve perfect security, so software organizations must plan for security response. The response process encompasses a security response team or center, which faces customers and security researchers, and the product team, which must be prepared to investigate and eliminate security vulnerabilities. To implement the SDL effectively, the product team must treat each vulnerability report as a learning experience and must attempt to find related vulnerabilities and fix them in security updates and to update its SDL processes based on the lessons learned from each vulnerability.

References

(Karger et al. 1991)   Karger, P. A., M. E. Zurko, D. W. Bonin, A. H. Mason, and C. E. Kahn. "A Retrospective on the VAX VMM Security Kernel," *Transactions on Software Engineering*, 17(11):1147–1165. November 1991.

(Eichlin and Rochlis 1989)   Eichlin, M. W., and J. A. Rochlis. "With microscope and tweezers: An analysis of the Internet virus of November 1988," *Proceedings of the IEEE Computer Society Symposium on Security and Privacy*, pp. 326–345, Oakland, CA, May 1989.

(CERT 2002)   Carnegie Mellon Software Engineering Institute, CERT Coordination Center. "CERT Advisory CA-2002-03 Multiple Vulnerabilities in Many Implementations of the Simple Network Management Protocol (SNMP)," *http://www.cert.org/advisories/CA-2002-03.html*. February 2002.

(Microsoft 2004a)   Microsoft Security Bulletin MS04-007. "ASN.1 Vulnerability Could Allow Code Execution (828028)," *http://www.microsoft.com/technet/security/Bulletin/MS04-007.mspx*. February 2004.

(Microsoft 2000a)   "Information on Cross-Site Scripting Security Vulnerability," *http://www.microsoft.com/technet/archive/security/news/crssite.mspx?mfr=true*. February 2000.

(Microsoft 2005)   Microsoft Security Bulletin MS05-029. "Vulnerability in Outlook Web Access for Exchange Server 5.5 Could Allow Cross-Site Scripting Attacks (895179)," *http://www.microsoft.com/technet/security/Bulletin/ms05-029.mspx*. June 2005.

(eWeek 2005)   Roberts, Paul F. "Microsoft Scraps Old Encryption in New Code," *http://www.eweek.com/article2/0,1895,1859751,00.asp*. September 2005.

(Microsoft 2000b)   "Outlook Email Security Update Now Available," *http://www.microsoft.com/presspass/features/2000/jun00/06-08outlook.mspx*. Microsoft PressPass, June 2000.

(Naraine 2004)   Naraine, Ryan. "Malware Hacker Attack Linked to Spammers," *http://www.internetnews.com/security/article.php/3373581*. InternetNews.Com, June 2004.

(Koetzle et al. 2004)   Koetzle, Laura, Charles Rutstein, Natalie Lambert, and Stephanie Wenninger, Forrester Research. "Is Linux More Secure Than Windows?" *http://www.forrester.com/Research/Document/Excerpt/0,7211,33941,00.html*. March 2004. Or *http://download.microsoft.com/download/9/c/7/9c793b76-9eec-4081-98ef-f1d0ebfffe9d/LinuxWindowsSecurity.pdf*.

(SecurityFocus 2005)   BugTraq, *http://www.securityfocus.com/archive/1/description*.

(Cartwright 2002)   Cartwright, John. [Full-Disclosure] Mailing List Charter, *http://lists.grok.org.uk/full-disclosure-charter.html*. Created July 2002.

(Microsoft 2003a)   Microsoft Security Bulletin MS03-026. "Buffer Overrun in RPC Interface Could Allow Code Execution (823980)," *http://www.microsoft.com/technet/security/Bulletin/MS03-026.mspx*. July 2003.

(Microsoft 2003b)   Microsoft Security Bulletin MS03-039. "Buffer Overrun in RPCSS Service Could Allow Code Execution (824146)," *http://www.microsoft.com/technet/security/Bulletin/MS03-039.mspx*. September 2003.

(Microsoft 2004b)   Microsoft Security Bulletin MS04-012. "Cumulative Update for Microsoft RPC/DCOM (828741)," *http://www.microsoft.com/technet/security/Bulletin/MS04-012.mspx*. April 2004.

(ZDNet 2006)   Espiner, Tom. "Microsoft to lift lid on hacker conference," *http://news.zdnet.co.uk/0,39020330,39257971,00.htm*. March 2006.

(Microsoft 2006)   Microsoft Security Bulletin MS06-001. "Vulnerability in Graphics Rendering Engine Could Allow Remote Code Execution (912919)," *http://www.microsoft.com/technet/security/Bulletin/MS06-001.mspx*. January 2006.

(Microsoft 2001)   Microsoft Security Bulletin MS01-017. "Erroneous VeriSign-Issued Digital Certificates Pose Spoofing Hazard," *http://www.microsoft.com/technet/security/Bulletin/MS01-017.mspx*. March 2001.

Chapter 16

Stage 11: Product Release

Congratulations, your product is complete! Release of the product as a CD or DVD or as a Web download requires completion of the Security Development Lifecycle (SDL) process for security and privacy as defined in this book.

 Important It is assumed that your company has a formal "sign off" process for releasing software to users. Such criteria often include the requirement that no bugs of a specific severity exist and that the software is in compliance with various legal requirements, such as the U.S. Rehabilitation Act Section 508 (Microsoft 2005).

To sign off on the software, the central security and privacy team must agree that the SDL has been followed satisfactorily. There really should be no surprises because the final security review (FSR) stage of the SDL should have uncovered any lingering issues. And, as we said in Chapter 14, "Stage 9: The Final Security Review," there should be few if any surprises during the FSR process if the team has performed the appropriate SDL due diligence throughout the software's development.

Finally, to better facilitate debugging security vulnerabilities reported to you, we strongly advise you to upload debugging symbols to a central, internal site that can be easily accessed by your engineers. Debuggers use symbols to turn addresses and numbers into human-readable function names and variable names. This debug symbol requirement applies to all publicly released binaries.

Now the hard work begins: maintaining software and handling security bugs. That's next.

References

(Microsoft 2005) "Microsoft and Section 508," *http://www.microsoft.com/enable/microsoft/section508.aspx*. September 2005.

Chapter 17

Stage 12: Security Response Execution

This chapter summarizes the real-world challenges associated with responding to security vulnerabilities. It amplifies and complements the guidance provided in Chapter 15, "Stage 10: Security Response Planning." This chapter also outlines what a software organization should do if it has not heeded the guidance in Chapter 15.

Following Your Plan

If you've faithfully followed the advice in Chapter 15, the reporting of a new security vulnerability is *almost* a non-event. Of course, hearing about a vulnerability in a product that you've worked hard to make secure is never pleasant, and you must use the lessons learned to avoid repeating the mistake. But if you have a response plan, your task is to do what you said you'd do in the plan rather than solve the problem from scratch. The following sections provide additional guidance for the execution phase of your security response process.

Stay Cool

Your team has probably worked hard on the security of the product that's the subject of the vulnerability report, and you think you've done a pretty good job. So one natural reaction to a vulnerability report is to blame the messenger. Our advice is simple: don't do that.

The security researcher who reported the vulnerability might have reported it to you responsibly (privately), or he might have reported it to a public mailing list. He might be very cooperative with your security response team (or the individual you've designated to handle security response cases if your organization is small and vulnerability reports are infrequent) or be rude and abusive as he berates you for the stupidity that led to the vulnerability in your product. In any case, your objective is to do the best you can to protect the security of your customers, and that objective should guide your actions in dealing with the researcher.

> **Important**   Never lose sight of the most important goal of the security response process: protecting your customers.

No matter how hard it is, your response team should be polite and cooperative and should treat the researcher with respect. If he made a private report, you should be appreciative and try to encourage that behavior in the future. If the vulnerability was disclosed irresponsibly, for example to a mailing list, you should still try to establish communications with the researcher. You should assume that anyone who is capable of discovering one vulnerability in your software is capable of discovering more, so your objective should be to build a relationship so as to get or keep the researcher on the path of cooperation and responsible disclosure.

Building cooperative relations with researchers can pay unexpected dividends: researchers communicate with each other, and a good relationship with one might lead others to treat you as a member of the community and cooperate with you as well. (A bad relationship with one researcher might lead others to treat your organization as untrustworthy and to report vulnerabilities in your products irresponsibly as a matter of course.) Building a good reputation is not easy: Many researchers believe that they are doing the vendor's security quality assurance (for free), and some have been prejudiced against all vendors by the slow or poor-quality response of vendors who would rather blame the messenger than fix problems in their products. The approach of cooperating with researchers maximizes the chances that your development and test teams will be able to find and fix all of the related vulnerabilities in your product and release only high-quality updates.

Losing your temper at a researcher might be tempting, but it leads to the likelihood of irresponsibly disclosed vulnerabilities, bad press, and risk for your customers. You certainly don't want that—especially not risk for your customers.

Take Your Time

If you're really serious about security and you have not experienced a response case before, you might naturally be tempted to work superfast to get the vulnerability fixed and the update out. This is another "don't." The response process encompasses numerous steps—you know that because you've put together a plan—and they are all included for a reason. If you shortcut any step, especially building a quality fix, searching for related vulnerabilities, or testing the fix, you are likely to regret doing so. Here are some specific reasons why being thorough can be more important than being fast:

- If you fail to take the time to build a quality fix, you'll likely release an update that introduces a compatibility problem or you'll overlook the root cause of the vulnerability that was reported. Doing so is a sure way to necessitate a re-release of your update. And if there's one thing your customers dislike more than applying a security update, it's having to apply additional updates to fix the same problem.

- Failing to take the time to search for related vulnerabilities exposes you to the risk that the researcher who reported the first vulnerability, or one of his peers, will be back the week after you release your update with a new report that looks almost like the last one. Your customers are likely to wonder why your product has so many similar problems. Releasing an update for a vulnerability very similar to one you just fixed is not quite as bad as releasing an update that fails to fix the first vulnerability, but it's not a good thing either.

- Failing to test the update exposes your customer to the risk that your update will break their systems or applications. This is probably the case that your customers would dislike most.

Your response plan must identify a process for releasing high-quality updates that fix the vulnerabilities they are supposed to fix. It's important to take the time to stick to the plan as long as circumstances allow you to do so.

Watch for Events That Might Change Your Plans

The recommendation to watch for events that might change your plans is the flip side of the suggestion to take your time. If someone begins to exploit a vulnerability in your software, you must mobilize your emergency response process and go as fast as possible to protect your customers. If you don't notice that the vulnerability is being exploited, you might continue with your routine process while your customers' systems are being "0wned." You need to know the severity and impact of a vulnerability and the severity, spread, and impact of any exploitation or attack.

Becoming aware that a vulnerability is being exploited is neither an easy nor a routine task, and no prescription guarantees that you'll notice exploitation. Error reports or intrusion-detection logs from customers might provide a clue, as might a surge in visible Web site defacements. And of course, an inquiry from a law-enforcement agency is a good clue that something is amiss.

It's a good idea to be proactive about detecting exploitation of product vulnerabilities. Watching the security mailing lists such as Bugtraq, Full-Disclosure, and NTBugtraq and paying attention to customer problem reports are good ideas, but there are other things you can do. If you have an e-mail alias such as *secure@microsoft.com* for reporting security vulnerabilities, your response team might receive reports of exploitation at that alias. Security researchers might hear about attacks that you miss and be willing to share information with you. (See the section titled "Stay Cool" earlier in this chapter; this is another good reason to maintain good relations with the researcher community.) You can also join a security response organization whose members share information about the security of the Internet and about evolving problems. The Forum of Incident Response and Security Teams is an international organization whose members cooperate to improve the safety and security of the Internet (FIRST 2006). The Information Technology Information Sharing and Analysis Center is another such organization (IT-ISAC 2006).

Follow Your Plan

If you have expended the time and effort to build a security response plan, you're well positioned to deal with any vulnerability report that might reach your product team. Of course, there are always surprises, so your team might still have to scramble occasionally, but you should always pay attention to your plan; after all, that's why you made it.

Making It Up as You Go

Your software organization should have a security response plan. If you don't have one, we recommend that you refer to Chapter 15 and begin now to build your plan. But just suppose that a bad vulnerability report reaches your organization tomorrow morning—before you can get your plan fully in place and your people trained on the process. What should you do? The following sections identify a couple of important suggestions that might help you get by in the absence of a full response plan.

Know Who to Call

Your organization probably can't get very far toward building and releasing a security update without people to build and test a fix. So the first thing you'll need is a list of the people to contact to get your response process moving. For security emergencies, Microsoft's Software Security Incident Response Process (SSIRP) maintains 24-hour contact information for multiple people in each role in each product team. To release a "routine" security update, you'll need to be able to reach people during normal working hours. If you're faced with a security response situation and you have no plan, it's a good idea to list all the roles needed to build, test, package, and release a security update. Then notify people in those roles about what's going on and what they'll need to do.

Be Able to Build an Update

You need not only people to release a security update, you also need something to update. By definition, a vulnerability in a fielded product will affect code that you've already shipped, possibly code that you shipped years ago. Your development team is probably working on a new version of your product, but you need to build, test, and package an update for the version on your customers' computers. That means you need the source code, build tools, and test suite for the old version, and you need people who know how to build an update or the documentation to tell them how.

If you need to build an update for a version that's several years old, you might have to search your libraries to find the right source code, but it's very important that you do so. Customers—especially enterprise customers—dislike being forced to upgrade versions on short notice to install a security update. If you can't find the source code, you will either have to figure out another way to update the old version—perhaps by working back from the current version—or have to face your customers with the (unacceptable) choice of upgrading to a newer version in which you have been able to eliminate the vulnerability.

Be Able to Install an Update

As we discussed in Chapter 15, there might have been a time when it was acceptable to release an update in the form of a compressed package of files and a readme file that tells the user where to copy the files. It's not clear that that time ever existed for consumer software, but it might have existed for business and system software. In any case, that time is now gone, and, if at all possible, you'll need to release your update with an installer that can place the new files on the system and do whatever initialization is required to provide customers with a working fix that eliminates the vulnerability.

If your response team is scrambling to release an emergency update and has no way to release an installer, you can consider doing without, but you should be prepared for customer dissatisfaction and a lower rate of installation of the update than you might otherwise achieve. Aggressive communication about the update, the need to install it, and the specifics of deploying it without an installer can help to compensate for the absence of an installer, but this option is clearly second choice.

Know the Priorities When Inventing Your Process

The time to start thinking about a response process is *not* after a critical vulnerability has been reported to your team. But if you must invent your response process "in real time," the guidance in the previous sections should help you decide what to do first: people, product code, and installer technology are the things you can't do without when you respond to a vulnerability report.

As we've said numerous times, it's much better if you don't have to build a response process in real time; that's why we recommend that you read Chapter 15 and develop a security response plan before you need one.

Knowing What to Skip

Both this chapter and Chapter 15 emphasize the need to develop a security response plan and execute it. But it's also important to remember that there can be times when responding fast is more important than executing all of the steps of the plan.

We talked about urgent response when we discussed the Microsoft Windows Metafile Format (WMF) vulnerability in Chapter 15. In that case, the Microsoft Security Response Center (MSRC) released a complete and tested update in advance of the normal "second Tuesday of the month" release cycle, released security advisories to keep customers informed, and provided workaround information until the update was ready. But in a very serious emergency, the following options—which are more complete than an advisory or workaround but short of releasing a comprehensive update—might merit consideration:

- If a vulnerability is being exploited, or if you believe that it's likely to be exploited before you can do a full search for related vulnerabilities, you might decide to release an initial update that addresses only the most obvious or critical vulnerabilities and then follow it with a more complete update. You might have to consider this option fairly frequently in the course of executing your response process.

- If a vulnerability is being exploited and causing significant harm to customers or the Internet infrastructure, you might be forced to skip much of the update-quality process to protect as many customers as possible as soon as possible. This case might require you to consider releasing an update that has not been fully tested or releasing updates for different versions or languages at different times. This sort of step is definitely not to be taken lightly, but it might be justified by an extremely serious attack of the scope of the Code Red or Nimda worm. Of course, the better prepared your product team is to build, test, and package an update quickly, the less likely you are to be faced with such a choice.

A decision to release an incomplete or partially tested update is a major break from the normal response process and can be a major mistake, depending on circumstances. The recommendation to "watch for events that might change your plans" applies especially in this case. The press and some security experts often overstate the severity, impact, and level of exploitation of vulnerabilities and attacks, and we've frequently seen them get it very wrong. Independently watching customer support calls, Internet mailing lists, the press, and the observations of other response teams can help you be aware of what is really going on and avoid making a mistake that will be expensive for your customers' operations and your reputation.

Summary

The most important aspect of security response execution is to have a response plan in place and to follow it. Having a plan will help you to avoid missteps and to make the right decisions without fear of overlooking something and without wasting time deciding what to do next. If you don't have a plan or comprehensive documentation, the minimum resources you'll need are the people who will build, test, and package an update and the source code for the software you're going to update.

Whether you're executing a response plan or trying to do without, having an independent (and accurate) picture of the severity, spread, and impact of the vulnerability or attack you're dealing with is vital to making the right decisions. To get this sort of picture, you need to have independent sources of information. These sources range from customer reports to the press and Internet newsgroups to information shared by researchers and the findings and observations of other response teams. Information is vital to making the right decisions, executing your response successfully, and protecting your customers.

References

(FIRST 2006)   Forum of Incident Response and Security Teams. *http://www.first.org/*.

(IT-ISAC 2006)   Information Technology: Information Sharing and Analysis Center. *https://www.it-isac.org/*.

Part III
SDL Reference Material

Integrating SDL with Agile Methods

Like them or not, Agile methods and processes such as Extreme Programming (XP) and Agile processes such as Scrum are gaining popularity (Extreme Programming 2006, Schwaber 2004). Microsoft has also adapted its Microsoft Solutions Framework to include Agile methods (Microsoft 2006).

We're not going to debate the merits of these rapid-development processes, but groups within Microsoft, such as those in MSN and Windows Live, have integrated Agile methods into their development processes to good benefit. What sets the MSN and Windows Live projects apart from most Microsoft projects is that MSN projects are not huge development efforts such as Microsoft Windows or Microsoft Office. Complex to a degree, they have an important goal: rapidly developed small releases. Examples of projects delivered by MSN using Agile methods include

- MSN Messenger 7.5

- MSN Tabbed Browsing for Microsoft Internet Explorer

- MSN Anti-Phishing add-in

- MSN Support tools

- Internet Access RADIUS Service

Note that some of these products were built using only Agile methods and others experimented with various ideas from Agile methods.

The rest of this chapter is split in two parts, the first looking at Security Development Lifecycle (SDL) concepts and applying them to Agile methods, and the second looking at Agile methods with regard to adding SDL concepts. Please note that the goal of this chapter is not to cover every aspect of all Agile methods. Rather, it is to choose where it makes sense to augment the rules and practices of Agile methods with more security discipline and best practices.

Using SDL Practices with Agile Methods

In this first section, we'll look at the core SDL practices and consider how these can be used with Agile methods.

Security Education

Regardless of what software development method you employ, security education is critical. No development method will create secure software if the people building the software do not use simple security best practices. We've heard people claim that <*insert popular development method*> produces bug-free software. This might be true—and of course, it is true if you know nothing about security bugs, because you wouldn't recognize a security bug if you had no idea what one was.

Hence, you should follow the standard SDL policy and train all engineers about security issues at least once a year. In the overall cost of software development, the cost of education (in terms of time and effort) is tiny, and the risk of security errors being introduced is large.

> **Tip**   We appreciate that everyone developing software is in a hurry these days, but please do not skimp on security and privacy education.

Because of the less structured environment fostered by Agile development, the MSN teams push for more time spent on education and training. As a result, one of the MSN group's new requirements is that at least one hour be spent every two weeks on training and education. Of course, security is not the only possible subject that could be covered, but it is an important component.

> **Important**   We would argue that security education is more critical in the Agile environment because more decision-making power is placed in the hands of the product owner and development team.

One could justifiably argue that the XP concept of pair programming would aid with security education. But if neither member of a pair understands security, chances are that neither will notice a security bug. It is our opinion that all engineers should have classroom-style or online security education. It really is that important.

Project Inception

Contrary to popular belief, Agile methods do require some up-front groundwork. From an SDL perspective, the team must understand who the security go-to person is. This person is the *security coach*.

> **Note**   The SDL concept of "security advisor" translates nicely to an Agile "security coach."

Another part of XP is the notion of moving people around. If you adhere to this principle, consider moving the security coach around so you will force more people to take a security leadership position. However, do not take unnecessary risks in choosing the security person: this person has to make the best-possible security decisions for the product.

Establishing and Following Design Best Practices

Design, according to the traditional software-engineering definition, does not exist in most Agile methods. Rather, as the application develops or is iterated, the design is also iterated. Of course, you could always make serious design mistakes early in the product's life, but the goal of Agile development is to understand these mistakes early, in conjunction with customers, and make incremental changes for the next iteration. Often an iteration, or *sprint* (in Scrum parlance), might be only 14 or 30 days long.

Another aspect of many Agile methods, including Extreme Programming, is *simple design*. The software should include only the code that is necessary to achieve the desired results, as communicated by the customer. Simple design has a valuable security side effect: if you keep the design simple, you increase the chance that the design is secure. Complex software is difficult, if not impossible, to make totally secure. Also, smaller and more modular software is likely to be architecturally more secure.

The core of the Agile design philosophy is the *user story*. A user story is a short text that describes how the system is supposed to solve a problem or support a business process. User stories should encompass the customer's security concerns. Developers sign up for stories, and it's not unreasonable to expect one or more stories to focus solely on the security of the system. But a story about security should focus on threats perceived by the customer, which we will discuss next.

> **Best Practices**   For some development projects, procuring an on-site customer might be impossible. Very large projects, such as development of an operating system or a Web server, are examples. In cases like these, consider using personas, which you create based on real customer data, to help prioritize features and maintain focus on target customers (Kothari 2004). Above all, personas must be believable! You can also dedicate an employee to play the role of each of the assigned personas in person during meetings.

Risk Analysis

When building an application using Agile methods, you will probably not have a data flow diagram (DFD). In some software projects, there is a design sprint, and a deliverable from the design sprint could be a DFD.

But at some point, you will know that component A will communicate with component B using, say, sockets, and that component B uses a database to persist the data over, say, Open Database Connectivity (ODBC). Figure 18-1 shows an example of this arrangement.

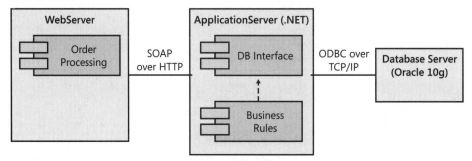

Figure 18-1   A portion of a story showing interaction among various components.

With this small diagram in hand, you can easily apply the risk analysis process using the following mapping:

- Code portions of the diagram are processes.
- Users are external entities.
- Any place where data is persisted is a data store.
- Interaction between code or data stores is a data flow.
- Interaction between users or external entities and code is a data flow.

Now you can apply the STRIDE threat taxonomy versus DFD elements described in Chapter 9, "Stage 4: Risk Analysis," and ask the customer questions such as the following:

- Does it concern you that an authenticated user or attacker can read any data from the Sales Order database?
- Will you be concerned if a valid user is denied access or degraded in her use of the application server?
- Does it concern you that anonymous users can read and change the network traffic between the application server and the database server?

If the answer to any of these questions is yes, that answer becomes part of the story. If not, make a note in the story that the customer is not concerned.

Best Practices   Translation from threats in the threat model to questions to ask the customer is the job of the security coach.

Take a closer look at the question sentences:

- "Anonymous," "authenticated user," and "valid user" are examples of roles or trust levels.

- "Read" is a synonym for information disclosure (I in STRIDE). "Change" means tampering (T in STRIDE). Denied or degraded service is an example of denial of service (D in STRIDE).

- "Sales Order database" and "application server" are example processes you need to defend from attack. Always remember that a customer's machine is an asset that always requires protection.

You can apply this simple analysis method to all parts of the Object Management Group's UML (Unified Modeling Language) diagram. In short, rather than thinking of potential security issues in an ad hoc manner, this method combines the analytical threat-modeling technique with rapid Agile development methods.

Creating Security Documents, Tools, and Best Practices for Customers

Agile methods are often criticized for having very little user-oriented documentation. At the very least, you should provide important security best practices in online Help files and within the application's user interface. Better still, if you are using the risk analysis process described in Chapter 9, you can use the security notes to help derive customer-facing documentation. That being said, it all depends on whether this is what the customer wants. So ask your customers what they want. Chances are that if you have a substantial user base (such as that of MSN Messenger 7.x), you should simply do the right thing by providing security best-practice documentation because no customer actively wants users to make security mistakes.

Secure Coding and Testing Policies

Agile methods support the notions of coding practices and requiring constant testing. In the case of coding practices, you should adopt secure coding best practices defined by SDL, such as the following:

- Requiring coding best practices.

- Not using banned application programming interfaces (APIs). (See Chapter 19, "SDL Banned Function Calls.")

- Using only appropriate cryptographic algorithms. (See Chapter 20, "SDL Minimum Cryptographic Standards.")

- Using static analysis tools such as those included with Microsoft Visual Studio 2005. (See Chapter 21, "SDL Required Tools and Compiler Options.")

Better yet, don't just define and use the coding rules; if you use Microsoft Visual Studio 2005 Team System, set up check-in policies and testing policies that enforce your rules (Microsoft 2005a, Microsoft 2005b).

Testing is a little more involved. Extreme Programming mandates that if you find a bug, you should write a test; this mandate applies to security bugs also. For example, if you find an integer overflow such as the following in your C/C++ code, you must build a security test that triggers this bug.

```
void * RenderEngine::AllocArbitraryBlob(int qty, int size) {
    if (qty && size)
        return GlobalAlloc(0,qty * size);
    else
        return NULL;
}
```

You must fix the code and rerun the test. The test should not fail. Rerun the test on every new build of your code. In CppUnit-like pseudocode (Wikipedia 2006, CppUnit 2006), your test might look like the following code example:

```
// Instantiate the class under test.
RenderEngine *e = new RenderEngine();

// Zero quantity or size is a no-op.
CPPUNIT_ASSERT(e->AllocArbitraryBlob(0,10) == NULL);
CPPUNIT_ASSERT(e->AllocArbitraryBlob(10,0) == NULL);

// An overflow should fail with NULL.
CPPUNIT_ASSERT(e->AllocArbitraryBlob(0x1fffffff,0x10) == NULL);

// A signed versus unsigned overflow should fail with NULL.
CPPUNIT_ASSERT(e->AllocArbitraryBlob(0x1fffffff,-1) == NULL);
CPPUNIT_ASSERT(e->AllocArbitraryBlob(-1,0x1fffffff) == NULL);

// This should succeed; NULL means there was an int overflow.
CPPUNIT_ASSERT(e->AllocArbitraryBlob(0x1fffff,1) != NULL);

// This should succeed too.
// And we need to verify that the return buffer size is correct.
void *ptr = e->AllocArbitraryBlob(0x200,0x20);
CPPUNIT_ASSERT(0x200*0x20 <= GlobalSize(ptr));
GlobalFree(ptr);
```

Then you would make the code fix:

```
inline void * RenderEngine::AllocArbitraryBlob(size_t qty, size_t size) {
    size_t alloc = qty * size;

    if (alloc ==0)
        return NULL;

    // Function is inlined, so 'size' is typically a constant
```

```
// and the division is optimized away at compile-time
if (MAX_INT / size <= qty)
    return GlobalAlloc(GPTR,alloc);
else
    return NULL;
}
```

When you rerun the tests, they should all succeed with the defensive code in place. You should build tests like this for all bugs, including security bugs.

Finally, fuzz testing lends itself well to Agile methods. If you have code that parses any input, you should build fuzz tests for all the entry points. These should be run daily, just like every other test.

Security Push

Within most Agile methods, there is no concept of specialized coding events such as those focusing on usability or security. However, a critical tenet of Extreme Programming is refactoring, which concerns itself with improving the internal representation of the code to make it cleaner, easier to read and maintain, higher quality, and, in our opinion, more secure (Fowler 2005). Secure software is by definition quality software, after all. One could argue there is no need for security pushes when Agile methods are used, except in one particular case: the security push, as defined in the SDL, focuses almost exclusively on legacy code. Code that has not been touched in three or more years probably has security bugs because

- The security landscape evolves substantially for good and for ill, but mostly for ill.
- Security tools advance quickly for good and for ill.
- People generally get better at finding security bugs, for good and for ill.

If the legacy code handles sensitive or personally identifiable data or is exposed to the Internet, *all* the legacy code should be reviewed in a series of "refactoring spikes" until all the code is reanalyzed, new tests are built, and bugs are fixed. More information about refactoring is provided later in this chapter.

If you use Scrum, you should also consider adding legacy code cleanup work to the product backlog every couple of sprints. The product backlog is a list of all the desired changes to the product being developed. Work items are taken from the product backlog and added to the sprint backlog by the product owner. If this is the first time your product has been subjected to security rigor, you should make the previous code cleanup work a major component of the backlog.

The MSN team has a mini-security push prior to a Release Candidate in which there is a group security code review and a dedicated test cycle for security testing. This amounts to one day for a two-week sprint or two days for a month-long sprint.

> **Tip** Some proponents of Agile methods at Microsoft indicate that having a series of one-day "security days" in the middle of the development schedule is beneficial.

Final Security Review

The Final Security Review (FSR), as discussed in Chapter 14, "Stage 9: The Final Security Review," is the point at which you verify the product is ready to ship from a security and privacy standpoint. Agile methods cannot employ a full-fledged FSR because of time constraints, but it does not mean you cannot do an FSR! For code developed using Agile methods, we propose the following minimum set of FSR requirements:

- All developers working on this iteration have attended security training within the last year.

- Unfixed security-related bugs are in fact appropriate to leave in this release. If the customer is well defined, the customer should have the final say.

- All customer security stories have been implemented correctly and signed off by the customer.

- All secure-coding best practices have been adhered to.

- All code-scanning tools have been used, and appropriate bugs have been fixed.

- All security-related tests have been run and bugs fixed.

- All parsed data formats have fuzz tests.

- If you are using managed code, such as C# or Microsoft Visual Basic .NET, results from tools like FxCop are evaluated and, if need be, fixed.

- Compilers used meet the minimum SDL requirements. (See Chapter 21.)

- If you are using Visual Studio, all C/C++ code is compiled with */GS* and linked with */SafeSEH*.

It's important that all security-related user stories be evaluated to make sure they are implemented correctly and meet the customer's needs.

All of the items in this list should be on a Big Visible Chart (BVC), also called an Information Radiator (Jeffries 2004). An important part of Extreme Programming is communication, and BVCs are a good way to very openly communicate what is expected of the engineering team.

Finally, because of the highly iterative nature of Agile methods, you can break an FSR into small "feature FSRs." In other words, rather than putting the entire software product through the FSR process every time you iterate, perform smaller FSRs on one or two features every sprint until the entire product is reviewed. The review order is determined by risk, and the riskiest features are reviewed first.

Product Release

An important part of the scheduling process when you use Extreme Programming is the release plan. This plan should include which security-related stories must be delivered to customers before you can consider the current iteration complete. When all these stories are complete, the product is ready for release to the customer.

Security Response Execution

The Security Response Execution stage is unique to SDL and is not apparent in Agile methods. Agile methods support the concept of rapid iterations that have well-defined and customer-supported features and the notion that any bugs found in one iteration can be fixed in the next iteration. But here is the problem: security bugs are not typical bugs. They might very well lead to emergencies that can put the customer at risk, which means you need to have a plan in place to handle potential security bugs at once. The preferred way to treat this situation is as a spike. You use a spike solution when you are working in a new problem domain or with a new technology you do not understand. We would argue that newly discovered security bugs fit both of these conditions. They are new problems in that the instance of this bug is new to you and your customer, and it's something you might not yet understand how to fix correctly. Another reason to use a spike is time; remember, if a security bug is publicly known, the chance that the vulnerability could be used to attack your customer increases over time until the customer applies the fix, mitigation, or workaround. Therefore, we recommend that the spike have two major components:

1.   A viable workaround as soon as possible.

2.   A real code-level or architecture-level remedy.

As a first step, determining an appropriate workaround might include tasks like these:

- Enabling a firewall rule
- Turning off some functionality
- Employing another security feature

When creating the real remedy, which might be a design or code change, it's important that you create a test to detect the defect first. Then make the fix and rerun the test to verify that the fix works.

Here is where Extreme Programming and SDL might be perceived to diverge. A spike is supposed to be a very discrete event focusing on solving one technical problem, but in the case of a security defect, the chances are good that the same type of bug exists in more than one place in the code. Because of the way security researchers find security bugs, they *will* find the other bugs—guaranteed! So when you find a security bug, you should form a spike that includes a security expert, make the appropriate and correct code fix (and the test), and then find the other defect variants within the same code area. Don't forget to create small tests of all the bugs.

Once the fix is complete and deemed acceptable, you must issue a fix and provide guidance to your customers.

Core values of Agile methods include learning from mistakes and being adaptive rather than predictive. These notions apply to security bugs, too; you must apply a root-cause analysis to answer the following questions:

- Why did this mistake occur?

- What do we need to change to make sure this mistake never happens again? The answers to this might include better testing, more education, and changes to and enforcement of the best practices.

- Can a tool be created to search for the mistake in future code?

- Where else could this mistake have occurred?

You should apply your new knowledge to all future iterations to reduce the chance that the same mistake is made again (and again!).

Augmenting Agile Methods with SDL Practices

In this short section, we'll look at some of the Agile doctrines and see how they can be augmented with security best practices from SDL. The following list identifies the Agile doctrines that we'll look at:

- Planning

    1. User stories

    2. Release planning

    3. Small releases and iterations

    4. Moving people around

- Design

    1. Simplicity

    2. Spike solutions

    3. Refactoring

- Coding

    1. Constant customer availability

    2. Coding to standards

    3. Coding the unit test first

    4. Pair programming

5.   Integrating often

6.   Leaving optimization until last

- Testing all bugs

Let's look at the specific doctrines in detail.

User Stories

User stories should include the customer's security requirements. As previously noted, such stories must be based not on intuition but on real-world threats. Use the risk- and threat-modeling method outlined in the "Risk Analysis" section in this chapter to understand these threats and articulate them to customers.

In his book *User Stories Applied: For Agile Software Development*, Mike Cohn suggests adding "Constraints" to user stories (Cohn 2004). A constraint is something that must be obeyed and is fundamental to the business. For example, from a security perspective, a story might include directives such as these:

- "The software must not divulge the data in the Orders database to unauthorized users."

- "All software add-ins must have valid digital signatures in order to run within the system."

- "The client must always authenticate the validity of the server."

For a software product to be complete, all user stories should be complete. By "complete" we mean

- All code and test code for each story is checked in.

- All unit tests for each story are written and passed.

- All applicable functional tests for each story are identified, written, and passed.

- Product owner has signed off.

And, from an engineering practices perspective, "complete" means the following steps have been taken:

- All appropriate security best practice has been adhered to, or exceptions granted.

- The latest compiler versions are used.

- All code scanning tools have been run over all code.

- All bugs from the code scanning tools are fixed or postponed.

- There is no use of banned functionality.

Small Releases and Iterations

It is easier to secure a small code delta than a large code delta. It is common to see coding bugs of all types on the boundary of old and new code; if this boundary is kept small, bugs can be found relatively easily. The doctrine of small releases is good for security, too. Another benefit of small iterations is that you can prioritize security defenses. Critical defenses can be added to the code in the current iteration, and less-important defenses can be added to later iterations if needed. Small iterations also address the notion of not adding functionality earlier than it's needed.

We have learned the hard way that one drawback of introducing a new security defense is that the chance of also introducing functional regressions is very high. Be forewarned.

Moving People Around

In general, competent security specialists are scarce and hard to hire. Be prepared to wait to hire the right person. Once you have hired an effective security person, encourage him to teach security to others in the team. A critical component of security skills is education: have the guru teach and mentor others in the team.

Note that although moving people around is a good idea, the authors have yet to see any team do it.

 Best Practices   Security should be a skill common to all software developers, not confined solely to just a select group of specialists.

Simplicity

A simple application is more secure than a complex application, period. Complexity is an enemy of security. Of course, in the real world, this truism is a little more subtle. We can always write simple software that would never get the job done. In fact, most code today is complex because business processes are complex and have thorny, but necessary, requirements that add complexity to the code, such as responsiveness, timeliness, robustness, transaction processing, offline and online capabilities, integration with older systems, and so on. But at the micro-level, your code can be simple and easy to understand and, hence, to maintain. Where possible, strive for simple designs and easy-to-understand code.

Spike Solutions

Invariably, you'll hit security roadblocks, perhaps security bugs or your own uncertainty on the best way to implement or take advantage of a security feature. A spike solution is a great method to determine the best way to resolve security dilemmas. Take two developers off the core project to work on the security solution.

Refactoring

At Microsoft, we often systematically review older code, looking for security bugs; if issues are found, the code is fixed. In some cases, design issues or erroneous coding patterns are found, and these patterns are fixed. This concept is very similar to that of *refactoring*, which is a technique for restructuring or changing an existing body of code without changing its interface or external behavior. You must consider security bugs as part of your refactoring process. Examples of security refactoring include

- Replacing banned APIs with safer APIs; for example, replacing strcpy with StringCchCopy or strcpy_s. (See Chapter 19.)

- Replacing weak crypto algorithms with more up-to-date and secure versions. (See Chapter 20.)

- Making cryptographic code more agile by removing hard-coded algorithm names, key sizes, and other cryptographic-related settings. (See Chapter 20.)

- Replacing integer arithmetic used in memory allocations and array indexing with safer code.

There are challenges with refactoring for the sake of refactoring—most notably, defects, usually called regressions, could be entered into the code base (Garrido and Johnson 2002).

Constant Customer Availability

The customer is a key contributor (some say the only contributor) to user stories. The customer must also provide the security requirements for the stories. You can make sure nothing is missing from user stories by building threat models for components within the application and validating that no threats are missing from the customer's stories. However, to many customers, security is an unspoken requirement. You really have to probe customers to learn how much security they'd like to buy. Customers won't mention it—they'll just say "Make it secure!" (which, of course, is meaningless).

 Important It's imperative that you always consider how the software can be misused.

When security issues arise, the customer must be consulted once the threats are thoroughly understood. At the meeting to review the threats, use a spike to determine the appropriate remedy.

Coding to Standards

Secure coding standards must be adhered to, and source-code analysis tools must be used regularly to help catch various security bugs. Refer to Chapter 11, "Stage 6: Secure Coding Policies," for secure coding ideas. The beauty of coding to standards is that you can reduce (not eliminate) the chance that new bugs, including security bugs, are entered into the system in the first place.

 Important Development and test tools for security play an important role in an Agile environment due to the absence of specifications.

Coding the Unit Test First

The "Coding the Unit Test First" doctrine is especially true of fuzz tests; for any protocol you parse, or for any payload you read and respond to, you should build a fuzz generator for that protocol or payload. Refer to Chapter 12, "Stage 7: Secure Testing Policies," for fuzz-testing concepts. The author of this chapter (Howard) believes security can be significantly improved if unit security testing becomes part of per-function or per-module unit before the application is assembled.

Pair Programming

At Pairprogamming.com, the practice is described as follows:

Two programmers working side-by-side, collaborating on the same design, algorithm, code or test. One programmer, the driver, has control of the keyboard/mouse and actively implements the program. The other programmer, the observer, continuously observes the work of the driver to identify tactical (syntactic, spelling, etc.) defects and also thinks strategically about the direction of the work. On demand, the two programmers can brainstorm any challenging problem. Because the two programmers periodically switch roles, they work together as equals to develop software. (Pair Programming 2006)

Having a person observe while another codes is an effective way to detect security bugs as they are entered or, better yet, to prevent them from being entered in the first place. You can help team members develop security skills by pairing them with the security expert.

Integrating Often

Integrating programmers' small code updates often will help you find security bugs faster than waiting for large code changes.

Leaving Optimization Until Last

There can be a conflict between optimization and security. Optimization itself doesn't necessarily lead to security bugs, but in our experience, making large changes to the code late in the process always leads to errors in the system. Beware.

When a Bug Is Found, a Test Is Created

In the authors' opinion, creating a test whenever a bug is found is wise because doing so helps prevent the bug from reentering the code base (a regression). Every time you identify a security bug, create a test case to find and fix the bug. Then rerun the test on every subsequent version to make sure the bug is indeed fixed.

Summary

To date, there is very little guidance for development teams wanting to augment Agile methods, such as Scrum and Extreme Programming, with security discipline. Based on our conversations with Agile proponents, most of the SDL best practices and requirements can be easily incorporated into Agile practice. Doing so can only be beneficial for those using Agile methods.

References

(Extreme Programming 2006)   "Extreme Programming: A Gentle Introduction," *http://www.extremeprogramming.org/*.

(Schwaber 2004)   Schwaber, Ken. *Agile Project Management with Scrum*. Redmond, WA: Microsoft Press, 2004.

(Microsoft 2006)   "MSF for Agile Software Development," *http://msdn.microsoft.com/vstudio/teamsystem/msf/msfagile/*. March, 2006.

(Kothari 2004)   Kothari, Nikhil. "Applying personas," *http://www.nikhilk.net/Personas.aspx*. January 2004.

(Microsoft 2005a)   Visual Studio 2005 Team Server Check-in Policy. "Walkthrough: Customizing Check-In Policies and Notes," *http://msdn2.microsoft.com/en-us/library/ms181281.aspx*. MSDN, 2005.

(Microsoft 2005b)   Michaelis, Mark. "Introducing Microsoft Visual Studio 2005 Team System Web Testing," *http://msdn.microsoft.com/library/en-us/dnvs05/html/VS05TmSysWebTst.asp*. MSDN, September 2005.

(Wikipedia 2006)   "XUnit," *http://en.wikipedia.org/wiki/XUnit*.

(CppUnit 2006)   "CppUnit Wiki," *http://cppunit.sourceforge.net/cppunit-wiki*.

(Fowler 2005)   Fowler, Martin. "Refactoring Home Page," *www.refactoring.com*.

(Jeffries 2004)   Jeffries, Ron. "Big Visible Charts," *http://www.xprogramming.com/xpmag/BigVisibleCharts.htm*. October 2004.

(Cohn 2004)   Cohn, Mike. *User Stories Applied: For Agile Software Development*. Reading, MA: Addison Wesley Professional Co., 2004.

(Garrido and Johnson 2002)   Garrido, Alejandra, and Ralph Johnson. "Challenges of Refactoring C Programs," *https://netfiles.uiuc.edu/garrido/www/papers/refactoringC.pdf.* May 2002.

(Pair Programming 2006)   Williams, Laurie. "What is pair programming?" *http://www.pairprogramming.com/.*

Chapter 19
SDL Banned Function Calls

When the C runtime library (CRT) was first created about 25 years ago, the threats to computers were different; machines were not as interconnected as they are today, and attacks were not as prevalent. With this in mind, a subset of the C runtime library must be deprecated for new code and, over time, removed from earlier code. It's just too easy to get code wrong that uses these outdated functions. Even some of the classic replacement functions are prone to error, too.

Following is a partial list of Microsoft security bulletins that could have been prevented if the banned application programming interfaces (APIs) that led to the security bug had been removed from the code:

Microsoft Bulletin Number	Product and Code	Function
MS02-039	Microsoft SQL Server 2000	sprintf
MS05-010	License Server	lstrcpy
MS04-011	Microsoft Windows (DCPromo)	wvsprintf
MS04-011	Windows (MSGina)	lstrcpy
MS04-031	Windows (NetDDE)	wcscat
MS03-045	Windows (USER)	wcscpy

You can get more info on these security bulletins at *http://www.microsoft.com/technet/security/current.aspx*. Note that many other software vendors and projects have had similar vulnerabilities.

The Banned APIs

This list is the SDL view of what comprises banned APIs; it is derived from experience with real-world security bugs and focuses almost exclusively on functions that can lead to buffer overruns (Howard, LeBlanc, and Viega 2005). Any function in this section's tables must be replaced with a more secure version. Obviously, you cannot replace a banned API with another banned API. For example, replacing strcpy with strncpy is not valid because strncpy is banned, too.

Also note that some of the function names might be a little different, depending on whether the function takes ASCII, Unicode, _T (ASCII or Unicode) or multibyte chars. Some function names might include *A* or *W* at the end of the name. For example, the StrSafe StringCbCatEx function is also available as StringCbCatExW (Unicode) and StringCbCatExA (ASCII).

Banned String Copy Functions and Replacements

Banned APIs	StrSafe Replacement	Safe CRT Replacement
strcpy, wcscpy, _tcscpy, _mbscpy, StrCpy, StrCpyA, StrCpyW, lstrcpy, lstrcpyA, lstrcpyW, strcpyA, strcpyW, _tccpy, _mbccpy	String**Copy or String*CopyEx	strcpy_s

*   For StrSafe, * should be replaced with Cch (character count) or Cb (byte count).

Banned String Concatenation Functions and Replacements

Banned APIs	StrSafe Replacement	Safe CRT Replacement
strcat, wcscat, _tcscat, _mbscat, StrCat, StrCatA, StrCatW, lstrcat, lstrcatA, lstrcatW, StrCatBuffW, StrCatBuff, StrCatBuffA, StrCatChainW, strcatA, strcatW, _tccat, _mbccat	String*Cat or String*CatEx	strcat_s

Banned sprintf Functions and Replacements

Banned APIs	StrSafe Replacement	Safe CRT Replacement
wnsprintf, wnsprintfA, wnsprintfW, sprintfW, sprintfA, wsprintf, wsprintfW, wsprintfA, sprintf, swprintf, _stprintf	String*Printf or String*PrintfEx	sprintf_s

Banned "n" sprintf Functions and Replacements

Banned APIs	StrSafe Replacement	Safe CRT Replacement
_snwprintf, _snprintf, _sntprintf, nsprintf	String*Printf or String*PrintfEx	_snprintf_s or _snwprintf_s

Banned Variable Argument sprintf Functions and Replacements

Banned APIs	StrSafe Replacement	Safe CRT Replacement
wvsprintf, wvsprintfA, wvsprintfW, vsprintf, _vstprintf, vswprintf	String*VPrintf or String*VPrintfEx	_vstprintf_s

Banned Variable Argument "n" sprintf Functions and Replacements

Banned APIs	StrSafe Replacement	Safe CRT Replacement
_vsnprintf, _vsnwprintf, _vsntprintf, wvnsprintf, wvnsprintfA, wvnsprintfW,	String*VPrintf or String*VPrintfEx	vsntprintf_s

Banned "n" String Copy Functions and Replacements

Banned APIs	StrSafe Replacement	Safe CRT Replacement
strncpy, wcsncpy, _tcsncpy, _mbsncpy, _mbsnbcpy, StrCpyN, StrCpyNA, StrCpyNW, StrNCpy, strcpynA, StrNCpyA, StrNCpyW, lstrcpyn, lstrcpynA, lstrcpynW, _fstrncpy	String*CopyN or String*CopyNEx	strncpy_s

Banned "n" String Concatenation Functions and Replacements

Banned APIs	StrSafe Replacement	Safe CRT Replacement
strncat, wcsncat, _tcsncat, _mbsncat, _mbsnbcat, StrCatN, StrCatNA, StrCatNW, StrNCat, StrNCatA, StrNCatW, lstrncat, lstrcatnA, lstrcatnW, lstrcatn, _fstrncat	String*CatN or String*CatNEx	strncat_s

It is common wisdom to replace functions like strcpy with the counted "n" version, such as strncpy. However, in our experience, the "n" functions are also hard to secure (Howard 2004), so we have banned their use in new code.

Banned String Tokenizing Functions and Replacements

Banned APIs	StrSafe Replacement	Safe CRT Replacement
strtok, _tcstok, wcstok, _mbstok	None	strtok_s

Banned Makepath Functions and Replacements

Banned APIs	StrSafe Replacement	Safe CRT Replacement
makepath, _tmakepath, _makepath, _wmakepath	None	_makepath_s

Banned Splitpath Functions and Replacements

Banned APIs	StrSafe Replacement	Safe CRT Replacement
_splitpath, _tsplitpath, _wsplitpath	None	_splitpath_s

Banned scanf Functions and Replacements

Banned APIs	StrSafe Replacement	Safe CRT Replacement
scanf, wscanf, _tscanf, sscanf, swscanf, _stscanf	None	sscanf_s

Banned "n" scanf Functions and Replacements

Banned APIs	StrSafe Replacement	Safe CRT Replacement
snscanf, snwscanf, _sntscanf	None	_snscanf_s

Banned Numeric Conversion Functions and Replacements

Banned APIs	StrSafe Replacement	Safe CRT Replacement
_itoa, _itow, _i64toa, _i64tow, _ui64toa, _ui64tot, _ui64tow, _ultoa, _ultot, _ultow	None	_itoa_s, _itow_s

Banned gets Functions and Replacements

Banned APIs	StrSafe Replacement	Safe CRT Replacement
gets, _getts, _gettws	String*Gets	gets_s

Banned IsBad* Functions and Replacements

Banned APIs	
IsBadWritePtr, IsBadHugeWritePtr, IsBadReadPtr, IsBadHugeReadPtr, IsBadCodePtr, IsBadStringPtr	These functions can mask errors, and there are no replacement functions. You should rewrite the code to avoid using these APIs. If you need to avoid a crash, wrap your usage of the pointer with __try/__except. Doing this can easily hide bugs; you should do this only in areas where it is absolutely critical to avoid a crash (such as crash recovery code) and where you have a reasonable explanation for why the data you're looking at might be invalid. You should also not catch all exceptions, but only types that you know about. Catching all exceptions is just as bad as using IsBad*Ptr.
	For IsBadWritePtr, filling the destination buffer using memset is a preferred way to validate that output buffers are valid and large enough to hold the amount of space that the caller claims they provided.

Banned OEM Conversion Functions and Replacements

Banned APIs	Windows Replacement
CharToOem, CharToOemA, CharToOemW, OemToChar, OemToCharA, OemToCharW, CharToOemBuffA, CharToOemBuffW	WideCharToMultiByte

Banned Stack Dynamic Memory Allocation Functions and Replacements

Banned APIs	Windows Replacement
alloca, _alloca	SafeAllocA

For critical functions, such as those accepting anonymous Internet connections, strlen must also be replaced:

Banned String Length Functions and Replacements

Banned APIs	StrSafe Replacement	Safe CRT Replacement
strlen, wcslen, _mbslen, _mbstrlen, StrLen, lstrlen	String*Length	strlen_s

Why the "n" Functions Are Banned

The classic C runtime "n" functions (such as strncpy and strncat) are banned because they are so hard to call correctly. The authors have seen numerous errors calling these functions in an attempt to make code more secure. Note that we're not saying the replacements are perfect, but issues with the current "n" functions include non-null termination of overflowed buffers and no error returns on overflow.

The newer StrSafe and Safe CRT functions are more consistent on failure.

Important Caveat

Simply replacing a banned function call with a better replacement does not guarantee that the code is secure. It's possible to misuse the replacement function, most commonly by getting the destination buffer size wrong.

 Best Practices   Review all instances of replaced function calls, and verify that the destination buffer size is correct.

Choosing StrSafe vs. Safe CRT

There is an overlap between these two sets of replacement C runtime functions. Which you choose depends on your specific situation; the following table should help you make the decision. In some cases, you might have little choice but to use one over the other; for example, if your code calls itoa a great deal, there is no replacement in StrSafe, but there is in Safe CRT. You would need to either code around the itoa call or use Safe CRT.

	StrSafe	Safe CRT
Distribution Method	Web (msdn.microsoft.com)	Microsoft Visual Studio 2005
# Headers	One (StrSafe.h)	Numerous (various C runtime headers)
Library Version Available	Yes	Yes
Inline Version Available	Yes	No
Industry Standard	No	Not Yet (Secure C Lib Functions)
Kernel Mode	Yes	No
Return Type	HRESULT (user mode) or NTSTATUS (kernel mode)	Varies by function (errno_t)
Requires Code Changes	Yes	Yes
Main Focus	Buffer overrun issues	Various, including buffer overruns

Using StrSafe

To use StrSafe in your C or C++ code, simply add the following header:

```
#include "strsafe.h"
```

This will make the functions inline. If you want to use the library version, strsafe.lib, add the following to your code:

```
#define STRSAFE_LIB
#include "strsafe.h"
```

Note that all the StrSafe functions include Rtl versions for kernel use.

StrSafe Example

The following code

```
void Function(char *s1, char *s2) {
    char temp[32];
    strcpy(temp,s1);
    strcat(temp,s2);
}
```

when converted to StrSafe might look like this:

```
HRESULT Function(char *s1, char *s2) {
    char temp[32];
    HRESULT hr = StringCchCopy(temp,_countof(temp),s1);
    if (FAILED(hr)) return hr;
    return StringCchCat(temp,_countof(temp),s2);
}
```

Using Safe CRT

The Safe CRT is included with Visual Studio 2005. When you compile code using this compiler, it will automatically warn you of the deprecated functions in the code. Also, in some cases, the compiler will change some function calls to safe function calls if the destination buffer size is known at compile time and CRT_SECURE_CPP_OVERLOAD_STANDARD_NAMES is #defined in the code.

For example, the following code

```
int main(int argc, char* argv[]) {
    char t[10];
       ...
    if (2==argc)
       strcpy(t,argv[1]);

       ...
    return 0;

}
```

is changed by the compiler to this:

```
int main(int argc, char* argv[]) {
    char t[10];
    ...
```

```
    if (2==argc)
        strcpy_s(t,_countof(t),argv[1]);


    ...
    return 0;
}
```

Safe CRT Example

The following code

```
void Function(char *s1, char *s2) {
    char temp[32];
    strcpy(temp,s1);
    strcat(temp,s2);
}
```

when converted to the Safe CRT might look like this:

```
errno_t Function(char *s1, char *s2) {
    char temp[32];
    errno_t err = strcpy_s(temp,_countof(temp),s1);
    if (!err) return err;
    return strcat_s(temp,_countof(temp),s2);
}
```

Other Replacements

If you are using C++, you should seriously consider using the std::string template class rather than manipulating buffers directly.

Many *nix variants, including OpenBSD and some Linux operating systems, include support for string copy replacements strlcpy and strlcat (Miller and de Raadt 1999).

Tools Support

The Visual Studio 2005 compiler has built-in deprecations for these functions; all C4996 compiler warnings should be investigated to make sure that the function in question is not on the preceding banned list. Also, look out for code that disables this warning, such as *#pragma warning(disable:4996)*.

On the CD   The companion disc accompanying this book includes a header file named banned.h listing all the banned APIs. If you add this as the first header file in your application, it will detect all banned API instances. It works and has been tested with Microsoft Visual C++ 2003 and 2005 compilers and GNU GCC 3.3.x.

ROI and Cost Impact

Removing banned APIs is one way to reduce potential security bugs with very little engineering effort. As you can see at the start of this document, some Microsoft security bulletins would not have been necessary if banned APIs had not been used.

Metrics and Goals

The metric to track is the number of banned APIs in former code and in new code. The quantity should be zero for new code and should follow a glide path down over time for earlier code.

> **Important**   This list of banned APIs is not static—over time, new functions will be added as new vulnerabilities are discovered and replacement APIs created.

References

(Howard, LeBlanc, and Viega 2005)   Howard, Michael, David LeBlanc, and John Viega. *19 Deadly Sins of Software Development*. New York, NY: McGraw-Hill, 2005. Chapter 1, "Buffer Overruns."

(Howard 2004)   Howard, Michael. "Buffer Overflow in Apache 1.3.xx fixed on Bugtraq—the evils of strncpy and strncat," *http://blogs.msdn.com/michael_howard/archive/2004/10/29/249713.aspx*. October 2004.

(Miller and de Raadt 1999)   Miller, Todd C., and Theo de Raadt. USENIX Annual Technical Conference, "strlcpy and strlcat – Consistent, Safe String Copy and Concatenation," *http://www.usenix.org/events/usenix99/full_papers/millert/millert_html/index.html*. June 1999.

Chapter 20
SDL Minimum Cryptographic Standards

As cryptographic research evolves and computers become faster, some cryptographic algorithms, security protocols, cryptographic key strengths, and usage are no longer deemed secure enough for software products.

To put this in perspective, the Electronic Frontier Foundation book *Cracking DES* claims that a specially built $1 million computer in 1993 would take, on average, about 3.5 hours to find a Data Encryption Standard (DES) key (Electronic Frontier Foundation 1998). According to Moore's Law, $1 million in 1998 could crack a DES key in about 35 minutes. If you don't have a spare million, spend $10,000 and you could break the key in 2.5 days. In 2006, CPU speeds are faster than in 1998, and memory is much cheaper.

This chapter outlines guidance and standards for writing new code or updating existing code covered by SDL, code which should be upgraded if advances in cryptographic research find algorithms or key sizes inadequate.

High-Level Cryptographic Requirements

The following sections describe at a very high level the basic SDL cryptographic requirements and best practices.

Cryptographic Technologies vs. Low-Level Cryptographic Algorithms

Whenever possible, use an established security standard rather than creating your own solution. For example, use SSL/TLS, IPSec, or WS-Security for protecting ephemeral on-the-wire data rather than creating your own authentication, key exchange, encryption, and integrity solutions from cryptographic primitives.

> **Best Practices**   Projects are required to use standard protocols rather than low-level cryptography when possible. If you cannot use a standard protocol, have the design reviewed by the central security team.

Use Cryptographic Libraries

Do not create your own cryptographic libraries, and certainly do not create your own cryptographic algorithms. For .NET code, you should use the class libraries defined in System .Security.Cryptography namespace (Microsoft 2006a). For C/C++ code, you should use CryptoAPI (Microsoft 2006b). For scripts (VBScript or JavaScript), you should use CAPICOM (Microsoft 2001).

For correct function and method-call usage, please refer to the references section at the end of this chapter.

> **Best Practices**   Projects are required to use standard cryptographic libraries rather than create unique cryptographic libraries or algorithms. Standard cryptographic libraries are operating system components specifically tasked with creating such functionality for use by others.

Cryptographic Agility

Do not hard-code the cryptographic algorithm(s) used by your application within the application code. Instead, store the cryptographic primitive(s) used in a configurable store—for example, in the registry or in an XML configuration file—where they can be updated quickly by the customer in the event of a sudden and unpredictable change in cryptographic technology. Note that tampering with any data store used in this way can compromise application behavior. Therefore, to protect the cryptographic primitives, appropriate mitigations—such as a strong access control policy that allows only trusted users to manipulate the data—should be defined for the data store. It's also worthwhile to add the cryptographic algorithms used by the payload. For example, the following could represent an encrypted and MACd data blob (RFC 2104). Note that it might look as though you are providing a lot of useful information to an attacker, but you aren't—the strength of an encryption algorithm, such as AES, lies solely in the quality and protection of the encryption.

```
<?xml version="1.0" encoding="utf-8"?>
<blob version="1.2">
  <encryption>
    <alg id="AES"
         keySize="256"
         IV="LqIfly+GYOORE3KnBjw41g=="
         mode="CBC"
         padding="PKCS7"/>
    <data>qAuGOVVIpQBVd ...snip... ml3yt1ngkY8=</data>
  </encryption>
```

```
<authentication>
  <alg id="HMACSHA56" />
  <data>1y1xAI9CywYQPvau71j6eRDqgfND1y1a5Hdf02xAp20=</data>
</authentication>

</blob>
```

Best Practices   Do not hard-code cryptographic algorithms in your code. Projects using cryptographic functions must be cryptographically "agile" to provide a way to upgrade the algorithms over time.

Default to Secure Cryptographic Algorithms

Use strong cryptographic algorithms by default. If a weak algorithm is needed for backward compatibility with older software or to comply with an industry standard, it should be a fallback, not a default, and it should be available only on an "opt-in" basis. Silently falling back to weak cryptography is considered bad practice; users should be notified if they are falling back to a weaker algorithm. System and network administrators should have the means to control whether applications can use weak algorithms in their administrative domains. Table 20-1 in the next section defines which cryptographic algorithms are acceptable for defaults.

Best Practices   If a project uses multiple cryptographic algorithms to maintain backward compatibility, it must not default or silently fall back to the cryptographic algorithms that are listed as ". . . Must Be Replaced" in Table 20-1.

Cryptographic Algorithm Usage

This section focuses on how different algorithms should be approached in new and earlier code. The SDL requirements dictate that

- New code uses only algorithms and key lengths from the rightmost column.

- Algorithms listed in the middle column are to be used only for backward compatibility.

- Algorithms and key lengths listed in the left column are not to be used in shipping products without an exception from the central security team.

Using any cryptographic algorithms that are not listed in the middle or right-hand columns requires an exception from your central security team. Be aware that the United States federal government mandates the use of specific cryptographic algorithms (NIST 2005).

Table 20-1   Cryptographic Algorithm Usage Guidance

Algorithm Class	Algorithms and Key Sizes That Must Be Replaced	Algorithms and Key Sizes Okay for Existing Code	Required Algorithms and Key Sizes for New Code
Symmetric Block Cipher	DES, DESX, RC2, Skipjack	3DES (112 bit or 168 bit)	AES (>= 128 bit)
Symmetric Stream Cipher	SEAL, CYLINK_MEK, RC4 (<128 bit)	RC4 (reviewed, see below, and >= 128 bit)	None—use a block cipher
Asymmetric Cipher	RSA or Diffie-Hellman (DH) (<1024 bit)	RSA or DH (1024-2047 bit)	RSA or DH (>=2048 bit) Elliptic Curve Cryptography (ECC) (>=256 bit)
Hash (includes Hashed Message Authentication Codes [HMAC])	SHA0, MD2, MD4 and MD5	SHA1	SHA256, SHA384 and SHA512 (also referred to as the SHA2 algorithms)
MAC key length	<112 bit	112–127 bits	>=128 bits

Symmetric Block Ciphers and Key Lengths

For symmetric block encryption algorithms, a minimum key length of 128 bits is required for new code (KeyLength 2006). The only block encryption algorithm recommended for new code is AES. (AES-128, AES-192, and AES-256 are all acceptable.) Two-key (112-bit) or three-key (168-bit) 3DES are currently acceptable if already in use in existing code. However, transitioning to AES is highly recommended. DES, DESX, RC2, and SKIPJACK are no longer considered secure; continued use of these algorithms should be for opt-in backward compatibility only.

Best Practices   For projects using symmetric block ciphers, AES is required for new code, and two- or three-key 3DES is permissible for backward compatibility. All other symmetric block cipher usage, including RC2, DES, DESX, and SKIPJACK, can be used only for decrypting old data.

Symmetric Stream Ciphers and Key Lengths

For symmetric stream ciphers, there is currently no recommended algorithm—you should use a block cipher, such as AES, with at least 128 bits of key material. Existing code that uses RC4 should be using a key size of at least 128 bits, and your application's use of RC4 should be reviewed by a cryptographer. This last point is very important—there are numerous subtle errors that can arise when using stream ciphers such as RC4. Refer to the "References" section of this chapter for other material outlining some of the common errors.

Best Practices   The RC4 stream cipher should be used with extreme caution, and any use of the algorithm should be reviewed by a cryptographer.

Best Practices   All stream cipher usages must undergo a security review. RC4 with 128-bit length key or greater is permissible, but only after a security review. All other usage, including RC4 <128 bit key, is permissible only for decrypting old data.

Symmetric Algorithm Modes

Symmetric algorithms can operate in a number of modes, most of which link together the encryption operations on successive blocks of plaintext and ciphertext. The electronic code book (ECB) mode of operation should not be used without signoff from the central security team. Cipher-block-chaining (CBC) is the recommended mode of operation for block ciphers. If, for interoperability reasons, you believe that you need to use another chaining mode, you should talk to the security team.

Best Practices   Projects using symmetric encryption algorithms must use CBC.

Asymmetric Algorithms and Key Lengths

For RSA-based asymmetric encryption and digital signatures, the minimum acceptable key length is 1024 bits, and 1024-bit signature keys should be used only for signatures with validity periods of one year or less. New code should use RSA keys of at least 2048 bits in length.

For DSA-based digital signatures, only 1024-bit keys should be used (the maximum allowed by the DSA standard) and then only for short-lived signatures (less than one year).

For key exchange and digital signatures that are based on elliptic curve cryptography (ECC), the three NIST-approved curves—P-256, P-384, and P-521—are all acceptable.

For key agreement, Diffie-Hellman is recommended, with 2048-bit keys for new code and 1024-bit keys for backward compatibility. Keys of 512 bits or fewer are not to be used at all.

Best Practices   For projects using asymmetric algorithms, ECC with >=256-bit keys or RSA with >=2048-bit keys is required for new code. RSA with >=1024-bit keys is permissible for backward compatibility. RSA <1024-bit keys can be used only for decrypting old data. ECC-based key exchange and digital signatures must use one of the three NIST-approved curves—P-256, P-384, and P521 are all acceptable. For key agreement, Diffie-Hellman is recommended, with >=2048-bit keys for new code, >=1024-bit keys for backward compatibility, and no keys using <1024 bits.

Hash Functions

No new code should use the MD4 or MD5 hash algorithms because hash collisions have been demonstrated for both algorithms, which effectively "breaks" them in the eyes of the crypto-graphic community. Continued use of SHA-1 is permissible in existing code for backward compatibility purposes and, as described in the next Best Practices reader aid, for new code running on certain down-level platforms. The SHA-2 family of hash functions (SHA-256, SHA-384, or SHA-512) is currently the only group that is generally recommended. The SHA-2 hash functions are available in .NET code and in unmanaged Microsoft Win32 code targeting Windows Server 2003 SP1 and Windows Vista.

Note that hash function agility—the ability to switch to another hash function without updating your code—is part of the cryptographic agility requirement discussed earlier in this chapter. Absent a backward compatibility requirement, code that uses SHA-1 must migrate to SHA-2 once SHA-2 is available on the platform.

Best Practices   For .NET code, use of a SHA-2 hash function is required. For new native Win32 code shipping to Windows Server 2003 SP1 or Windows Vista, use of a SHA-2 hash function is required. For new native Win32 code shipping to earlier operating systems (including Windows 95, Windows 98, Microsoft Windows NT 4, and Windows 2000), use of SHA-1 is permitted. This exemption automatically expires if a service pack containing SHA-2 support ships on the platform in question. Continued use of SHA-1 is permissible for backward compatibility. All others hash functions, including MD2, MD4, and MD5, should not be used.

Message Authentication Codes

The most common and well-known message authentication code (MAC) function is the HMAC, which uses a hash function and secret MAC key for message authentication. It uses an underlying hash function (MD5, SHA-1, or SHA-2) and a secret key of a specified length. The strength of an HMAC relies on the strength of the underlying hash function and the length of the secret.

Best Practices   For HMAC usage, SHA-2 with >=128-bit keys is required for new code. SHA-1 with >=128-bit keys is permissible for backward compatibility. All other keys lengths <112 bits or hash functions, including MD2, MD4, or MD5, should not be used.

Data Storage and Random Number Generation

In this section, I will discuss issues related to cryptography, including sensitive data storage and generating random numbers.

Storing Private Keys and Sensitive Data

Keys, secret data, and passwords should be protected using the Data Protection API (DPAPI). Applications must not embed private keys, encrypted or not, in code.

> **Best Practices**   Projects must use DPAPI to store secret data and passwords.

Generating Random Numbers and Cryptographic Keys

Security code and code using cryptographic algorithms require random numbers that exhibit unpredictability. Pseudorandom functions, such as the C runtime function rand or system functions such as GetTickCount, should therefore never be used in such code. Instead, one of the following functions or methods should be used:

- CryptGenRandom (for C/C++ code)
- rand_s (new C runtime library function that calls CryptGenRandom)
- RNGCryptoServiceProvider (for .NET code)
- GetRandom (CAPICOM for script languages)

> **Best Practices**   If a project is using random numbers for cryptographic purposes, it must use CryptGenRandom, rand_s, RNGCryptoServiceProvider, or GetRandom.

Generating Random Numbers and Cryptographic Keys from Passwords or Other Keys

It's sometimes necessary to use a password or other secret data to derive cryptographic keys, typically combined with random data such as a nonce or a salt. Using a password directly as an encryption key is not allowed. Direct hashing of the password should never be used to derive session (ephemeral) keys. Direct hashing of the password should not be used to derive long-term (static) secret or private keys.

The supported way to derive cryptographic keys from passwords or other secret data is to use a well-defined and analyzed key derivation function (KDF) (RFC 2898) such as Crypt-DeriveKey in CAPI and PasswordDeriveBytes or Rfc2898DeriveBytes for .NET code.

> **Best Practices**   If a project derives cryptographic keys from passwords, it needs to use a key derivation function.

References

(Electronic Frontier Foundation 1998)   "Cracking DES," *http://cryptome.org/cracking-des.htm*. First published by O'Reilly & Associates, May 1998.

(Microsoft 2006a)   Microsoft Corporation. .NET Framework Developer's Guide, "Cryptographic Services," *http://msdn.microsoft.com/library/en-us/cpguide/html/ cpconCryptographicServices.asp*. MSDN.

(Microsoft 2006b)   Microsoft Corporation. "Microsoft CryptoAPI System Architecture," *http://msdn.microsoft.com/library/en-us/seccrypto/security/cryptoapi_system_architecture.asp.*

(Microsoft 2001)   Lambert, John. Microsoft Corporation. "Introducing CAPICOM," *http:// msdn.microsoft.com/library/en-us/dnsecure/html/intcapicom.asp.* MSDN, May 2001.

(RFC 2104)   Internet Engineering Task Force, Network Working Group. RFC 2104: "HMAC: Keyed-Hashing for Message Authentication," *http://www.ietf.org/rfc/rfc2104.txt.* February 1997.

(NIST 2005)   National Institute of Standards and Technology. Guideline for Implementing Cryptography in the Federal Government, *http://csrc.nist.gov/publications/nistpubs/ 800-21-1/sp800-21-1_Dec2005.pdf.*

(KeyLength 2006)   KeyLength.com. "Cryptographic Key Length Recommendation," *http:// www.keylength.com.*

(RFC 2898)   Internet Engineering Task Force, Network Working Group. RFC 2898: "PKCS #5: Password-Based Cryptography Specification, Version 2.0," *http://www.ietf.org/rfc/ rfc2898.txt.* September 2000.

Chapter 21

SDL-Required Tools and Compiler Options

This chapter outlines the SDL-mandated security-related tools to be used during the development and testing processes. We focus on tools that are publicly available from Microsoft developer Web sites (such as MSDN) and Microsoft Visual Studio 2005.

Required Tools

At a minimum, the following tools are required during the development process:

- PREfast (Microsoft 2005)
- FxCop (GotDotNet 2006a)
- Application Verifier (Microsoft 2003)
- Minimum compiler and build tool versions

Let's look at each tool in more detail.

PREfast

A product of Microsoft Research, PREfast is a static analysis tool used to detect coding defects in C and C++ code. A subset of these defects is security bugs. PREfast was first made publicly available as part of the Microsoft Windows Server 2003 Driver Development Kit (DDK). The most "usable" version of PREfast is the one in Visual Studio 2005 that is accessible easily through a simple compiler option, */analyze*. Figure 21-1 shows where to set this option.

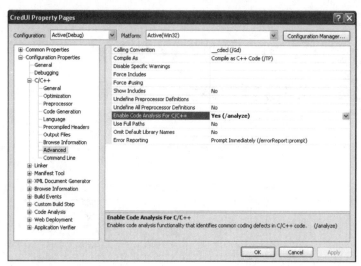

Figure 21-1   Setting the */analyze* option in Visual Studio 2005.

The warnings described in Table 21-1 should be triaged and fixed appropriately in your code.

Table 21-1   Defective-Code Warnings

Warning Number	Description	Sample Defective Code

6011	Dereferencing NULL pointer <ptr>.	<pre>char *p = NULL;
		if (argc == 2)
		    p = argv[1];
		*p = 'A';</pre>

6029	Possible buffer overrun in call to <function>.	<pre>char buff[80];
		DWORD cbLen, cbRead;
		if (!ReadFile (hFile, &cbLen,
		                sizeof (cbLen),
		                &cbRead, NULL)) {
		    return;
		}
		if (!ReadFile (hFile, buff, cbLen,
		                &cbRead, NULL)) {
		    // Error!
		    // Need to check that cbLen <= 80
		    return;
		}</pre>

6053	Call to <function> might not zero-terminate string <variable>.	<pre>char buff[N];
		strncpy(buff, input, N);
		// if strlen(input) > N, buff will not
		// be zero-terminated
		return strlen(buff);
		// possible crash here</pre>

Table 21-1   Defective-Code Warnings

Warning Number	Description	Sample Defective Code
6057	Buffer overrun because of number of characters or bytes mismatched in call to <function>.	```TCHAR buff[128];
LoadString(hInst,
uID,
buff,
sizeof (buff));
// wrong in Unicode case```
6059	Misuse of length parameter in call to <function>.	```char arr[10];
arr[9] = 0;
strncpy(arr, arg1, 9);
strncat(arr, arg2, 10);
// wrong: this says to copy 10 chars```
6063	Format string mismatch.	```char buff[5];
sprintf(buff, "%s %s", "a");```
6067	Format string mismatch.	```char buff[5];
sprintf(buff,
"%s %s",
"a",1);```
6200 and 6201	Buffer overrun for [stack] buffer <variable>.	```char buff[5];
buff[sizeof(buff)] = '\0';```
6202 and 6203	Buffer overrun for [stack] buffer <variable> in call to <function>.	```char charArray[5];
int intArray[5];
memset ((void *)charArray, 0,
sizeof(intArray));```
6204	Possible buffer overrun in call to <function>.	```char buff[10];
strcpy(buff, ptr);```
6248	Setting the DACL of a SECURITY_DESCRIPTOR to NULL will result in an unprotected object.	```SetSecurityDescriptorDacl(pSD,
TRUE,
NULL,
FALSE);```
6255	_alloca indicates failure by raising a stack overflow exception. Consider using an exception handler.	```_alloca(10);```
6259	Labeled code is unreachable.	```switch (i & 3) {
case 0:
case 1:
case 2:
case 3:
// Reachable
break;
case 4:
// Not reachable
break;
default:
break;
}```

Table 21-1 **Defective-Code Warnings**

Warning Number	Description	Sample Defective Code
6260	sizeof * sizeof is usually wrong.	```size_t a = sizeof (L"String")` ` * sizeof (WCHAR);```
6263	Using _alloca in a loop. This can quickly overflow the stack.	```char *b;` `do {` ` b = (char *)_alloca(9);` ` ...` `} while (1);```
6268	Incorrect order of operations.	`int *ptr = (int *)(char *)p + offset;`
6276	Cast between semantically different string types.	```LPWSTR pSrc = (LPWSTR)"a";` `WCHAR szBuffer[2];` `wcscpy(szBuffer,pSrc);```
6277	Dangerous call to <function>: NULL application name and unquoted path. This will result in security vulnerability if the path contains spaces.	```CreateProcess(NULL,` ` "c:\\program files\\foo.exe arg1",` ` ...);```
6281	Incorrect order of operators.	```int x = 3, y = 7, z = 13;` `if (x & y != z) {}```
6282	Incorrect operator.	`while (a = 5) {}`
6287	Redundant code. The left and right subexpressions are identical.	`if ((x != 1) || (x != 1)) {}`
6288	Incorrect operator: Mutual inclusion over && is always FALSE. Was || intended?	`if ((x == 1) && (x == 2)) {}`
6289	Incorrect operator: Mutual exclusion over || is always TRUE. Was && intended?	`if ((x != 1) || (x != 2)) {}`
6290	Bitwise operation on logical result. The ! character has higher precedence than &. Use && or (!(x & y)) instead.	`if (!x & y) {}`
6291	Bitwise operation on logical result. The ! character has higher precedence than |. Use || or (!(x | y)) instead.	`if (!x | y) {}`
6296	Ill-defined FOR loop. Body executed only once.	`for (size_t i = 0; i < 100; i--) { }`

Table 21-1 Defective-Code Warnings

Warning Number	Description	Sample Defective Code
6298	Using a read-only string \<pointer> as a writable string argument. This will attempt to write into static read-only memory and cause random crashes.	```CreateProcessA(NULL, "MyApp.exe -?", // RW NULL, NULL, FALSE, 0, NULL, NULL, &Si, &Pi);```
6299	Explicitly comparing a bit field to a Boolean value will yield unexpected results.	```if (a.flag == 1) {} // Should be -1```
6305	Potential mismatch between sizeof and countof quantities.	```struct S {int a; int b;} *p = (S*)p2; int cb = sizeof(struct S); p += cb; // should be p+=1;```
6306	Incorrect call to \<function>.	```va_list v; va_start(v, pformat); printf(pformat, v); // should be vprintf va_end(v);```
6308	Leaking memory.	```char *c; c = (char *)malloc(10); if (c) c = (char *)realloc(c,512);```
6334	The sizeof operator applied to an expression with an operator might yield unexpected results.	```char a[10]; size_t x = sizeof (a + 1); // should be sizeof(a) + 1```
6383	Buffer overrun because of conversion of an element count into a byte count.	```LPTSTR dest = (LPTSTR)malloc(x * sizeof (TCHAR)); if (dest) _tcsncpy(dest, src, x * sizeof (TCHAR)); // drop the * sizeof```

FxCop

FxCop is a code-analysis tool that checks .NET-managed code assemblies for conformance with the Microsoft .NET Framework design guidelines, including common security issues specific to managed code. The following FxCop security rules (GotDotNet 2006b) should be triaged and fixed appropriately:

- *AllowPartiallyTrustedCallers* attribute (APTCA) methods should call only APTCA methods.

- APTCA types should extend only APTCA base types.

- Array fields should not be read-only.

- Call GC.KeepAlive when using native resources.

- Catch non-CLSCompliant exceptions in general handlers.

- Do not declare read-only mutable reference types.

- Do not indirectly expose methods with link demands.

- Method security should be a superset of type.

- Override link demands should be identical to base.

- Pointers should not be visible.

- Review declarative security on value types.

- Review deny-only and permit-only usage.

- Review imperative security.

- Review Structured Query Language (SQL) queries for security vulnerabilities.

- Review suppress-unmanaged code security usage.

- Review visible event handlers.

- Seal methods that satisfy private interfaces.

- Secure asserts.

- Secure GetObjectData overrides.

- Secure late-binding methods.

- Secure serialization constructors.

- Secured types should not expose fields.

- Specify marshaling for PInvoke string arguments.

- Static constructors should be private.

- Type-link demands require inheritance demands.

- Wrap vulnerable finally clauses in an outer try.

Figure 21-2 shows FxCop in Visual Studio 2005.

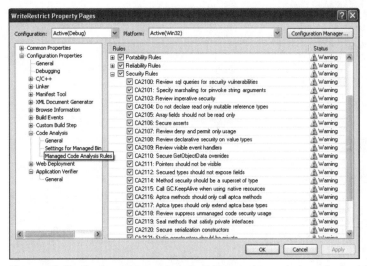

Figure 21-2   Setting managed-code FxCop code-analysis options within Visual Studio 2005.

Application Verifier

Application Verifier (AppVerif) is a runtime verification tool for unmanaged (in other words, not .NET) code. It assists developers in quickly finding subtle programming errors that can be extremely difficult to identify with normal application testing. AppVerif helps you create reliable applications by monitoring an application's interaction with the Windows operating system and profiling its use of kernel objects, the registry, the file system, and Microsoft Win32 application programming interfaces (APIs; these include heap, handles, locks, and more). AppVerif, originally designed to help uncover application errors early—especially application compatibility issues—works by intercepting function calls from the application under test and looking for erroneous behavior.

Microsoft offers two versions of AppVerif. One is included with Visual Studio 2005, and the other is available as a free download. Each has advantages over the other; the version built into Visual Studio 2005 is easier to use because it's simply part of the build-and-execution process (just build your application and select Debug and then Start by using AppVerif). The standalone downloadable version has a higher learning curve but provides many more security-related options and performs a more comprehensive review of your code. Figures 21-3 and 21-4 show the Visual Studio 2005 AppVerif options and the standalone version of AppVerif.

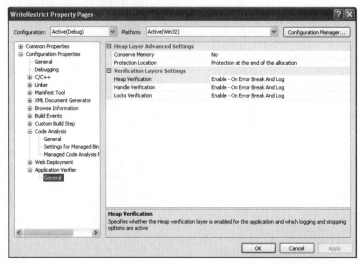

Figure 21-3   AppVerif configuration options in Visual Studio 2005.

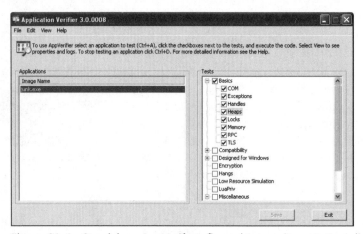

Figure 21-4   Standalone AppVerif configured to monitor a test application at run time.

From the command-line prompt, you can also set up an application to run under AppVerif by entering the following code:

```
appverif /verify MyApp.exe
```

The */verify* option will enable all the base checks:

■ **Handles**   Detects erroneous use of handles, including NULL, closed, and uninitialized handles.

■ **Locks**   Checks for issues that might lead to deadlocks when you use synchronization methods such as the critical section method.

■ **Exceptions**   Detects first-chance exceptions. This helps ensure that applications do not use structured exception handling to hide access violations.

■ **Heap**   Checks for heap overruns and underruns, double-free, and corruption.

> **Best Practices**   It is *highly* recommended that you perform all your tests by using AppVerif. Doing so helps detect numerous subtle and hard-to-find defects quickly. This recommendation applies especially to malformed input tests such as fuzz tests.

When you are finished running all your tests, you can enter the following command to turn off checking:

```
appverif /n MyApp.exe
```

You must run your application with all base checks enabled; this is what the Visual Studio 2005 version does. If using the standalone version, also enable all Security checks.

Minimum Compiler and Build Tool Versions

As security threats evolve, tool vendors should continue to add defenses to the tools used to build software. Microsoft has done this continually over the last few years by upgrading the core set of compilers and ancillary tools, especially those found in the core development suite, Microsoft Visual Studio. Table 21-2 outlines the required minimum versions for various development tools and the rationale for each tool version.

Table 21-2 Minimum Development-Tool Versions

Tool	Minimum version	Recommended version and version benefit
C/C++ compiler (cl.exe)	Visual Studio .NET 2003 13.10.3077.0	Visual Studio 2005 14.00 Improved stack-based buffer overrun detection (Microsoft 2004)
Linker (link.exe)	7.10.3077.0	8.0 Improved exception handling support (*/SafeSEH*) (Microsoft 2006)
RPC and COM IDL compiler (midl.exe)	6.0.361.1	6.0.366 Improved RPC run-time stub code
Microsoft Visual C# compiler (csc.exe)	Visual Studio .NET 2003 7.10	Visual Studio 2005 8.00
Microsoft Visual Basic (vbc.exe)	Visual Studio .NET 2003 7.10	Visual Studio 2005 8.00

Unmanaged Compiler Flags

All unmanaged code (Win32 C and C++) must be compiled with the */GS* flag and linked with the */SafeSEH* flag. It is highly recommended that prerelease debug code be compiled with the */RTC1* and */RTCc* run-time check options. These options perform the tasks described in the following table.

Flag	Description
/RTC1	The same as */RTCsu*: ■ Detects overrun and underrun of local arrays. ■ Performs stack-pointer verification. ■ Sets local variables to nonzero, which can help you find bugs that don't appear in debug mode.
/RTCc	Reports when a value is assigned to a smaller data type. Can help find some forms of integer arithmetic issues caused by data truncation.

Finally, for new code, you should consider using the */W4* warning level. Again, this can help you detect some forms of subtle issues. New code should compile with no warnings at this level.

References

(Microsoft 2005)   "PREfast Step-by-Step," *http://www.microsoft.com/whdc/DevTools/tools/PREfast_steps.mspx*. April 2005.

(GotDotNet 2006a)   Microsoft Corporation. FxCop download, *http://www.gotdotnet.com/team/fxcop*.

(Microsoft 2003)   "Microsoft Application Verifier," *http://www.microsoft.com/technet/prodtechnol/windows/appcompatibility/AppVerif.mspx*. TechNet, May 2003.

(GotDotNet 2006b)   Microsoft Corporation. FxCop Documentation, "Security Rules," *http://gotdotnet.com/team/fxcop/Docs/Rules/Security.html*.

(Microsoft 2004)   Gregory, Kate, Gregory Consulting. "Security Checks at Runtime and Compile Time," *http://msdn.microsoft.com/library/en-us/dv_vstechart/html/securitychecks.asp*. MSDN, April 2004.

(Microsoft 2006)   Visual C++ Linker Options, "/SafeSEH (Image Safe Exception Handlers," *http://msdn.microsoft.com/library/en-us/vccore/html/vclrfsafesehimagehassafeexception-handlers.asp*. TechNet, 2006.

Chapter 22

Threat Tree Patterns

In Chapter 9, "Stage 4: Risk Analysis," we mentioned threat trees that reflect common attack patterns and help application designers think about security conditions in the system. This chapter itemizes the threat tree patterns and discusses what you should think about when designing and testing an application.

Chapter 9 presented an important table—Table 9-5, "Mapping STRIDE to DFD Element Types"—that is repeated here. The table shows the threat types (STRIDE) that apply to each data flow diagram (DFD) element type.

DFD Element Type	S	T	R	I	D	E
External Entity	X		X			
Data Flow		X		X	X	
Data Store		X	†	X	X	
Process	X	X	X	X	X	X

The dagger mark (†) in this table indicates a specific kind of data store, notably a data store that records logging or auditing data. This kind of data store is subject to repudiation threats because an attacker might attempt to cover his tracks by modifying or erasing the data.

For each valid intersection in the table, a threat tree shows the possible security-related preconditions for that STRIDE category. The leaf nodes of each tree can aid in secure design and security testing.

In this chapter, we'll look at each tree as well as associated design and security questions. Note that some trees cascade. For example, the tree in Figure 22-1 shows the conditions that could lead to spoofing threats against an external entity or a process. The circle at the right in Figure 22-1 shows tampering threats against the authentication process. This means that someone can indirectly spoof, say, a user by attacking the process that determines whether the user is who she claims to be. In some scenarios, this is a valid attack path.

For every threat in your threat models, you should consult this chapter for the appropriate threat tree and its accompanying table—each threat tree is followed by a related table—to confirm that you have considered all the appropriate design and testing concepts.

Spoofing an External Entity or a Process

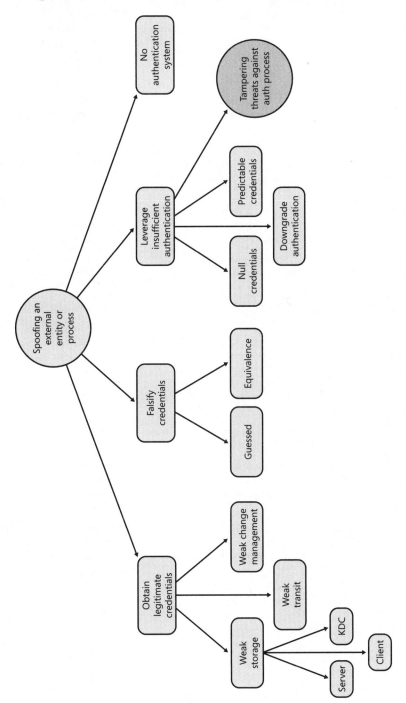

Figure 22-1   Threat tree for spoofing an external entity or a process.

Table 22-1   Design and Test Considerations: Spoofing External Entity or Process

Leaf Node	Design	Test
Weak server-credential storage	Are credentials held at the server? If yes, how are they protected?	Probe any place where credentials may be stored to see if the credentials are well protected. Determine how the information is encrypted and where the encryption keys are stored. Set a known credential and then scour storage for that credential.
Weak client-credential storage	Are credentials held at the client? If yes, how are they protected?	See above.
Weak key-distribution-center (KDC) storage	Do you have a key-distribution center? If yes, how are the credentials protected?	See above.
Weak credential transit	How are credentials transmitted between two endpoints?	Update or set a known credential and then listen on the wire for that credential.
Weak credential-change management	What is the protocol for updating a credential? How secure is it? Who reviewed it?	Set a known credential and then listen on the wire for that credential.
Guess credential	What is the credential complexity policy? Is it adequate? Is there an incorrect credential time-out?	Try brute-forcing credentials.
Credential equivalence	Could two or more credentials be treated to the same credential?	This is hard to test without using an exhaustive key-space attack.
Null credential	Does your application support a null credential or an account with no password?	Try making an anonymous connection or a connection with no password.
Downgrade authentication	Does your application support an older and less-secure authentication scheme? If yes, is the scheme enabled by default? If yes, why?	Build a client or server that negotiates with the older protocol and then revisit the spoofing threat tree using the downgraded scheme.

Table 22-1   Design and Test Considerations: Spoofing External Entity or Process

Leaf Node	Design	Test
Predictable credential	How random is the credential? A good example of a predictable credential is a cookie-based authentication scheme that uses incrementing values to identify users.	If the endpoint creates a credential, connect, look at the cookie, and then connect with another computer and look at the credential. Can you see a pattern in the credential?
No authentication scheme	Do you really need to forgo an authentication scheme?	Determine the amount of data an unauthenticated user could gather or which assets that user could access. Can that user access more than he or she should?

Tampering with a Process

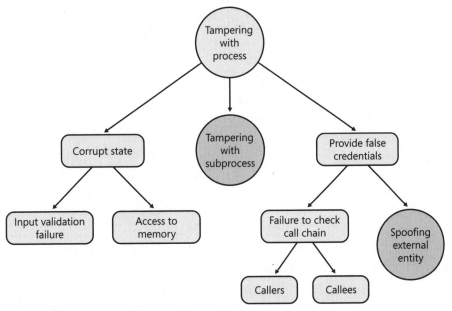

Figure 22-2   Threat tree for tampering with a process.

Table 22-2   Design and Test Considerations: Tampering with a Process

Leaf Node	Design	Test
Input validation failure	Is all input verified for correctness?	Fuzz testing is an effective testing technique for input validation issues.
Access to memory	This is hard to defend against, but for some processes, perhaps you need to defend against corruption of internal state. Examples of memory access issues include protecting against local administrators using debuggers. If you do not want to defend against this scenario, call the scenario out as an assumption in the threat model: you're not protecting your application from administrators with debuggers!	Using a debugger, determine what privileges are required to corrupt the internal application state. Again, this attack might be out of scope, so verify that it is out of scope in the threat model.
Callers	Do you trust code that calls your code? For example, do you have a LinkDemand (Microsoft 2005a) on your code that does not require the caller's caller to have the permissions you are link demanding?	Try mounting a luring attack (Brown 2001).
Callees	Do you trust the code you call? For example, your code may call code that uses CodeAccessPermission.Assert insecurely (Microsoft 2005b).	If the application has extensibility mechanisms, build a component that uses Assert to use a permission in an insecure manner.

Tampering with a Data Flow

You'll notice that the threat tree in Figure 22-3 references the message and the channel. The message is the data that travels across a channel, and you can opt to protect the message itself from attack or to use a protected channel. For example, you could decide to use an application-level digital signature on the message to protect the message, or you could use SSL/TLS (Secure Sockets Layer/Transport Layer Security) to provide integrity protection through the use of message authentication codes.

Finally, there is some philosophical debate in the author's team about whether tampering with a data flow requires you to tamper with the message *and* the channel or the message *or* the channel. For the moment, we're leaving it as an "or" condition.

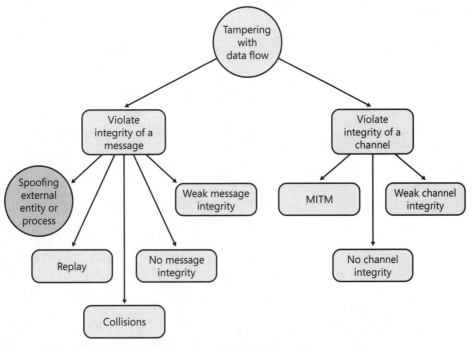

Figure 22-3   Threat tree for tampering with a data flow.

Table 22-3   Design and Test Considerations: Tampering with a Data Flow

Leaf Node	Design	Test
Replay	Is the dataflow defended (hashed, MAC'd, or signed) using antireplay defenses such as time stamps or counters?	Replay valid messages.
Collisions	See above.	See above.
No message integrity	Why is there no message integrity? Does this component's DFD include an unmitigated threat that should be fixed?	Fuzz the messages.
Weak message integrity	How good is the message-integrity algorithm, technology, or protocol? Is it appropriate?	See above.
Violated channel through man-in-the-middle (MITM)	Is the channel protected by an appropriate integrity technology?	Fuzz the channel.
No channel integrity	Why is there no channel integrity? Does this component's DFD include an unmitigated threat that should be fixed?	See above.
Weak channel integrity	How good is the channel-integrity algorithm, technology, or protocol? Is it appropriate?	See above.

Tampering with a Data Store

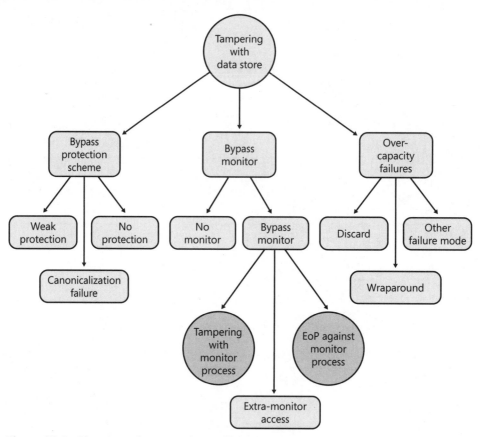

Figure 22-4   Threat tree for tampering with a data store.

Table 22-4   Design and Test Considerations: Tampering with a Data Store

Leaf Node	Design	Test
No protection	Why is there no protection scheme? Is this by design?	There is nothing to test.
Canonicalization failure	Does any code rely on a name, such as a file name, to determine access? If yes, make sure the code looks for only valid names and does not filter out illegal names.	Try malforming names, trailing dots, trailing spaces, device names, and so on (Howard, LeBlanc, and Viega 2005).

Table 22-4   Design and Test Considerations: Tampering with a Data Store

Leaf Node	Design	Test
Weak protection	Look at the permissions on all objects to determine whether they offer the correct level of protection.	Determine whether compromising the data store as a subject associated with the permission set could lead to application failure. You have a problem if the application consuming the data store fails and has higher privilege than the subject that is able to tamper with the data store.
No monitor	Is the data store on a system that does not support access checks or semantic checks? An example of a semantically different data is numeric versus alphabetic data; they are both made of ASCII or Unicode characters, but they each have a different meaning.	For semantic checks, test to determine whether type checks exist.
Extra-monitor access	Is all access to the data store throttled through one entry point? Is all access totally mediated?	Can you access the data store without following the process governing access? For example, if an application has logic to grant or deny access to the store, can you access the data store through other means, such as FTP or file sharing?
Discard	When the data store is full, is data discarded? If so, why?	Observe what happens when the data store is flooded.
Wraparound	When the data store is full, is data written to the beginning of the data store? If so, why?	See above.
Other failure mode	When the data store is full, is data dropped and not written to the store? Does the application crash? In some cases, a crash may be appropriate if a critical security log is full.	See above.

Repudiation

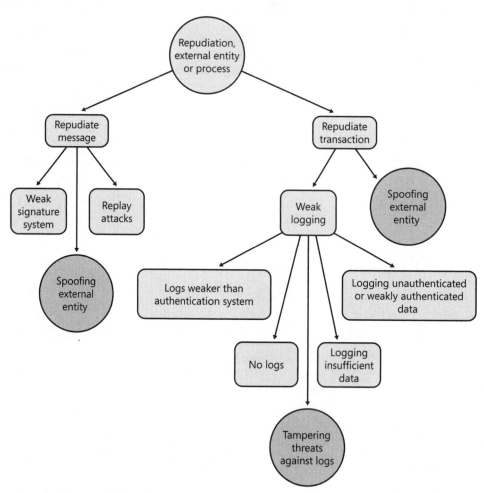

Figure 22-5   Repudiation threat tree.

Table 22-5   Design and Test Considerations: Repudiation

Leaf Node	Design	Test
Weak signature system	If you are using digital signatures, is the system strong? Consider having a security expert or cryptographer review the design. Where are the private keys stored, and how well protected are they?	Can you access the private keys associated with the signatures? Make sure each signature covers every bit of data you intend it to, and make sure that the signature is invalid when any bit of data is changed. For an example of this kind of failure: (GNU Privacy Guard 2006).
Replay attacks	See "Replay" in Table 22-3.	See "Replay" in Table 22-3.
No logs	Why are there no logs?	There is nothing to test.
Logs weaker than the authentication system	The logging system should be written to only by trusted code, and less-trusted users should be unable to write directly to the log files.	Try writing to the log files directly.
Logging unauthenticated or weakly authenticated data	Data written to logs should be reliable and generated by the application performing the logging.	Try generating requests of the application performing logging to determine whether you can write arbitrary data that might make it difficult to understand the data. A good example of this kind of issue is found in Apache 1.3.x (CVE 2003).
Logging insufficient data	It's important to log appropriate data to aid in supporting repudiation claims. Are you logging enough data? You might want to talk to a computer-forensics expert or computer-auditing expert to determine an appropriate level of logging.	There is nothing to test.

Information Disclosure of a Process

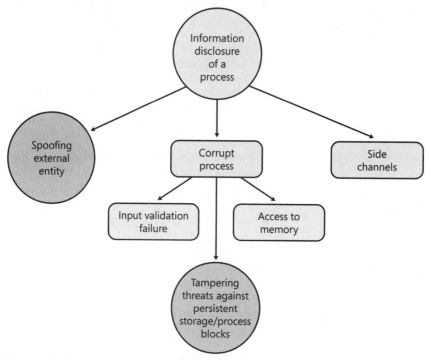

Figure 22-6   Threat tree for information disclosure of a process.

Table 22-6   Design and Test Considerations: Information Disclosure of a Process

Leaf Node	Design	Test
Input validation failure	See "Input validation failure" in Table 22-2.	See "Input validation failure" in Table 22-2.
Access to memory	See "Access to memory" in Table 22-2.	See "Access to memory" in Table 22-2.
Side channels	Could any side channels (Wikipedia 2006) disclose data? An example of a side channel is the existence of a special file, which means the process handles certain sensitive data. For a discussion of other examples of side channels: (CERT 2001, Anley 2002, CERT 2002a, CERT 2003, Lucas 2005, SecuriTeam 2005, Mimoso 2006).	Side channels can be hard to test for; a best practice is to review past side-channel exploitations (see the list in the Design column in this table) to determine whether they could occur in your software.

Information Disclosure of a Data Flow

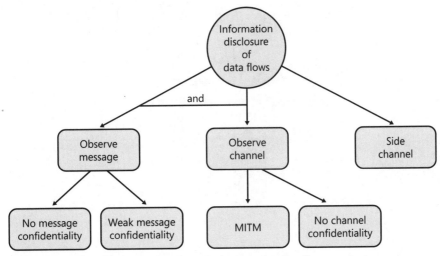

Figure 22-7   Threat tree information disclosure of a data flow.

Table 22-7   Design and Test Considerations: Information Disclosure of a Data Flow

Leaf node	Design	Test
No message confidentiality	Why is there no message confidentiality? What is the impact if the data is disclosed?	Can you view any sensitive data that should be protected?
Weak message confidentiality	Is the data well defended? What cryptographic algorithms are used, and where are the keys stored?	Can you access the keys, or is the encryption really "encraption"?
Channel observable through man-in-the-middle (MITM)	If a rogue listener can be placed between two endpoints on the data flow, can the listener read the data?	Build a man-in-the-middle tool, perhaps a proxy, to listen and potentially read the data.
No channel confidentiality	Why is there no channel confidentiality? What is the impact if the data is disclosed?	Can you view sensitive data that should be protected?
Side channels	See "Side channels" in Table 22-6.	See "Side channels" in Table 22-6.

Information Disclosure of a Data Store

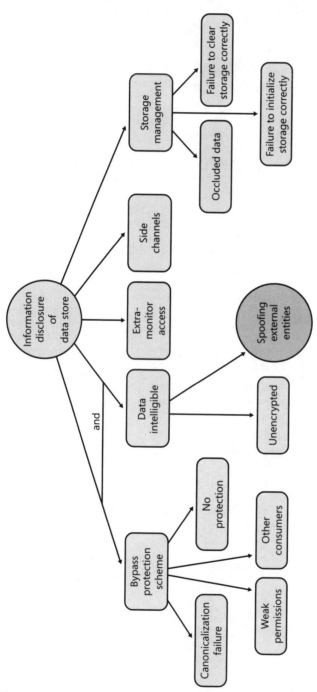

Figure 22-8 Threat tree for information disclosure of a data store.

Table 22-8   Design and Test Considerations: Information Disclosure of a Data Store

Leaf Node	Design	Test
Canonicalization failure	See "Canonicalization failure" in Table 22-4.	See "Canonicalization failure" in Table 22-4.
Weak protection	See "Weak protection" in Table 22-4.	See "Weak protection" in Table 22-4.
Other consumers	Are there data-store consumers other than this application (for example, indexing or searching applications)?	Can you use other methods (such as search engines) to reveal the protected data?
No protection	See "No protection" in Table 22-4.	See "No protection" in Table 22-4.
No encryption	If the data is not encrypted, are other protections good enough?	Is the data viewable in the data store when accessed using a simple hex-dump tool?
Extra-monitor access	See "Extramonitor access" in Table 22-4.	See "Extramonitor access" in Table 22-4.
Side channels	See "Side channels" in Table 22-6.	See "Side channels" in Table 22-6.
Occluded data	Does your application support undo or recovery operations? Does it support object properties that might contain sensitive data? If so, how will you erase this data? For a good reference for dealing with these issues: (National Security Agency 2006).	If the application supports "hiding" data, enter some known text, hide the data, and then search the file on disk for the data. Although the data might not be visible in the application, it might be visible when you perform a binary scan.
Failure to initialize storage correctly	Is storage in the data store set to a known value before use? If not, why? Setting data to a known value is rarely a performance issue.	If possible, set a known data value in the uninitialized data store. Then when the application runs, find out if you can still read the data.
Failure to clear storage correctly	Is storage in the data store set to a known value after use? If not, why? Setting data to a known value is rarely a performance issue.	Set data to a known value. When the application has finished using the data, scour the data store to see if the data is still there. For interesting examples of failure to scrub data correctly: (Howard 2002, Chow et al. 2005).

Note   Some information disclosure threats can be privacy issues if the data being disclosed is private or personally identifiable information (PII). Refer to Chapter 8, "Stage 3: Product Risk Assessment," for more information on the subject.

Denial of Service Against a Process

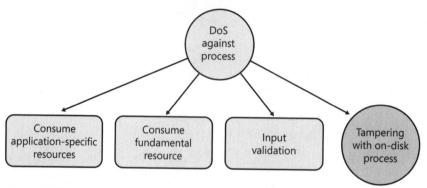

Figure 22-9   Threat tree for denial of service against a process.

Table 22-9   Design and Test Considerations: Denial of Service Against a Process

Leaf Node	Design	Test
Application-specific resource consumption	Are there limits on application-specific resource consumption? Can unprivileged users consume large quantities of such resources? For a good example of malicious resource consumption: (CERT 2002b).	Identify all application-specific resources and determine what privilege level is required to consume the resources. There are issues if low-trust or anonymous users can consume large quantities of application-specific resources.
Fundamental resource consumption	Are there limits on fundamental resource consumption, such as memory, CPU, network bandwidth, or disk space? Can unprivileged users consume large quantities of such resources?	Attempt to consume large quantities of fundamental resources as an untrusted user.
Input validation	Is all input validated for correctness? Input validation is a broader variation of the canonicalization issues noted previously, because even valid input could trigger infinite recursions or cause the application to consume large amounts of CPU time.	Do intelligent fuzz testing.

Denial of Service Against a Data Flow

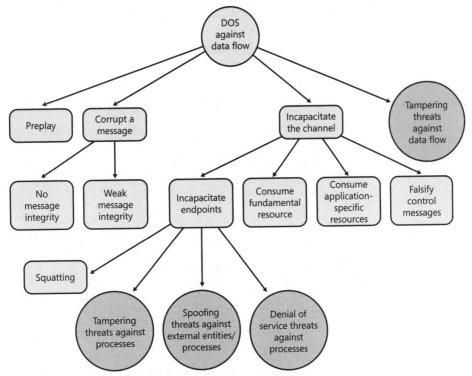

Figure 22-10   Threat tree for denial of service against a data flow.

Table 22-10   Design and Test Considerations: Denial of Service Against a Data Flow

Leaf Node	Design	Test
Preplay	An adversary makes a preplay attack when she performs an action before the valid application does so. How does your application respond to such attacks? How do you ensure that the action is performed by a valid user and not an attacker?	Build tests that perform partial communication. Then have another computer or process inject the continuation of the protocol.
No message integrity	See "No message integrity" in Table 22-3.	See "No message integrity" in Table 22-3.
Weak message integrity	See "Weak message integrity" in Table 22-3.	See "Weak message integrity" in Table 22-3.
Squatting	Can the data flow name (pipe name, for example) be hijacked or squatted?	Get a list of all the data flow names used by the application, create all these names ahead of time, and then start the application to see if the data flows are valid.

Table 22-10   Design and Test Considerations: Denial of Service Against a Data Flow

Leaf Node	Design	Test
Fundamental resources consumption	See "Fundamental resources consumption" in Table 22-9.	See "Fundamental resources consumption" in Table 22-9.
Application-specific resources consumption	See "Application-specific resources consumption" in Table 22-9.	See "Application-specific resources consumption" in Table 22-9.
Falsified control messages	Does the application use any messages to control the flow of data across the data flow? Is there a state-machine or transition diagram (Young 2000) used to determine the correct flow order? If so, how well is the state-machine followed?	Get a list of control messages used by the application protocols and then fuzz them. Don't fuzz the message data; just fuzz the control messages, or create out-of-order messages or incorrect messages. Also, if there is a state-machine, try to build messages that violate the normal transition flow.

Denial of Service Against a Data Store

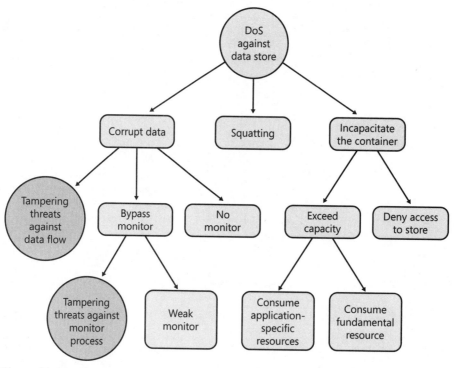

Figure 22-11   Threat tree for denial of service against a data store.

Table 22-11   Design and Test Considerations: Denial of Service Against a Data Store

Leaf Node	Design	Test
Weak protection	See "Weak protection" in Table 22-4.	See "Weak protection" in Table 22-4.
No protection	See "No monitor" in Table 22-4.	See "No monitor" in Table 22-4.
Squatting	See "Squatting" in Table 22-12.	See "Squatting" in Table 22-12.
Fundamental resources consumption	See "Fundamental resources consumption" in Table 22-9.	See "Fundamental resources consumption" in Table 22-9.
Application-specific resources consumption	See "Application-specific resources consumption" in Table 22-9.	See "Application-specific resources consumption" in Table 22-9.
Deny access to store	What happens if the application is denied access to the data store? Is there a permission on the object that allows untrusted users to deny access to or lock the file?	Try denying access to the file (for example, in Microsoft Windows, by setting an Everyone Deny-All ACE to the data store), or try locking the data source.

Elevation of Privilege

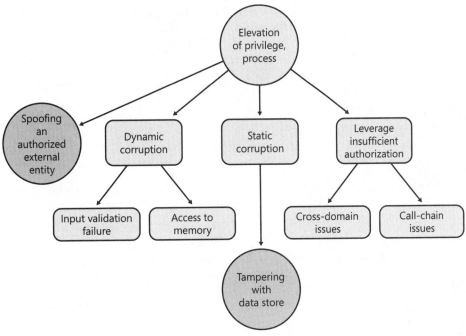

Figure 22-12   Threat tree for elevation of privilege.

Table 22-12   **Design and Test Considerations: Elevation of Privilege**

Leaf Node	Design	Test
Input validation failure	See "Input validation failure" in Table 22-2.	See "Input validation failure" in Table 22-2.
Access to memory	See "Access to memory" in Table 22-2.	See "Access to memory" in Table 22-2.
Cross-domain issues	Applications that host potentially malicious script from the Internet enforce a security model, often called the cross-domain security model or same-origin policy. All Web browsers do this, as do application frameworks like Java and Microsoft .NET Framework. The cross-domain security model prevents script and code that originated from one domain from interacting with content from another domain. The intention is to prevent script from a malicious Web site from having access to content from Hotmail.com in the security context of the user accessing Hotmail.com.	Can the application host multiple instances of a Web browser rendering engine? If so, can script running in one instance of the Web browser manipulate the other Web browser instance? If your application has an object model accessible to script running in a Web browser, how can malicious script from the Internet abuse the object model?
Call-chain issues	See "Callers" and "Callees" in Table 22-2.	See "Callers" and "Callees" in Table 22-2.

References

(Microsoft 2005a)   .NET Framework Developer's Guide, "Demand vs. LinkDemand," *http:// msdn2.microsoft.com/en-us/library/3ky50t49.aspx*. MSDN, 2005.

(Brown 2001)   Brown, Keith. "Security in .NET: Enforce Code Access Rights with the Common Language Runtime," *http://msdn.microsoft.com/msdnmag/issues/01/02/cas/*. *MSDN Magazine*, February 2001.

(Microsoft 2005b)   .NET Framework Developer's Guide, "Using the Assert Method," *http:// msdn2.microsoft.com/en-us/library/91wteedy.aspx*. MSDN, 2005.

(Howard, LeBlanc, and Viega 2005)   Howard, Michael, David LeBlanc, and John Viega. *19 Deadly Sins of Software Development*. New York, NY: McGraw-Hill, 2005. Chapter 15, "Improper File Access."

(GNU Privacy Guard 2006)   Koch, Werner. "GnuPG does not detect injection of unsigned data," *http://lists.gnupg.org/pipermail/gnupg-announce/2006q1/000216.html*. March 2006.

(CVE-2003-0020)   Common Vulnerabilities and Exposures. "Terminal Emulator Security Issues," *http://cve.mitre.org/cgi-bin/cvename.cgi?name=CVE-2003-0020.*

(Wikipedia 2006)   "Side channel attack," *http://en.wikipedia.org/wiki/Side-channel_attack.*

(CERT 2001)   US-CERT. "Vulnerability Note VU#959207, Lotus Notes Java VM leaks file existence through timing difference in ECLs," *http://www.kb.cert.org/vuls/id/959207.* May 2001.

(Anley 2002)   Anley, Chris, NGSSoftware. "(more) Advanced SQL Injection," *http://www.ngssoftware.com/papers/more_advanced_sql_injection.pdf.* June 2002.

(CERT 2002a)   US-CERT. "Vulnerability Note VU#156123, Microsoft Office Web Components allow arbitrary user to determine whether local file exists via Chart component 'Load' method," *http://www.kb.cert.org/vuls/id/156123.* September 2002.

(CERT 2003)   US-CERT. "Vulnerability Note VU#888801, SSL/TLS implementations disclose side channel information via PKCS #1 v1.5 version number extension," *http://www.kb.cert.org/vuls/id/888801.* April 2003.

(Lucas 2005)   Lucas, Michael W. "Information Security with Colin Percival," *http://www.onlamp.com/pub/a/bsd/2005/07/21/Big_Scary_Daemons.html.* July 2005.

(SecuriTeam 2005)   SecuriTeam Blog. "Side-channel attacks and listening to keyboards," *http://blogs.securiteam.com/index.php/archives/89.* September 2005.

(Mimoso 2006)   Mimoso, Michael, SearchSecurity.com. "Crypto panel takes on RFID, bashed hash functions," *http://searchsecurity.techtarget.com/originalContent/0,289142,sid14_gci1166550,00.html.* February 2006.

(National Security Agency 2006)   "Report # I333-015R-2005, Redacting with Confidence: How to Safely Publish Sanitized Reports Converted from Word to PDF," *http://www.nsa.gov/notices/notic00004.cfm?Address=/snac/vtechrep/I333-TR-015R-2005.PDF.* February 2006.

(Howard 2002)   "Some Bad News and Some Good News," *http://msdn.microsoft.com/library/en-us/dncode/html/secure10102002.asp.* MSDN, October 2002.

(Chow et al. 2005)   Chow, Jim, Ben Pfaff, Tal Garfinkel, and Mendel Rosenblum,   Stanford University Department of Computer Science. "Shredding Your Garbage: Reducing Data Lifetime Through Secure Deallocation," *http://www.stanford.edu/~blp/papers/shredding.html/.* 14th USENIX Security Symposium, July/August 2005.

(CERT 2002b)   US-CERT. "Vulnerability Note VU#539363, State-based firewalls fail to effectively manage session table resource exhaustion," *http://www.kb.cert.org/vuls/id/539363.* October 2002.

(Young 2000)   Young, Warren. Winsock Programmer's FAQ. "Debugging TCP/IP," *http://tangentsoft.net/wskfaq/articles/debugging-tcp.html.*

Index

Number

3DES, 254. *See also* DES

A

access control lists. *See* ACLs
access controls, code setting, 173
access, restricting, 106
access violations, not using structured exception handling to hide, 267
accessibility, increasing attack surface, 82
accounts
    adding users to the local administrator's group, 137
    creating with limited privileges, 84
acknowledgements to security researchers, 200
ACLs (access control lists)
    configuring, 108
    creating an empty, 149
    examples of weak, 85
    reviewing, 85
    verifying for every object, 176
ActiveX code vs. .NET, 85
ActiveX controls
    arguments to, 163
    larger attack surface of, 85
    marked safe for scripting, 85
    marked safe for scripting vs. not, 87
    reviewing methods and properties on, 96
    SiteLocked, 86
    uninstalling XCP DRM software, 85–86
ActiveX developer, restricting to the SiteLocking control, 86
ad hoc remote queries, 88
adaptability under Agile methods, 234
AdjustTokenPrivileges, calling, 84
administrator
    as all-powerful in Windows, 107
    vs. authenticated user access, 87
    not handling any user requests in IIS6, 84
    operating a computer as, 7
    running code, 87
administrators. *See also* network administrators
    accessibility to authenticated users vs., 121
    giving help in controlling systems, 134
Administrators group, excluding, 84
adversaries, making security researchers into, 200
AES block encryption algorithm, 254
Agile design philosophy, 227
Agile doctrines, listing of, 234–235
Agile environment, development and test tools, 238

Agile methods, 22
    augmenting the rules and practices of, 225
    augmenting with SDL practices, 234–239
    integrating SDL with, 225–239
    no employing full-fledged FSR, 232
    up-front groundwork required by, 226
    using SDL practices with, 226–234
Alert and Mobilize phase of the SSIRP, 207
Allchin, Jim, 12, 45
_alloca in a loop warning in PREfast, 262
AllowPartiallyTrustedCallers attribute (APTCA)
    increasing the attack surface of code, 86
    security rule in FxCop, 263
    strong-named assemblies marked with, 86
always-on computer, automatic updates enabled, 135
amplification of DoS threats, 124
analysis tools. *See* source-code analysis tools
analytical threat-modeling technique, 229
/analyze compiler option in Visual Studio 2005, 259
/Analyze feature in Visual Studio 2005, 33
analyze step of the model-building process, 104
anonymous access
    vs. authenticated user access, 86
    blocking by default, 198
anonymous data, 96
anonymous Internet attacks, 4
anonymous network-facing interfaces, 175
anonymous users
    accessibility to, 121
    consuming resources, 284
    products primarily accessed by, 105
antivirus vendors, 207
Apache
    attacks on, 11
    as the most compromised Web server on the Internet, 133
    privilege model on *nix, 84
    version 2.0 having more security bugs than Apache 1.3, 20
apache account, 84
APIs (application programming interfaces)
    banned, 242–245
    dangerous, 158
    Microsoft security bulletins involving banned, 241
    miscellaneous parsers and, 154
    not using banned, 229
    replacing banned with safer, 237
Application Compatibility Toolset, AppVerif in, 158
application vendors, unaware of security issues, 5
Application Verifier. *See* AppVerif test tool

model-building process, 104
modes for symmetric algorithms, 255
modules, modeling smaller, 104
monetary value, assigning to the risk of disclosing data, 6
Moore's Law, 251
moving people around doctrine, 236
MS-DOS, designed as single-user operating systems, 27
MSDN (Microsoft Developer Network)
    documentation in, 138
    programming language-specific guidance, 138
MSF for Agile Software Development, 22
MSN
    Anti-Phishing add-in, 225
    Messenger 7.5, 225
    projects as rapidly developed small releases, 225
    projects delivered using Agile methods, 225
    Support tools, 225
    Tabbed Browsing for Microsoft Internet, 225
    teams, 226, 231
MSRC (Microsoft Security Response Center)
    anticipating press questions, 203
    content produced by, 202
    dealing with all externally discovered vulnerabilities, 190
    identifying duty officers, 200
    initiating press outreach, 205
    initiating the Watch phase of SSIRP, 206
    maintaining emergency contact information, 209
    preceded by the Security Response Team, 30
    reaching out to the press proactively, 203
    releasing and testing updates, 221
    security bulletin rankings, 121
    Security Bulletin Rating System, 196
    working with partners, 207
multilayer defenses, 82
multiprocess DFD element type, 110
Must Fix bug bar category, 163, 164
Must Investigate bug bar category, 163, 164
MySQL ALTER TABLE/RENAME Forces Old Permission Checks, 146
MySQL, security bugs, 146

N

n-byte data format for a PNG chunk, 156
n functions
    as hard to secure, 243
    reasons for banning, 245
n scanf functions, 244
n sprintf functions, 243
n string concatenation functions, 243
n string copy functions, 243
names of functions, 242
national governments, seeking to steal secrets or disrupt systems or networks, 193
National Vulnerability Database, 44
native authentication schemes, 108

negative values, setting numeric data to, 156
.NET code
    vs. ActiveX code, 85
    cryptography class libraries defined in, 252
    SHA-2 hash functions available in, 256
.NET common language runtime. See CLR
.NET Framework
    checking managed code assemblies for conformance, 263
    making as secure as possible, 34
    security updates addressing externally discovered vulnerabilities, 47–48
    ship schedule delayed for, 47–48
Netscape, early discoveries of vulnerabilities in, 29
network accessibility
    reducing, 87
    reducing in SQL Server 2005, 89
    restricting by a configuration switch, 83
network administrators, 176. See also administrators
network connections. See also connections
    open vs. closed, 86
network entry points. See also entry points
    restricting, 176
network fuzzing. See fuzzing
network protocol format, building malformed packets based on, 160
network protocols
    building fuzzers for complex, 161
    fuzzing, 160–163
    parsing, 154
    reaching deep parts of, 160
    using standard, 251
Network Service
    account in IIS6, 84
    main SQL Server process running as, 88
    using in place of Local System, 84
network traffic, fuzzing, 160
Neumann, Peter, 20
Nimda worm, 33, 133
*nix
    bad design constructs including symbolic-link errors, 149
    creating a special group for the application, 84
    daemon processes, 83
    reviewing code setting permissions, 85
    variants, 248
NNTP, turning off by default, 87
nobody account, 84
noise, mistaking for real bugs, 146
non-repudiation, 115
non-repudiation services
    mitigation technique against repudiation, 125
    mitigation technique technologies, 126
non-security fix, 199
nonce, 257
Not a Security Bug predefined value, 72, 73
Not acceptable (1) rating for a threat model, 129

Michael Howard

Michael Howard, CISSP, is a Senior Security Program Manager in the Security Technology Unit at Microsoft. He is the author of many security articles and books, including the award-winning *Writing Secure Code* and *19 Deadly Sins of Software Security*, writes regularly for industry magazines, and is a co-editor of IEEE Security and Privacy. He is part of the team responsible for defining and delivering security education, defining the Security Development Lifecycle, researching new threats and defenses, and working with Microsoft product groups to help them build more secure software. He is the inventor of four patents in the field of software security.

Steven B. Lipner

Steven B. Lipner, CISSP, is Senior Director of Security Engineering Strategy in the Security Technology Unit at Microsoft. He is responsible for the definition and updating of the Security Development Lifecycle, which Microsoft applies to improve the security and privacy of its products. Mr. Lipner is also responsible for Microsoft's policies and strategies for the security evaluation of its products, and for the development of programs to provide improved product security to Microsoft customers. Mr. Lipner has over thirty years' experience as a researcher, development manager, and general manager in IT security. He is named as co-inventor on eleven patents in the field of computer and network security. Mr. Lipner holds S.B. and S.M. degrees from the Massachusetts Institute of Technology and attended the Harvard Business School's Program for Management Development. He is a member of the United States Information Security and Privacy Advisory Board, a Certified Information Systems Security Professional, and a member of the ISC^2 Americas Advisory Board.

Additional Resources for Web Developers
Published and Forthcoming Titles from Microsoft Press

Microsoft® Visual Web Developer™ 2005 Express Edition: Build a Web Site Now!
Jim Buyens • ISBN 0-7356-2212-4

With this lively, eye-opening, and hands-on book, all you need is a computer and the desire to learn how to create Web pages now using Visual Web Developer Express Edition! Featuring a full working edition of the software, this fun and highly visual guide walks you through a complete Web page project from set-up to launch. You'll get an introduction to the Microsoft Visual Studio® environment and learn how to put the light-weight, easy-to-use tools in Visual Web Developer Express to work right away—building your first, dynamic Web pages with Microsoft ASP.NET 2.0. You'll get expert tips, coaching, and visual examples at each step of the way, along with pointers to additional learning resources.

Microsoft ASP.NET 2.0 Programming
Step by Step
George Shepherd • ISBN 0-7356-2201-9

With dramatic improvements in performance, productivity, and security features, Visual Studio 2005 and ASP.NET 2.0 deliver a simplified, high-performance, and powerful Web development experience. ASP.NET 2.0 features a new set of controls and infrastructure that simplify Web-based data access and include functionality that facilitates code reuse, visual consistency, and aesthetic appeal. Now you can teach yourself the essentials of working with ASP.NET 2.0 in the Visual Studio environment—one step at a time. With *Step by Step*, you work at your own pace through hands-on, learn-by-doing exercises. Whether you're a beginning programmer or new to this version of the technology, you'll understand the core capabilities and fundamental techniques for ASP.NET 2.0. Each chapter puts you to work, showing you how, when, and why to use specific features of the ASP.NET 2.0 rapid application development environment and guiding you as you create actual components and working applications for the Web, including advanced features such as personalization.

Programming Microsoft ASP.NET 2.0
Core Reference
Dino Esposito • ISBN 0-7356-2176-4

Delve into the core topics for ASP.NET 2.0 programming, mastering the essential skills and capabilities needed to build high-performance Web applications successfully. Well-known ASP.NET author Dino Esposito deftly builds your expertise with Web forms, Visual Studio, core controls, master pages, data access, data binding, state management, security services, and other must-know topics—combining definitive reference with practical, hands-on programming instruction. Packed with expert guidance and pragmatic examples, this *Core Reference* delivers the key resources that you need to develop professional-level Web programming skills.

Programming Microsoft ASP.NET 2.0
Applications: *Advanced Topics*
Dino Esposito • ISBN 0-7356-2177-2

Master advanced topics in ASP.NET 2.0 programming—gaining the essential insights and in-depth understanding that you need to build sophisticated, highly functional Web applications successfully. Topics include Web forms, Visual Studio 2005, core controls, master pages, data access, data binding, state management, and security considerations. Developers often discover that the more they use ASP.NET, the more they need to know. With expert guidance from ASP.NET authority Dino Esposito, you get the in-depth, comprehensive information that leads to full mastery of the technology.

Programming Microsoft Windows® Forms
Charles Petzold • ISBN 0-7356-2153-5

Programming Microsoft Web Forms
Douglas J. Reilly • ISBN 0-7356-2179-9

CLR via C++
Jeffrey Richter with Stanley B. Lippman
ISBN 0-7356-2248-5

Debugging, Tuning, and Testing Microsoft .NET 2.0 Applications
John Robbins • ISBN 0-7356-2202-7

CLR via C#, Second Edition
Jeffrey Richter • ISBN 0-7356-2163-2

For more information about Microsoft Press® books and other learning products, visit: **www.microsoft.com/books** *and* **www.microsoft.com/learning**

Additional Resources for C# Developers

Published and Forthcoming Titles from Microsoft Press

Microsoft® Visual C#® 2005 Express Edition: Build a Program Now!
Patrice Pelland ● ISBN 0-7356-2229-9

In this lively, eye-opening, and hands-on book, all you need is a computer and the desire to learn how to program with Visual C# 2005 Express Edition. Featuring a full working edition of the software, this fun and highly visual guide walks you through a complete programming project—a desktop weather-reporting application—from start to finish. You'll get an unintimidating introduction to the Microsoft Visual Studio® development environment and learn how to put the lightweight, easy-to-use tools in Visual C# Express to work right away—creating, compiling, testing, and delivering your first, ready-to-use program. You'll get expert tips, coaching, and visual examples at each step of the way, along with pointers to additional learning resources.

Microsoft Visual C# 2005 *Step by Step*
John Sharp ● ISBN 0-7356-2129-2

Visual C#, a feature of Visual Studio 2005, is a modern programming language designed to deliver a productive environment for creating business frameworks and reusable object-oriented components. Now you can teach yourself essential techniques with Visual C#—and start building components and Microsoft Windows®–based applications—one step at a time. With *Step by Step*, you work at your own pace through hands-on, learn-by-doing exercises. Whether you're a beginning programmer or new to this particular language, you'll learn how, when, and why to use specific features of Visual C# 2005. Each chapter puts you to work, building your knowledge of core capabilities and guiding you as you create your first C#-based applications for Windows, data management, and the Web.

Programming Microsoft Visual C# 2005 Framework Reference
Francesco Balena ● ISBN 0-7356-2182-9

Complementing *Programming Microsoft Visual C# 2005 Core Reference*, this book covers a wide range of additional topics and information critical to Visual C# developers, including Windows Forms, working with Microsoft ADO.NET 2.0 and Microsoft ASP.NET 2.0, Web services, security, remoting, and much more. Packed with sample code and real-world examples, this book will help developers move from understanding to mastery.

Programming Microsoft Visual C# 2005 *Core Reference*
Donis Marshall ● ISBN 0-7356-2181-0

Get the in-depth reference and pragmatic, real-world insights you need to exploit the enhanced language features and core capabilities in Visual C# 2005. Programming expert Donis Marshall deftly builds your proficiency with classes, structs, and other fundamentals, and advances your expertise with more advanced topics such as debugging, threading, and memory management. Combining incisive reference with hands-on coding examples and best practices, this *Core Reference* focuses on mastering the C# skills you need to build innovative solutions for smart clients and the Web.

CLR via C#, Second Edition
Jeffrey Richter ● ISBN 0-7356-2163-2

In this new edition of Jeffrey Richter's popular book, you get focused, pragmatic guidance on how to exploit the common language runtime (CLR) functionality in Microsoft .NET Framework 2.0 for applications of all types—from Web Forms, Windows Forms, and Web services to solutions for Microsoft SQL Server™, Microsoft code names "Avalon" and "Indigo," consoles, Microsoft Windows NT® Service, and more. Targeted to advanced developers and software designers, this book takes you under the covers of .NET for an in-depth understanding of its structure, functions, and operational components, demonstrating the most practical ways to apply this knowledge to your own development efforts. You'll master fundamental design tenets for .NET and get hands-on insights for creating high-performance applications more easily and efficiently. The book features extensive code examples in Visual C# 2005.

Programming Microsoft Windows Forms
Charles Petzold ● ISBN 0-7356-2153-5

CLR via C++
Jeffrey Richter with Stanley B. Lippman
ISBN 0-7356-2248-5

Programming Microsoft Web Forms
Douglas J. Reilly ● ISBN 0-7356-2179-9

Debugging, Tuning, and Testing Microsoft .NET 2.0 Applications
John Robbins ● ISBN 0-7356-2202-7

For more information about Microsoft Press® books and other learning products,
visit: **www.microsoft.com/books** *and* **www.microsoft.com/learning**

Additional Resources for Visual Basic Developers

Published and Forthcoming Titles from Microsoft Press

Microsoft® Visual Basic® 2005 Express Edition: Build a Program Now!
Patrice Pelland • ISBN 0-7356-2213-2

Featuring a full working edition of the software, this fun and highly visual guide walks you through a complete programming project—a desktop weather-reporting application—from start to finish. You'll get an introduction to the Microsoft Visual Studio® development environment and learn how to put the lightweight, easy-to-use tools in Visual Basic Express to work right away—creating, compiling, testing, and delivering your first ready-to-use program. You'll get expert tips, coaching, and visual examples each step of the way, along with pointers to additional learning resources.

Microsoft Visual Basic 2005 *Step by Step*
Michael Halvorson • ISBN 0-7356-2131-4

With enhancements across its visual designers, code editor, language, and debugger that help accelerate the development and deployment of robust, elegant applications across the Web, a business group, or an enterprise, Visual Basic 2005 focuses on enabling developers to rapidly build applications. Now you can teach yourself the essentials of working with Visual Studio 2005 and the new features of the Visual Basic language—one step at a time. Each chapter puts you to work, showing you how, when, and why to use specific features of Visual Basic and guiding as you create actual components and working applications for Microsoft Windows®. You'll also explore data management and Web-based development topics.

Programming Microsoft Visual Basic 2005 *Core Reference*
Francesco Balena • ISBN 0-7356-2183-7

Get the expert insights, indispensable reference, and practical instruction needed to exploit the core language features and capabilities in Visual Basic 2005. Well-known Visual Basic programming author Francesco Balena expertly guides you through the fundamentals, including modules, keywords, and inheritance, and builds your mastery of more advanced topics such as delegates, assemblies, and My Namespace. Combining in-depth reference with extensive, hands-on code examples and best-practices advice, this *Core Reference* delivers the key resources that you need to develop professional-level programming skills for smart clients and the Web.

Programming Microsoft Visual Basic 2005 Framework Reference
Francesco Balena • ISBN 0-7356-2175-6

Complementing *Programming Microsoft Visual Basic 2005 Core Reference*, this book covers a wide range of additional topics and information critical to Visual Basic developers, including Windows Forms, working with Microsoft ADO.NET 2.0 and ASP.NET 2.0, Web services, security, remoting, and much more. Packed with sample code and real-world examples, this book will help developers move from understanding to mastery.

Programming Microsoft Windows Forms
Charles Petzold • ISBN 0-7356-2153-5

Programming Microsoft Web Forms
Douglas J. Reilly • ISBN 0-7356-2179-9

Debugging, Tuning, and Testing Microsoft .NET 2.0 Applications
John Robbins • ISBN 0-7356-2202-7

Microsoft ASP.NET 2.0 *Step by Step*
George Shepherd • ISBN 0-7356-2201-9

Microsoft ADO.NET 2.0 *Step by Step*
Rebecca Riordan • ISBN 0-7356-2164-0

Programming Microsoft ASP.NET 2.0 *Core Reference*
Dino Esposito • ISBN 0-7356-2176-4

For more information about Microsoft Press® books and other learning products,
visit: **www.microsoft.com/books** *and* **www.microsoft.com/learning**

Additional Resources for Developers: Advanced Topics and Best Practices

Published and Forthcoming Titles from Microsoft Press

Code Complete, Second Edition
Steve McConnell • ISBN 0-7356-1967-0

For more than a decade, Steve McConnell, one of the premier authors and voices in the software community, has helped change the way developers write code—and produce better software. Now his classic book, *Code Complete*, has been fully updated and revised with best practices in the art and science of constructing software. Topics include design, applying good techniques to construction, eliminating errors, planning, managing construction activities, and relating personal character to superior software. This new edition features fully updated information on programming techniques, including the emergence of Web-style programming, and integrated coverage of object-oriented design. You'll also find new code examples—both good and bad—in C++, Microsoft® Visual Basic®, C#, and Java, although the focus is squarely on techniques and practices.

More About Software Requirements: Thorny Issues and Practical Advice
Karl E. Wiegers • ISBN 0-7356-2267-1

Have you ever delivered software that satisfied all of the project specifications, but failed to meet any of the customers expectations? Without formal, verifiable requirements—and a system for managing them—the result is often a gap between what developers think they're supposed to build and what customers think they're going to get. Too often, lessons about software requirements engineering processes are formal or academic, and not of value to real-world, professional development teams. In this follow-up guide to *Software Requirements*, Second Edition, you will discover even more practical techniques for gathering and managing software requirements that help you deliver software that meets project and customer specifications. Succinct and immediately useful, this book is a must-have for developers and architects.

Software Estimation: Demystifying the Black Art
Steve McConnell • ISBN 0-7356-0535-1

Often referred to as the "black art" because of its complexity and uncertainty, software estimation is not as hard or mysterious as people think. However, the art of how to create effective cost and schedule estimates has not been very well publicized. *Software Estimation* provides a proven set of procedures and heuristics that software developers, technical leads, and project managers can apply to their projects. Instead of arcane treatises and rigid modeling techniques, award-winning author Steve McConnell gives practical guidance to help organizations achieve basic estimation proficiency and lay the groundwork to continue improving project cost estimates. This book does not avoid the more complex mathematical estimation approaches, but the non-mathematical reader will find plenty of useful guidelines without getting bogged down in complex formulas.

Debugging, Tuning, and Testing Microsoft .NET 2.0 Applications
John Robbins • ISBN 0-7356-2202-7

Making an application the best it can be has long been a time-consuming task best accomplished with specialized and costly tools. With Microsoft Visual Studio® 2005, developers have available a new range of built-in functionality that enables them to debug their code quickly and efficiently, tune it to optimum performance, and test applications to ensure compatibility and trouble-free operation. In this accessible and hands-on book, debugging expert John Robbins shows developers how to use the tools and functions in Visual Studio to their full advantage to ensure high-quality applications.

The Security Development Lifecycle
Michael Howard and Steve Lipner • ISBN 0-7356-2214-0

Adapted from Microsoft's standard development process, the Security Development Lifecycle (SDL) is a methodology that helps reduce the number of security defects in code at every stage of the development process, from design to release. This book details each stage of the SDL methodology and discusses its implementation across a range of Microsoft software, including Microsoft Windows Server™ 2003, Microsoft SQL Server™ 2000 Service Pack 3, and Microsoft Exchange Server 2003 Service Pack 1, to help measurably improve security features. You get direct access to insights from Microsoft's security team and lessons that are applicable to software development processes worldwide, whether on a small-scale or a large-scale. This book includes a CD featuring videos of developer training classes.

Software Requirements, Second Edition
Karl E. Wiegers • ISBN 0-7356-1879-8

Writing Secure Code, Second Edition
Michael Howard and David LeBlanc • ISBN 0-7356-1722-8

CLR via C#, Second Edition
Jeffrey Richter • ISBN 0-7356-2163-2

For more information about Microsoft Press® books and other learning products,
visit: **www.microsoft.com/mspress** *and* **www.microsoft.com/learning**

Additional SQL Server Resources for Developers

Published and Forthcoming Titles from Microsoft Press

Microsoft® SQL Server™ 2005 Express Edition
Step by Step
Jackie Goldstein • ISBN 0-7356-2184-5

Teach yourself how to get database projects up and running
quickly with SQL Server Express
Edition—a free, easy-to-use
database product that is based
on SQL Server 2005 technology.
It's designed for building simple,
dynamic applications, with all
the rich functionality of the SQL
Server database engine and
using the same data access APIs,
such as Microsoft ADO.NET, SQL
Native Client, and T-SQL.
Whether you're new to database
programming or new to SQL Server, you'll learn how, when, and
why to use specific features of this simple but powerful database development environment. Each chapter puts you to work,
building your knowledge of core capabilities and guiding you
as you create actual components and working applications.

Microsoft SQL Server 2005 Programming
Step by Step
Fernando Guerrero • ISBN 0-7356-2207-8

SQL Server 2005 is Microsoft's
next-generation data management and analysis solution that
delivers enhanced scalability,
availability, and security features
to enterprise data and analytical
applications while making them
easier to create, deploy, and
manage. Now you can teach
yourself how to design, build, test,
deploy, and maintain SQL Server
databases—one step at a time.
Instead of merely focusing on
describing new features, this book shows new database
programmers and administrators how to use specific features
within typical business scenarios. Each chapter provides a highly
practical learning experience that demonstrates how to build
database solutions to solve common business problems.

Microsoft SQL Server 2005 Analysis Services
Step by Step
Hitachi Consulting Services • ISBN 0-7356-2199-3

One of the key features of SQL Server 2005 is SQL Server Analysis
Services—Microsoft's customizable analysis solution for business
data modeling and interpretation. Just compare SQL Server
Analysis Services to its competition to understand the great
value of its enhanced features. One of the keys to harnessing
the full functionality of SQL Server will be leveraging Analysis
Services for the powerful tool that it is—including creating a cube,
and deploying, customizing, and extending the basic calculations. This step-by-step tutorial discusses how to get started, how
to build scalable analytical applications, and how to use and administer advanced features. Interactivity (enhanced in SQL Server
2005), data translation, and security are also covered in detail.

Microsoft SQL Server 2005 Reporting Services
Step by Step
Hitachi Consulting Services • ISBN 0-7356-2250-7

SQL Server Reporting Services (SRS) is Microsoft's customizable
reporting solution for business data analysis. It is one of the key
value features of SQL Server 2005: functionality more advanced
and much less expensive than its competition. SRS is powerful,
so an understanding of how to architect a report, as well as how
to install and program SRS, is key to harnessing the full functionality of SQL Server. This procedural tutorial shows how to use the
Report Project Wizard, how to think about and access data, and
how to build queries. It also walks through the creation of charts
and visual layouts for maximum visual understanding of data
analysis. Interactivity (enhanced in SQL Server 2005) and security
are also covered in detail.

Programming Microsoft SQL Server 2005
Andrew J. Brust, Stephen Forte, and William H. Zack
ISBN 0-7356-1923-9

This thorough, hands-on reference for developers and database
administrators teaches the basics of programming custom applications with SQL Server 2005. You will learn the fundamentals
of creating database applications—including coverage of
T-SQL, Microsoft .NET Framework, and Microsoft ADO.NET. In
addition to practical guidance on database architecture and
design, application development, and reporting and data
analysis, this essential reference guide covers performance,
tuning, and availability of SQL Server 2005.

Inside Microsoft SQL Server 2005:
The Storage Engine
Kalen Delaney • ISBN 0-7356-2105-5

Inside Microsoft SQL Server 2005:
T-SQL Programming
Itzik Ben-Gan • ISBN 0-7356-2197-7

Inside Microsoft SQL Server 2005:
Query Processing and Optimization
Kalen Delaney • ISBN 0-7356-2196-9

Programming Microsoft ADO.NET 2.0 Core Reference
David Sceppa • ISBN 0-7356-2206-X

For more information about Microsoft Press® books and other learning products,
visit: **www.microsoft.com/mspress** *and* **www.microsoft.com/learning**

Microsoft®
Press

What do you think of this book? We want to hear from you!

Do you have a few minutes to participate in a brief online survey? Microsoft is interested in hearing your feedback about this publication so that we can continually improve our books and learning resources for you.

To participate in our survey, please visit:

www.microsoft.com/learning/booksurvey

And enter this book's ISBN, 0-7356-2214-0. As a thank-you to survey participants in the United States and Canada, each month we'll randomly select five respondents to win one of five $100 gift certificates from a leading online merchant.* At the conclusion of the survey, you can enter the drawing by providing your e-mail address, which will be used for prize notification *only*.

Thanks in advance for your input. Your opinion counts!

Sincerely,

Microsoft Learning

Learn More. Go Further.

To see special offers on Microsoft Learning products for developers, IT professionals, and home and office users, visit: *www.microsoft.com/learning/booksurvey*